Henry James Coleridge

The Life and Letters of St. Teresa

Volume 3

Henry James Coleridge

The Life and Letters of St. Teresa
Volume 3

ISBN/EAN: 9783743489264

Manufactured in Europe, USA, Canada, Australia, Japa

Cover: Foto ©Lupo / pixelio.de

Manufactured and distributed by brebook publishing software (www.brebook.com)

Henry James Coleridge

The Life and Letters of St. Teresa

Quarterly Series.

SIXTY-SEVENTH VOLUME.

THE LIFE AND LETTERS
OF ST. TERESA

VOL. III.

ROEHAMPTON:

PRINTED BY JAMES STANLEY.

THE LIFE AND LETTERS OF ST. TERESA.

BY

HENRY JAMES COLERIDGE.

OF THE SOCIETY OF JESUS.

VOLUME THE THIRD.

LONDON: BURNS AND OATES, LIMITED.
NEW YORK, CINCINNATI, CHICAGO: BENZIGER BROTHERS

1896.

PREFACE.

———

FEW words are needed to introduce the present volume, the last of a work which has cost more labour than appears on the surface, carried on through a number of years during which the writer has always had other matters of importance to occupy his time. The work, however, is now complete, as far as it is within his power to make it so, and if it reveals the character of St. Teresa to others as it has revealed it to her biographer, it will abundantly repay the labour that it has cost.

In a work begun several years ago, and carried on in the manner in which alone it has been possible to accomplish this, there will of necessity be found many small inaccuracies and mistakes which, it may be hoped, will be thought venial. It was not till the second volume had been commenced that it became manifest that the Letters of St. Teresa could not all be inserted in their integrity, and that therefore the plan of epitomizing and paraphrasing parts of their contents had to be adopted. The reader will probably agree that her Letters become almost more interesting as the story of St. Teresa's Life proceeds to its close, and that certain of her most attractive characteristics become more and more prominent. There are many good Lives of the Saint, but even in the best of them the materials contained in the Letters have not been fully used. Indeed, these seem often to light up parts of her life and character to an unexpected degree. No apology, therefore, need be made for the present work, which is now committed to the English reader in the hope that it will conduce somewhat to the glory of God and the honour of His Saint.

H. J. C.

31, Farm Street, Berkeley Square,
Octave of St. Teresa, 1888.

CONTENTS.

Contents. · xi

CHAPTER I.

Crisis of the Reform.

ALMOST at the same time when St. Teresa was writing her letter, imploring the aid of Father Paolo Henandez at Madrid, the chief friars of the Reform were taking a bold and most hazardous step to bring about a solution of their difficulties by their own action. When we last heard of Gratian and his friars,[1] they had gone to Madrid with the hope of explaining to the Royal Council the step which they had lately taken at Pastrana, in submitting entirely to the authority of the delegates of the Nuncio Sega, notwithstanding the support which they might have reckoned on from the secular magistrates, who were instructed by the King's authority, to defend them from molestation. This act, dictated mainly by the scruples and the timidity of Gratian, was likely to alienate, and did alienate from them, at least for the time, their only remaining defender, Philip, himself. He could no longer go on helping men who would not use his authority, and who thus exposed him to contempt and defeat. Gratian, Mariano, and Antonio of Jesus had therefore, as has been said, proceeded to the capital, hoping to show the King and the Royal

---

[1] Vol. ii. p. 374.

B 3

Council that they had not acted in disrespect or ungratefully. The Nuncio had at once put an end to their attempt by ordering them into prison in various monasteries, and we hear nothing more of their representations to Philip. This was in August or September, 1578. But the friars seem to have been released after a short detention. They probably satisfied the Nuncio that they would not proceed any further in the matter. The letter to Father Paolo Henandez, just now mentioned, seems to show that St. Teresa did net think that much would come of their visit to Madrid, and she rests her hopes, humanly speaking, on Henandez' intercession with the Nuncio. We know, however, that at the same time she wrote herself to the King. Her letter is unfortunately lost.

But, as it seems, some of the friars persuaded themselves that the time had now come for a last effort on their own part to gain a separate Province. They probably did not communicate with St. Teresa, as they already knew that she was certain to oppose any imprudent step. She had—too late—carried her point as to the despatch of two friars to Rome, who might represent there the interests of the Reform, and explain to the General and to the Holy See the case of its friars. Her last letter before this time to Gratian, of which we possess only a fragment, speaks of her approval of the Fathers chosen, and we have already spoken[1] of a long paper written by her which seems to have been meant for the guidance of the deputies. But, as has been said, the Reform was

[1] Vol. ii. p. 389.

now brought into a danger more extreme than any that had hitherto been incurred, by the act of its own chief friars. It appears that when the first Visitors of the Carmelite Order in Spain, Fra Pedro Hernandez and Fra Francisco Vargas, had been appointed by Pius V., several years before this time, they had made an order that, when the visitation of the Province was finished, the Discalced Friars were to assemble in chapter and elect a Provincial for themselves. This order had never been acted upon, its legality was probably questionable at any time, and now it could hardly be thought to have any authority whatever. The thought of getting rid of his own burthen had, from the first, pressed upon Gratian, and that desire was already sufficiently accomplished by his submission to the Nuncio. It seems to have been supposed that the powers given by the former Visitors might now be used for the purpose of supplying a new Provincial, and thus erecting a separate Province. Antonio of Jesus, the former Provincial of Castile before the beginning of the Reform, which he shared with St. John of the Cross the glory of having been the first to join, had been elected "Definitor" in the former Chapter of Almodovar, held two years before this time. Gratian seems to have suggested to him to call a Chapter at Almodovar. We have already seen what Teresa thought of the project, and her solid arguments against it,[1] which are given in her letter of April of this year to Father Gratian. It seems almost inconceivable that so imprudent a step should have seemed

---

[1] See vol. ii. p. 380.

even possible. But the Discalced Friars—or rather some of their very small number—felt like drowning men, who catch at a straw, and the Chapter was convened by Fra Antonio.

By a singular providence, his companion in the first Discalced monastery, St. John of the Cross, was able to be present at the Chapter, which was held on the 9th of October. The escape of the Saint from the monastery of Toledo, in which he was kept a prisoner with great rigour and severity, is an incident such as we do not often meet with in the lives of the saints. He was confined in a very small cell in a corridor, the door of which was kept locked, lest he should escape. He suffered terribly from the heat and bad air, he lost all appetite, and could not sleep. He appeared to be gradually dying under his treatment, giving all the while the most heroic example of humility, submission, charity, and gratitude for the least services which were rendered him, but without at all moving the hearts of the Superiors. One day when he was on his knees absorbed in prayer, the Prior came to his cell, and St. John did not notice him, thinking he was the Brother who acted as jailor. The Prior reproved him for his want of respect, and St. John begged his pardon. The Prior asked him what he was thinking of with so much recollection? "That to-morrow is the feast of our Lady's Assumption, and how much it would console me to be allowed to say Mass." But the Prior sternly refused, and turned away. St. John raised his heart to Heaven, and the Blessed Virgin consoled him by telling him that he should soon be out of his prison. He wondered how this could ever be, he was so well guarded, the locks were so strong, the walls so high. But his thoughts were directed to a window in the corridor, high above the ground outside, with the Tagus flowing underneath. His jailor had often shown him little kindnesses and indulgences, and let him walk up and down the corridor. Availing himself of this one day, he examined the window in question, and made up his mind to try. A night or two after, the door of the passage into the corridor was left unlocked, on account of the arrival, late at night, of two friars from a distance, who were placed in cells near that of St. John. He managed to tear the coverlet of his bed into strips, and thus make a rope, and succeeded, notwithstanding one alarm at which the strangers woke up, in getting to the window and letting himself down. He had to drop from a height, as his rope was far too short, but the fall did not hurt him, and after making his way over walls and enclosures, guided by a marvellous light, he found himself at last in a street, where, after waiting for dawn in an open court, he found some one to guide him to the convent of the Discalced Carmelite Nuns. He told his name to the astounded portress, and was at once taken to help a nun who was at the point of death. A canon of the Chapter sheltered him in his own house for a short time, and then sent him, well escorted, to Almodovar.[1]

[1] This account of the escape of St. John of the Cross is taken from the *Ensayo Historio* of Don Emmanuele Mugnoz Garnica (1875). We use, however, the Italian translation by the learned Barnabite, Francesco Alessandrino Piantoni, Rome, 1882.

St. John's escape must have taken place before
the middle of September, as it seems then to have
been known to St. Teresa, who appears to allude to
it in one of the short fragments to Gratian mentioned
in the last volume.[1]   St. John did his best at the
Chapter of Almodovar to prevent the foolish step for
which the Chapter had been convened.   He argued
that the powers of the Visitors were extinct, that a
separation between the Mitigated Friars and the
Reform could not be made by one of the parties
alone, that they had no power to create a new
Religious Order, and that the whole matter was in
the hands of the Pope.   But, notwithstanding the
reverence which his well known sanctity, increased
as it was by the too evident traces which he bore
about him of the kind of martyrdom which he had
lately suffered, St. John of the Cross spoke in vain.
Father Antonio of Jesus, who had convened the
Chapter, was elected Provincial.   It seems that, being
the oldest friar of the Reform, he had a foolish
ambition for the post.   Two Fathers were appointed
to go to Rome, Father Pedro de Angelis and Father
Juan de San Diego, and St. John of the Cross himself
was appointed Prior of the Monastery of Mount
Calvary in the place of the latter.   Some of the
chief friars were absent from the Chapter, Ambrosio
Mariano, Nicolo Doria, and others.   Doria, with
Father Juan de Jesus Roca, seems to have arrived
before the Chapter was dissolved, and to have tried
to have its acts annulled, but to no purpose.   Indeed,
Father Juan de Jesus was kept in confinement for a

---

[1] Vol. ii. p. 393.

month, in order that he might not go to Madrid to complain to the Nuncio. Father Antonio proceeded to Madrid with some other Fathers to ask the Nuncio to ratify the acts of the Chapter. They were received with the severity which might have been foreseen. Mgr. Sega at once annulled all that had been done, and put the Fathers in confinement, Gratian with the Carmelite Fathers at Madrid,[1] Antonio and Mariano in a monastery of Reformed Franciscans in the same place. He also ordered St. Teresa to retire to Toledo, and issued a Brief on the 16th of October subjecting the Reform to the Mitigated Friars.

It was this last measure that broke down St. Teresa's courage. It was the one blow which she had always dreaded most of all, and if the measures which it involved had been carried out, it is difficult to see how her Reform could have escaped entire destruction. We are told that when the news came she gave herself up to grief. At last, late in the evening, her companion, Anne of St. Bartholomew, persuaded her to go to the refectory to take some food before the night Office began. Teresa obeyed, and then Anne as well as herself saw our Lord standing by her at the table, breaking pieces of bread for her, and putting them to her mouth, bidding her eat, for He saw how much she suffered, and also to take courage, for what had

---

[1] Father Gratian was afterwards sent to Alcala de Henares, and remained there a considerable time. Fra Antonio was allowed to go to Roda, with Father Gabriel of the Assumption, who was Prior there. Antonio thus became able to help in the foundation of Villanueva de la Jara, of which we shall presently hear.

happened could not be otherwise. In the morning
her courage had returned, and she set herself and
her nuns to work with prayers and penances to obtain
help from Heaven, while at the same time she sent
letters in every direction to ask the aid of powerful
persons all over the country. Anne of Jesus helped
her in this. Teresa also wrote to the King, and her
biographers assure us that her letters had more effect
on him than all the other numerous applications
which he received.

One of these biographers, Yepez, tells us how calm
and confident she remained during this time of trial.
He says that he paid her a visit at Toledo one day,
and found Ambrose Mariano with her. Each had
that day received a letter from Gratian, in which he
spoke most despairingly of the condition of affairs.
Mariano was quite discouraged. What could four or
five friars do, left to themselves, almost unknown,
despised and forsaken, and without authority or
any one to protect them? Nevertheless, he says,
St. Teresa was full of calmness and confidence. She
was like a person who saw the land from the mast-
head, while all on deck were abandoned to despair.
She told her friends that it was necessary that they
should suffer, but the Order would not perish. He
afterwards learnt that she had been thinking whether
their adversaries could really wish the Reform to be
destroyed, and our Lord had answered her thought
by telling her that some of them would wish it, but
that it would not be so, but far differently. Yepez
says that from that time he never lost his confidence.[1]

[1] Yepez, ii. 28.

In truth, the four or five friars had made a terrible mistake in the Chapter of Almodovar, and were now reaping the fruits of their folly. But that folly was not to be punished by the destruction of so great a work of God as the Reform of St. Teresa. It may be questioned whether any but the more violent among the Friars of the Mitigation really wished this. They did not like the Reform, for it was by its very existence a silent reproach to themselves. The Mitigation was thoroughly sanctioned by Papal Bulls, and its friars had come into it, personally, in all good faith. They may have been relaxed in their lives and discipline, but the Mitigation itself could not be blamed. Many saints who are the glory of Religious Orders, have been found in such branches of great Institutes. St. Mary Magdalene of Pazzi was a "Mitigated" Carmelite, St. Joseph of Cupertino was a "Mitigated" Franciscan. The number might easily be increased. The Carmelite Order in Spain needed reform, but there must have been among its members countless great servants of God. Then, also, they had been hardly treated by the summary measures of the Apostolical Visitors. They must have been provoked beyond measure by the appointment of Gratian, although personally his manner of dealing with them was amiable and gentle. Some other of the chief men among the Reformed Friars were by no means gentle. Now the time of the Mitigated had come. The Apostolical Visitors were no longer in power, the Nuncio was now on their side, the King was no longer protecting the Discalced. These last had precipitated a crisis by their own foolish action.

But after all, St. Teresa might well ask, did they wish
her work to perish? Some did, but many did not.
The violent men were at the head, no doubt, and
they had been able to say that the General Chapter
was on their side, the General himself—who died
about this time, much to the grief of St. Teresa—
the Vicar Tostado, and the Papal Nuncio. But the
Friars of the Mitigation had taken up arms, as it
were, to defend their own homes and altars, and no
measure seemed too strong for them, when they were
put on the defence of what they had a right to defend.
But now it was not a question of self-defence. Now
that their assailants seem to be at their mercy, the
more reasonably minded among them must have had
no great appetite for an exterminating vengeance.

Moreover, in a country like Spain, full of ardent
and practical Catholics, and with the spirit of religious
zeal and religious revival in the very air, the general
feeling of pious and devout people could not go for
nothing. Lay Catholics very quickly catch the truth
when religious and ecclesiastical persons fall out in
public. It was an age of reform in religious Institutes,
which came by no means too soon. Reformers in
such Institutes are generally approved by the public,
while they are still opposed by some among the
Religious themselves. St. Teresa's name was very
great, and, if it influenced Philip II., it is not
wonderful that it had great weight on public opinion.
It did not prepossess good people in favour of the
Mitigation, that it was made so very great a crime
and so formidable a danger to return to a primitive
Rule. And, moreover, wherever the Reformed Car-

melites were known, they were respected and loved. It could hardly seem a service to God to stamp them out, in order that the older Carmelites might go on happily with the Mitigated Observance.

But, in fact, the short time during which the elder Carmelites had matters all their own way with the Reform, was long enough to make it evident to all prudent persons on the spot that, if the Reform was to exist at all, it must be set free at once. As soon as the Reformed Carmelites were placed under the jurisdiction of the Mitigation, and as soon as these last began to take active measures to assert their authority, visiting the houses, changing the Superiors, forbidding the reception of novices, and the like, the tide began to run in favour of their victims. Generally speaking, the friars and nuns of the Reformed Carmel seem to have made little actual resistance. Only in one place, as far as we know, was the royal order used which allowed the appeal to the help of the secular magistrates against any act done on the authority of the Nuncio. This was in Granada. Hurtado de Mendoza, Count of Tendiglia, a man whose name occurs more than once as distinguished in carrying out the measures taken against the Moors, had had a large share in the foundation of Granada, and took up the cause of the Reformed Friars. He went to Madrid to intercede with the Nuncio, but Sega would not listen to him, and the fiery Count broke out in reproaches. He did more, for he went to the Fiscal of the Royal Council, the man who had foiled Tostado, to see if anything could be done in defence of his friends. Without more ado, an order was obtained from the Royal Council suspending the execution of the Brief of the Nuncio of the 1st of October until the Discalced had been heard against it. This appears to have happened early in the year 1579.

As it does not seem that the Brief had been resisted anywhere but in Granada, it is probable that the order for its suspension had not any great effect on the immediate condition of affairs generally. But it had a considerable effect on Mgr. Sega. He was now, to some extent, in collision with the Royal Council, a collision which had been occasioned by the violence of the Friars of the Mitigation. Moreover, he was hurt by the language which the Count had used to him. He determined to complain to the King, and thus give Philip an occasion of speaking what was in his mind. He did not, meantime, in any way relax his severity against the Reform, though it is hardly possible to think that the few months which had passed since the issue of his Brief had not brought to him a number of powerful remonstrances from the friends of St. Teresa and her Reform, couched in language more respectful than that which Tendiglia had used. Philip received the complaint of the Nuncio with dignity. He saw that Tendiglia had gone beyond due bounds, and he promised that a fitting apology should be made to the representative of the Holy See.

At the same time, Philip added a few words of his own. He knew, he said, the enmity with which the Carmelite Friars of the Mitigation regarded those of the Reform, who were persons who professed austerity and perfection, and he therefore had some suspicion about the opposition with which they met. The Nuncio, as he heard, was also hostile to them. He was continually receiving complaints of his hard treatment of the Discalced, and he begged him to "protect the virtuous." At the same time Philip ordered the Count to be summoned back to Madrid, that he might make a due apology to the Nuncio. Tendiglia wrote to the President of Castile, the Bishop of Avila, a letter explaining his own action in protecting the Discalced, and the reasons he had for favouring them, and then set out to follow his letter to Madrid. The letter was full and calm, and was laid by the order of the King before the Nuncio. It either changed the mind of Sega, or, at least, prepared it for a change. When Tendiglia came to make his apology, he was received with great courtesy and kindness, and the Nuncio listened attentively to all that he had to say. Sega ended by saying that he would be very glad if the King would appoint some men of weight and learning, with whom he would willingly confer, with a view to the settlement of the questions now afloat as to the Carmelite Order.

The only thing that was now required was that the assessors thus asked for should be men who could really aid the Nuncio in judging the whole matter justly and equitably. The King appointed Luis de Manrique, his own chaplain and almoner, Father Lorenzo of Villa Vicencio, an Augustinian monk and preacher to the King, and two Dominican friars, Ferdinand de Castillo, also a royal preacher, and Pedro Hernandez, who had been Visitor of the Carmelites in Castile, and to whom St. Teresa was well known. He was now Provincial of the Dominicans. All four were men of high repute for virtue and learning. No better choice could have been made. The Carmelites had not long to wait for an immediate result of their meetings. The Nuncio issued letters on the 1st of April, by which the Discalced were exempted from the jurisdiction of the Mitigated Friars.

Fra Angelo de Salazar was appointed Superior and Vicar for the Discalced. Although himself one of the Mitigation, he knew the Discalced well, and had an immense respect for St. Teresa. One of Fra Angelo's first acts was to allow her to return from Toledo to Avila. He soon after visited all the houses in Castile, but was prevented by ill-health from doing the same in Andalusia. His acts while in authority were generally as kind and considerate as could be expected. The consultations with the Nuncio lasted into July. On the 15th of that month, the day before the feast of Our Lady of Mount Carmel, the Nuncio laid before the King a paper signed by them all, containing three articles. The first declared that the Reform of St. Teresa should be maintained and fostered, the second that the Discalced and Mitigated should not live together promiscuously, and the third, that the local Superiors of the Discalced were to be taken from among themselves alone. It was probably felt that the Nuncio had not the power to create a separate Province, or that, if he did so, the measure might afterwards be revoked. So the King was asked to use his intercession with the Holy Father for the creation of a separate Province of the Discalced alone. Thus St. Teresa gained the well founded hope that all for which she had striven and suffered so long would be granted to her, and the affairs of the Reform were placed on a better footing than even in the time of the Nuncio Ormaneto.

The result was, no doubt, mainly attained by the prayers and austerities of St. Teresa, her nuns, and the friars of the Reform, and their many pious friends. But when we look back on the history from a distance, it will hardly seem wonderful that the Saint whose life we are considering should have been so full of confidence to the last, even putting aside any preternatural communications which she may have received in prayer. The triumph of a good and reasonable cause is often secured by the momentary success of its enemies, who push matters to extremities. Nor must we leave out of sight the immense activity of Teresa and others in bringing the true state of the case before the King, as the person at once most able and most likely to be prevailed upon to help and protect them. The numberless letters of St. Teresa to great people, including some to the King himself, are lost, and we are thus inclined to forget the influence which was thus exercised in favour of the Reform.

It was at this time also, that another saintly soul among the Carmelite nuns became very prominent in the struggle of the Discalced for life. This was Anne of Jesus, now the Prioress at Veas, of whom we have already had to speak more than once. The

reader will remember that when Anne de Lobera
applied through her confessor for admission into the
new Carmel, St. Teresa wrote to say she welcomed
her rather as a companion and coadjutor in her work
than as an ordinary novice.[1]   The words were indeed
prophetic, and to some who knew both of these great
souls best, it seemed as if there were scarcely any
difference between Teresa and Anne.   Anne had
been first Mistress of Novices—before her own profession—at Salamanca, and she had formed her new
community at Veas in the perfect spirit of Teresa
herself.   Teresa was now drawing near to the close
of her glorious labours, and Anne was to be provi-
dentially brought forward as if to supply her place
when the time came for her to pass to her reward.
Teresa had, whenever she had the opportunity,
chosen out Anne as her particular confidant, and
even made her live in the same cell as herself.   It
is said that when the last great alarm came over the
Reform in consequence of the measures of the Nuncio
Sega, Teresa had written to Anne to ask her advice,
as was her constant practice, and that, after a fortnight spent in prayer and penance, Anne had
counselled the recourse to the King which was
finally made.   She exerted herself most energetically
in influencing all the great persons in the kingdom
to whom she was known, and had perhaps nearly
as great a part in the ultimate decision of Philip as
her great Mother in Religion.

The biographer of Anne of Jesus gives us a
most characteristic letter of hers, written before that

[1] See vol. i. p. 434.

change of mind on the part of the Nuncio which was the beginning of better things to the Reform. Mgr. Sega, as has been said, had placed the Discalced friars and nuns under the authorities of the Mitigation, and the visitations made by these last were the cause of extreme disturbance and misery to the Religious. The Mitigated Provincial of Castile seems to have fallen into the same mistake with St. Teresa herself, who had made the foundation at Veas without discovering that the town belonged to Andalusia. He had visited other convents, and wrote from Malagon to Anne of Jesus that he proposed to come next to Veas. She, he said, was the chief among the Prioresses,[1] and he should be delighted to see her, as well as all the others, return to the " parent stock," meaning the Mitigated. Doña Teresa de Ahumada and her adherents were to be considered as branches broken off, and it was most desirable that all Carmelites should be united in their sentiments and the same manner of life.

The letter of which we speak takes up the Provincial's words very cleverly.

May Jesus be with your Paternity [says Anne], and may He make you understand that you have done wrong in accusing us Discalced Carmelites of having separated ourselves from the stock. Our parent stock [she says] is Jesus Christ, our sovereign good. We have consecrated ourselves to Him, and we would give a thousand lives, if we had them, rather than leave Him. There is also a second stock on which our holy Religion is founded, that is our holy Father Elias. What has our Mother foundress,

---

[1] " La Capitana de las Prioras."

C 3

Teresa of Jesus, done? Desiring to unite herself most closely to the parent stock, inflamed with the desire of serving Jesus Christ, and supernaturally enlightened by His Divine Majesty, she cast her eye on this second stock, our father St. Elias, and seeing that she could not emulate him in his robe of camel skin, she cast aside fine cloth and stuff, to use rough and coarse serge, and then went on to approach as nearly as she could to her stock and father, Elias, by imitating his fasting, his retirement from the world, his penance, and his prayer. That is what we all of us are doing, and we would lose a thousand lives, rather than separate ourselves from this second stock. In my opinion, it is not we, but you, Reverend Father, and the other Calced Carmelites, that have separated yourselves from your stock, that is, your father St. Elias. For I see you wear fine habits, that you avoid solitude in order to see company, and that, instead of the continual prayer which is made so strict a law by our holy Rule, you occupy your minds on all that can distract you, and thus it is that you separate yourselves from Jesus Christ, Who is our principal and parent stock. For the rest, I take the liberty to remark to your Reverence that our convent belongs, not to Castile, but to Andalusia, and that, as your Paternity has no juris-diction out of Castile, you have nothing to do with us. Therefore, my Father, do not put yourself to any trouble to visit us. It would be a useless labour, for we do not recognize you as our Superior.[1]

It is not wonderful that after such a letter, the good Provincial did not present himself at Veas. Nor indeed, we are told, did his colleague of Andalusia. The date of the letter is not given by the author from whom we take it. Probably it was

[1] *Vie de la Mère Anne de Jesus.* Par le R. P. Berthold-Ignace de Ste. Anne. Malines: H. Dessain, 1876, vol. i. p. 250.

not written long before the new order of things began, when the Discalced were set free from the Superiors of the Mitigation. The whole letter breathes a confidence in the speedy termination of the trouble, which shows us how entirely its writer shared the feelings of St. Teresa herself.

Before that dawn of happier hopes for the Reform which was the immediate consequence of the change of mind in the Nuncio Sega, Teresa had set herself to work to renew the preparation for that mission of some representatives of the Discalced Carmelites to Rome of which we have already spoken. The mission had once been tried already, and failed. It will be remembered that at the unfortunate Chapter of Almodovar, which had provoked so much the resentment of the Nuncio, two friars had been appointed for this purpose, Father Pedro of the Angels and Father Juan of St. James. Their mission came to a disastrous end. As soon as they arrived at Naples on their way to Rome, Father Pedro ruined the whole project. Rossi, the General with whom St. Teresa had so often dealt, had lately died, and Father Caffardi, the Vicar appointed to discharge his office until the election of a new General, chanced to be in Naples. The simple Father Pedro thought that he might settle the whole affair with him, and thus save himself and his companion the trouble of a long negotiation with the Pope and the Cardinals. Without consulting his companion, he went to Father Caffardi and laid the whole case before him. Caffardi received him with great personal kindness. But he seized the opportunity before him without a moment

of scruple or of delay. He asked for all the papers
which Father Pedro had with him on the subject of
the mission with which he was charged, and they
were at once surrendered, never to be returned.

The Viceroy of Naples was Inigo Hurtado de
Mendoza, Marquis of Mondejar, who was the father
of the Conde de Tendiglia, the great friend of
the Discalced Friars. It does not appear that
the Marquis had any hostile intention towards the
Reform of which his son was so conspicuous a
defender. But he killed the religious spirit in Father
Pedro by his too great kindness. He took the two
friars into his own palace, while they waited at
Naples for fresh instructions from Spain. They
were treated with a magnificent hospitality, and a
number of servants waited on their every want.
Father Juan of St. James was intensely disgusted
with a kind of life so unlike that which they professed. But Father Pedro was overcome by the
comforts and comparative luxury of the palace. He
went on to Rome at last, but only to lose all his
labour, and the cause of the Discalced found no
support. He returned to Spain after a time, but
only to lay aside the habit of the Reform, as, it is
said, St. John of the Cross had foretold to him when
he was appointed to his mission, and died three years
after this time at Granada in the monastery of the
Mitigation. Anne of Jesus was at that time Prioress
of the newly founded convent of the Reform in that
city. He had sold the cloak which he had worn as
a Discalced friar, and Anne had bought it of the
purchaser, sending at the same time a message to

Father Pedro to look to his soul, as he was soon to die. He was struck by the message, and often asked to see her, but she constantly refused. One day, full of contrition, he entered the church of the convent, the door being accidentally open, and threw himself upon his knees to pray. He wept himself quite blind, and died a few days afterwards. It appears that Anne knew that it was to be so, and that her warnings and refusals to see him had been meant to make him enter into himself.

At the time of which we are writing, Teresa's exertions for the mission to Rome were more successful. She suggested that Father Juan de Jesus Roca, Prior of Mancera, should be the delegate, and her advice was followed, although Gratian is said to have resisted it. Father Diego of the Most Holy Trinity was allotted to Juan de Jesus as his companion, and they appear to have sailed from Alicante in the May of 1579, while the deliberations of the Commissaries appointed to assist the Nuncio were still going on. It was a dangerous mission. They might be stopped even before leaving Spain, as travelling without leave of their Superiors, by some of the Mitigation. They must have money for the journey, and they would need introductions and letters of recommendation from great personages in Spain to others in Italy whose aid they might need. All was provided speedily by Teresa and Anne of Jesus, whom the Saint consulted on this and on all other such matters. Anne of Jesus consulted theologians at Salamanca and at Alcala, who were unanimously of opinion that the general good of religion was a sufficient reason to justify a religious man in assuming the dress of a secular. Thus a possible scruple of conscience was avoided.

But a great deal more than this was required. The Conde de Tendiglia gave four hundred gold pieces towards the expenses, and also furnished letters of commendation to his father, the Viceroy at Naples. Anne of Jesus raised another sum equal to that given by the Count, by requesting the father of one of her novices to advance so much out of her dowry. Other convents contributed also, and Father Nicolas Doria gave a sum of eight thousand reals. Letters were also promised from the King and other great people. A friend of the Reform, Francisco Bracamante of Avila, furnished clothes and other things necessary that they might travel as secular gentlemen, and, to complete the disguise of the real object in view, made them his procurators to obtain at Rome for him a dispensation to marry one of his cousins. Teresa sent them to Veas on their road to the coast, that Anne might encourage them. They left her in high spirits, and with some of her gold pieces carefully sewn by her own hands into their garments.

It seems to have been on this occasion that St. Teresa wrote a joyous and grateful letter to Anne of Jesus, the language of which has seemed somewhat exaggerated and unlike her usual to the latest and most judicious editor of her works in Spain, who has therefore printed the letter, or rather the fragment, with a warning to his readers that it appears to him suspicious.

My daughter and my crown, I cannot enough thank God for the favour which He has done to me in bringing me your Reverence to this Order. It is as He did to the children of Israel, when He delivered them from Egypt. His Majesty provided them with a pillar which guided them, gave them light by night and by day shielded them from the sun, so it seems that He has done with our Order, and that your Reverence, my daughter, is this pillar which guides us and gives us light and defends us. Very judicious indeed has been all that your Reverence has done with those Fathers of ours, and it seems certain that God is in your soul, since you do all that you do with so much grace and success. May our Lord recompense you, for Whom you have done it, and grant the good issue which is fitting to all this business.[1]

It is very true that St. Teresa does not often speak in this way. But Anne of Jesus was a person whom she regarded as a second self in the affairs of the Order, and on this occasion she had shown an energy, a skill, and a devotion to the good cause which it was impossible to over-estimate or to praise too highly. Most unfortunately, we are deprived of the best evidence as to the authenticity of the letter, at least on internal grounds, from the fact that at a moment of danger St. Teresa had written to Anne to destroy all her letters to her. This fragment, therefore, which has escaped, cannot be compared with other letters addressed to her by Teresa. If the series had survived, they would probably have

---

[1] Letter ccxxvii. The expression, "hija mia e corona mia," is Scriptural, and there was no one in the Carmelite Order of whom it could be more fitly used by St. Teresa than Anne of Jesus (Philipp. iv. i. ; I Thess. ii. 19).

been almost a greater treasure to us than all the rest of her correspondence put together.

But we must not forget other letters of St. Teresa which belong to this period, and which we have passed over for the sake of putting the whole history consecutively. There are, however, a few important letters which belong to the interval between St. Teresa's letter to Father Henandez in October, 1578, and the appointment of the "assessors" to the Nuncio at the beginning of the next year. The first of these is to Father Gratian, and is dated from Avila, October 15th.[1] St. Teresa speaks with tender feeling of the death of the General Rossi, of which she had just heard. For the first day, she says, she could do nothing but weep. *Llorar que llorarás, sin poder hacer otra cosa,* and she thought of the great trouble they had given him, which certainly he did not deserve. He would have been all kindness, if they had dealt with him directly. We may remember how much she had tried to get the Fathers of the Reform to write to him, instead of acting solely upon the authority of the Nuncio. "May God forgive those who had always prevented it." Gratian had not let her influence him. God will turn all to good, but certainly she feels as she says, and also what he (Gratian) has had to suffer, for his last letters have been like "draughts of death." She blames, in her quiet way, the false step that had been taken in handing in the papers of his Visitation to the Council of Castile, instead of giving them to the Nuncio who had asked for them. It must have been counselled

[1] Letter ccxv.

by some one who has no care about what Gratian has to suffer. She has had enough experience of the bad policy of conducting matters of this sort violently and "against the stream." Then she is very much against the plan of sending friars to Rome under present circumstances, especially since the General's death, and she gives good reasons why. She even wishes a messenger to be sent to Almodovar, to stop the execution of the project, if Gratian and Mariano agree. It seems to have been too late, and we know the unfortunate issue of the mission. She fears that the line the Discalced Friars are now taking will only end in further sufferings to themselves. She says in conclusion that she was much pleased that they should not elect a Provincial, although Fra Antonio had told her they could not refrain from it without sin.[1]

This next letter on our list is a mere fragment, but like many of these fragments, it seems to have been preserved on account of the importance of its contents. It is undated, but seems certainly to belong to the time when Father Gratian, to whom it is addressed, was in "prison," that is, confined to one place, and (probably) not allowed to preach. Its object is to strengthen and console him, and it is

[1] "Harto me he holgado no hagan Provincial, que, segun lo que vuestra paternidad dice, es muy acertado, aunque, como me digo Fray Antonio, que so pena de pecar, no podia hacer otra coso ; no le contradije." It would seem from this that Gratian was opposed to the election of a Provincial, as well as Fathers Doria and Roca, and St. John of the Cross. Father Roca was put into "punishment" for a month because he opposed it. Gratian was certainly punished by the Nuncio for his part in the Chapter, but he may still have opposed the nomination of a Provincial.

very plain that he was either thinking himself of
leaving the Order, or had been urged to do so by
his friends. "May God give him," says St. Teresa,
"fortitude to remain firm in justice, although he find
himself in great troubles." She is not surprised that
those who love him wish to see him free from them,
and seek means for this: though it could not be well
to leave the Blessed Virgin in a time of such need.
She ventures to say that his mother would not give
such counsel, nor consent to such a change. "God
deliver us! It would be, not to avoid troubles, but
to put ourselves into them. Those we have now will
soon be over, with the love of God, while those we
might have by a change of Order would last all
our life." She goes on to urge him not to accept
the office of Visitor again, even if the Nuncio orders
it.[1]

If we rightly understand this fragment, there
would seem to have been some thought on Gratian's
part of retiring from the Order—at least he had
received the suggestion. There are many curious
facts about his history, and this is hardly the place
for discussing all the questions that may be raised
concerning him. But it might throw light upon
some of the obscure points if the fact here hinted
at could be ascertained. As it is, we can only be
sure that the proposal had been made, but St. Teresa's
manner of speaking does not lead us to understand that Gratian had shown any inclination to
accept it.

There are two letters[2] to Father Ambrose

---

[1] Letter ccxvi.   [2] Letters ccxvii. ccxviii.

Mariano a little later—in November, 1578. He was in Madrid, with the Calced Friars, and the letters are chiefly notes of caution. He is to remember that all his words are counted. There are two more[1] to their staunch friend, Roque Huerta, complaining of the extortions of the Calced Friars when the Nuncio's Brief was notified to the nuns of St. Joseph at Avila, and on the subject of the separate Province. In one of them she mentions a report that she was to be moved to another convent. "If it was one of theirs (the Mitigation), how much worse a life would she have to lead than St. John of the Cross! Perhaps they will send her an order of excommunication! But she does not merit so much suffering." Another letter, in December, consoles Doña Maria Dantisco on the sufferings of her son. She tells her that she knows he has long made it a special prayer that he may have great crosses to bear.

We now come to a long and beautiful letter to Father Gonzalo Davila, her confessor, as it appears, while at Avila, the date of which is uncertain, as is that of many of these fragments, and which is placed by some writers as early as May, 1578. Happily the date is of little importance. The letter contains a reference to a certain "fountain" for the College of the Fathers, about which they wished to have a visit of Fra Mariano, which seems to fix the date in the summer or autumn of 1578.

It is an answer to a request of Father Davila for some instruction on the manner of preserving recollection in the midst of great occupations.

[1] Letters ccxix. ccxx.

Father Davila was then Rector of the College at Avila.

The letter is as follows :

JESUS

Be with your honour! It is some time since I have had a mortification like that which the letter of your honour gives me to-day. I am not so humble as to wish to pass for one so proud. And your honour ought not to seek to show your own humility at such a cost to me. I never had a letter from your honour which I thought of tearing up so readily! I tell you that you know well how to mortify me and make me understand what I am, since it seems to your honour that I think I can myself teach others. God deliver me from it! I shouldn't like even to think of it.

But I see that the fault is mine, though I do not know whether it is not rather that I desire so much to see your honour well, and this weakness may be the cause of the foolish things I say to your honour, and the affection I bear to you, which makes me talk so freely, without thinking what I say. I sometimes even have a scruple about some things I talk of with your honour. If it was not the fear of being disobedient, I should not answer what you tell me, since it causes me great repugnance. May God accept it. Amen.

One of my great faults is to judge from myself in these matters of prayer. Your honour must not make any account of what I may say. God will give you greater light than a poor little woman like myself. When I consider the grace that God gives me of always keeping actually in His presence, and on the other hand, the great number of matters which I have to attend to and which must pass through my hands, there are no persecutions and troubles which disturb me so much. If it is a business which must be despatched by me, it has happened to me, and this very often, to go to bed at one or two in the morning, or even later, in order that my soul may not then be obliged to give itself to other cares, but to that which God makes constantly present to me. This has done my health much harm, and so it must be a temptation, though it seems to me that greater liberty of soul is the result. It is as if one had an affair of great importance and necessity, and got to the end of other matters quicker, in order that they may not hinder him from attending to what was most necessary. So I am very glad when I can leave matters to the Sisters, even though in a certain way they might be done better by myself. As this is not done with a bad motive, His Majesty supplies what is wanting, and I find I make evidently greater progress, the more I take pains to withdraw myself from business. Though I see this clearly, I am often negligent in taking pains about this, and certainly, I feel the loss, and see that I might be more and more diligent in the matter, and that it would be better for me.

This is not to be understood of grave matters which cannot be avoided, and in this also there may be a fault of mine. Your occupations are of this kind, and it would not be good to leave them in the power of other persons. So I think, but as I see your honour's health suffering, I could wish you had less to burthen you. Certainly it makes me praise our Lord when I see how seriously you take the business of your house. I am not so silly as not to see the great grace which our Lord gives you in this talent for business, and the great merit that it is. It fills me with envy, and I should like to have such a Superior. And as God gives you to my soul in this way, I could wish you to take as much care of it as you do of the fountain you mention. I am very glad to hear of it, as it is so necessary for the College, and whatever trouble your honour takes about it, the cause deserves it.

I have nothing more to say. I am sure I say the whole

truth to you, as if to God. I understand that all that is
done for the sake of discharging well the office of Superior
is so pleasing to Him, that when this is done He will give
in a short time what He might else take long to give. I
know it by experience, as I have said. Seeing your honour
so continually occupied, I thought in a general way what I
said to you, and the more I think of it, the more I see the
difference, as I say, between your honour and myself. I
shall take care in future not to utter my first thoughts, since
it costs me so much. When I see your honour in better
health, my temptation to check you will cease. May our
Lord make you better, as He can, and as I desire !

Your honour's servant,

TERESA DE JESUS.[1]

We have next two fragments which are taken
from letters to Veas, the one to the community, the
other to the Prioress, Anne of Jesus. They both
relate to the spiritual treasure which that convent
possessed in the presence of St. John of the Cross,
who paid them a visit on his way to the Monastery
of Mount Calvary, of which he was made Superior
after the Chapter of Almodovar, and became their
confessor. The last fragment was quoted by one
of the nuns in the Information for the Beatification
of St. John. The Prioress had made some complaint,
and St. Teresa tells her she is amused and surprised
that she can complain of anything when she has
St. John of the Cross with her, "a heavenly and
divine man. I can tell my daughter that since he
went there, there has not been in the whole of Castile
another like him, who kindles such fervour in the

[1] Letter ccxxii.

path to Heaven. You can't conceive how lonely I am without him. You must understand that you have a great treasure in having him there. All in the house should talk with him, and open the state of their souls to him. You will see what profit will follow, and you will get on very far in all that relates to spirit and perfection, for our Lord has given him a particular grace for this."[1]

She says much the same in the fewest possible words to Anne of St. Albert, the foundress of Caravaca,[2] in the two fragments which remain. The next is the short note to Anne of Jesus, which we have already quoted.[3] The next fragment is without date and address, but it is supposed to be an exhortation to Mary of St. Joseph, the Prioress of Seville, to be very patient during the troubles of her convent, and it seems particularly to refer to what she had to suffer from the priest, Garcia Alvarez. We shall have more to say of him presently, and the contents of this note will help us to understand St. Teresa's attitude towards him. Gratitude was one of her favourite virtues, as it seems to be of her spiritual children. " God cannot bear our showing ingratitude to one who has done us good. I remember when people tried to take us in about a house they were selling us, he showed us our mistake, and I can never forget the good he did to us, and the trouble from which he saved us, and I have always esteemed him a servant of God, and well intentioned. I know this is not a perfection of mine, being so grateful, it must

---

[1] Letters ccxxiii. ccxxiv.   [2] Letters ccxxv. ccxxvi.
[3] Letter ccxxvii.

be natural. If they gave me a sardine, they would bribe me!" This is another instance of the value of a fragment. The Spanish Editor thinks that Mary of St. Joseph may have destroyed the rest of the letter on purpose, because it may have spoken of the faults of the good Garcia Alvarez.[1]

Another fragment without date and address, but which, from internal evidence, belongs to this stage of the troubles of the Reform, is an answer to some ladies who had applied for admission into one of her convents. She is glad to hear of them, and their perseverance in their good intentions, it is a great grace, especially for those who are in "esa Babilonia" of the world, where all they hear tends rather to dissipation than to recollection. Her Order, she hears, for a year past and more, has been in such a state that it would give much pain to any one who did not understand how our Lord proceeds. But seeing that all tends to the purification of souls, and that our Lord will in the end favour His servants, she is not pained, but rather desires much that these troubles may increase, and praise God Who grants to them to suffer for the sake of justice. Let the ladies to whom she writes do the same, and trust in Him, and they will see their desires fulfilled when they do not think of it.

We pass over two other fragments,[2] which are both to Gratian, and do not sufficiently explain to what they refer.

---

[1] Letter ccxxviii.   [2] Letters ccxxx. ccxxxi.

NOTE TO CHAPTER I.

———

The letters mentioned in this chapter are as follows :

1. Letter of Anne of Jesus *to the Provincial of the Mitigated Friars in Castile.*

This letter is given in full at p. 17.

2. (ccxxvii.) Fragment of a letter *to Anne of Jesus.* Date uncertain.

Translated at p. 23.

3. (ccxv.) *To Father Jerome Gratian.* From Avila, October 15, 1578.

A full account of this letter is given at p. 24.

4. (ccxvi.) *To the same.* Undated.

This fragment is quoted at p. 26.

5. (ccxvii.) *To Father Ambrose Mariano,* at Madrid. From Avila, November, 1578.

6. (ccxviii.) *To the same.* From Avila, November, 1578.

These two short letters are mentioned at p. 26.

7. (ccxix.) *To Roque Huerta,* at Madrid. From Avila, end of December, 1578.

8. (ccxx.) *To the same.* Avila, December 28, 1578.

These two letters are mentioned at p. 27.

9. (ccxxi.) *To Doña Juana Dantisco.* Avila, December 28, 1578.

Mentioned at p. 27.

10. (ccxxii.) *To Father Gonzalo Davila, of the Society of Jesus,* at Avila. Avila, 1578. Uncertain date.

This letter is translated at pp. 28—30.

11. (ccxxiii.) *To the Prioress and Community at Veas.* Apparently towards the end of 1578.

12. (ccxxiv.) *To Anne of Jesus, Prioress of Veas.* Same date.

These two fragments are mentioned at p. 30.

13. (ccxxv.) *To Anne of St. Albert, Foundress at Caravaca.*

D 3

14. (ccxxvi.) *To the same.*

Two small fragments, mentioned at p. 31.

15. (ccxxvii.) *To Anne of Jesus, Prioress of Veas.* Date lost. A remarkable fragment, though suspected by some.

This fragment has been quoted before in this chapter, p. 23. It is doubted, but mainly on account of the warmth of its language, by Don Vicente de la Fuente, the great authority on the letters of St. Teresa. But in addition to what has been already said in explanation in the text, it may be remarked that St. Teresa is said to have had a vision of the drowning of the Egyptians in the Red Sea, and the preservation of the Israelites, which she understood to represent the crisis in the history of her Reform of which she is speaking in this fragment. This vision is related in the *Vita de St. Teresa* of Father Frederic of St. Antony, iv. 399. If she had this in her mind, the language of St. Teresa here is easily intelligible. See also Letters lxxvi. lxxvii. vol. ii. p. 279. She was, in truth, constantly using the imagery of this fragment.

16. (ccxxviii.) *To Mary of St. Joseph, Prioress at Seville* (in 1578).

This fragment is quoted at p. 32.

17. (ccxxix.) *To some ladies desirous of receiving the habit of Carmel.* Uncertain date.

Quoted at p. 32.

18. (ccxxx.) *To Father Jerome Gratian.* End of 1578 or beginning of 1579.

19. (ccxxxi.) *To the same.* Date uncertain. P. 32.

Two fragments, perhaps taken from more than one letter each.

CHAPTER II.

Troubles at Seville.

ONE cause of heavy anxiety to St. Teresa during this time was the convent at Seville, which was under great persecution. This convent was very dear to her, and it had certainly from the very beginning cost her a large portion of suffering. We have had to speak of this in the last volume, the letters in which tell but an imperfect tale of the whole trial which she had to go through. The convent was hardly ever without trouble from without or from within, and that of which we are now to speak had become serious long before the time which has now been reached. Although we have had a good many letters of St. Teresa addressed to the Prioress, Mary of St. Joseph, the correspondence is not complete enough to give us the full information which we might desire. We must go back almost to the beginnings of the convent to give a full account of the troubles which reached their height at the time of which we now speak.

After St. Teresa left Seville in May, 1575, it appears that an inexperienced and unlearned confessor—who seems to have been none other than the good Garcia Alvarez, already well known to

us[1]—was allowed to hear confessions in the convent.
He became very intimate with some of the young
novices—some of those, it seems, who had entered since
St. Teresa left—and spent long hours daily in hearing
their confessions and conversing with them in the
confessional. The Prioress was aware of the danger,
and after three or four months began to interfere to
put an end to it. The consequence was that either
the priest in question, or the nuns who had been so
devoted to him, or their friends, or the enemies of
the Reform, who were numerous and powerful in the
city, filled Seville with strange tales against her,
injuring her character to such an extent that no one
trusted her, and she could hardly get a confessor for
herself. St. Teresa was informed of it all by her,
and she induced her old friend, Father Hernandez
the Dominican, to help her, as well as Father Nicolas
Doria, who was not yet at that time a Carmelite.
The result was that the confessor was dismissed.

This was not done, however, without much reluctance on the part of St. Teresa, and, indeed, of the
others. They all felt the great obligation under which
the convent lay to the priest in question. But there

---

[1] No one else is named, and this seems the most probable account
of the story. One of the nuns who became so intimate with him was
the first novice, the same Sister Beatrix who has been so highly spoken
of by St. Teresa. See vol. ii. of this work, pp. 248—251, and again
p. 261 (as to Garcia Alvarez), and p. 269. We find St. Teresa, in
March and April, 1577, speaking against the communication of matters
of prayer—it would seem, to this confessor, except in the cases of
certain nuns of whom she felt sure (Letters cl. cliii.). But she was met
by the authority of something that Father Gratian had said on the
subject, and so recalled her injunction. She was particularly firm
against having those matters written down.

were many elements in the situation which made it
extremely critical. The Andalusians were an inflam-
mable race. They did not like the convent which had
been intruded upon them by "strangers" from Castile.
There were all the griefs of the Mitigated Friars which
had been so long brooding in their minds—the young
Visitor who had been put over them, as they thought,
by Court favour, without having ever been a subject
since his noviceship—and now the personal injury to a
respected priest of Seville, who had been forbidden to
hear confessions in the convent. Nothing but the
most consummate prudence could avoid an outbreak,
and certainly not all the Reformed Carmelites had
the prudence of Teresa. So matters appear to have
been until the time when, by order of the Nuncio,
the monasteries and convents of the Reform were
made subject to the Friars of the Mitigation.

The Provincial of the Mitigation in Andalusia
did not like Mary of St. Joseph, who was a loyal
subject of St. Teresa and of Father Gratian. The
banished confessor was immediately reinstated. Now
came his time for revenge, if he sought it. At all
events, the two nuns who were so devoted to him
were either persuaded, or, perhaps, deluded into re-
viving the calumnies against the Prioress, as well as
extending the charges to others, and even to Father
Gratian and to St. Teresa herself. The accusations were made before the Holy Office, the nuns
were examined for hours together, and the whole
city was filled with the scandal. When St. Teresa
heard of it she said, "If they are to lie, let them
do so in such a way that no one will believe what

they say." The charges, whoever may have been the original author of them, were of the very worst character. The Prioress, Mary of St. Joseph, was deposed, and a young nun, who was a partisan against her, put in her place as Vicaress. The nuns were all in alarm lest they should be committed to the prisons of the Inquisition.

All power being now in the hands of hostile persons, it was not possible for St. Teresa and the nuns to communicate by letters in the ordinary way. But she could not bear to leave them unaided, and we find her writing early in the year 1579, three months or so after the decree of the Nuncio, to her friend the Prior of the Carthusians at Seville, hoping through his means to get a letter at least read to the nuns. We may give an account of her letter to the Prior, as well as that which she enclosed for the nuns themselves. The letter is dated January 31, 1579.[1]

Teresa begins by asking the Prior what he thinks of the affairs of the Convent of the glorious St. Joseph, and how they have treated and are treating his children there. They have long been suffering spiritual troubles and vexations from those who ought to comfort them. Her opinion is that if they have been asking for crosses, God has certainly satisfied them. Blessed be His Name for ever! She feels little pain for those of them whom she had taken with her to Seville—sometimes she is full of gladness, because they must gain so much by the war waged against them by the devil. But she is troubled for those who have entered since, because,.

[1] Letter ccxxxii.

at the time when they ought to be gaining peace and becoming familiar with the spirit of the Order, they are disturbed and upset, and thus much damage may be done to their souls, as yet new to religious life.

She says that she had urged the Prioress to communicate all her sufferings to his Paternity, but she seems not to have had the courage to do so. She herself would find great consolation if she could talk with him openly, but she does not dare to commit what she has to say to paper, nor would she write so much as she has, if it were not that she had a most faithful carrier for her letter. This was a lad in search of a place, if his Paternity knew any one who could help him. He was a native of Avila, unable to reside there on account of the severity of the climate. He had been servant to a canon, a friend of hers, who assures her that he is virtuous and faithful, can write well and keep accounts. She implores the Prior, if he can, to do her this favour for the love of God, and to be his security if he gets a place, as she is sure her informant would have told her nothing of him that was not true. She was pleased when the application was made to her, as it gave her an occasion of writing to his Paternity.

She asks him to arrange that the ex-Prioress (Mary of St. Joseph), and the other nuns she had brought from Castile, may read the letter she sends them. His Paternity probably knows that Mary has been deprived of her office, a new Superior appointed, —one of those lately entered,—and other harsh measures inflicted on her, one of which was that all Teresa's letters to her had been sent to the Nuncio. The poor nuns had no one to give them counsel. All her learned friends at Avila are astonished at the things the nuns have been made to do under pain of excommunication. She fears that they have burthened their consciences very much in the examination, without meaning it, of course. But there are things in the Process which she knows to be enormous falsehoods. She was there herself at the time referred to, and nothing of what is said occurred. But she is not surprised at the faults into which they have fallen, as one nun was six hours under examination, and some were of such poor intelligence as to sign whatever was required. The nuns at Avila had learnt that lesson, at least, to see what they signed, and so there was nothing against them.[1] Our Lord, she says, has tried them in every way, for a year and a half. But she is most confident that He will take the part of His servants, friars and nuns, and that all the entanglements which the devil has contrived in that house will be exposed to light. St. Joseph will bring out the truth in full clearness, what those nuns are who came from Castile, for as for the others, she does not know them. Only she knows that they are too much trusted by those who have to deal with them, which has been the cause of so many evils.

---

[1] " Hános acá aprovechado, para mirar lo que firmabamos, y así no ha habído qué decir." She refers, apparently, to the persecution that fell on the nuns of the Incarnation in consequence of her election, or on the nuns of St. Joseph's after the Nuncio's decree subjecting them to the " Mitigated " Friars.

She then implores his Paternity for the love of God not to desert them, but to help them in their tribulation by his prayers, for they depend entirely on God, and on earth they have no one with whom to find comfort. But His Majesty, Who knows them, will help them, and will give to his Paternity the charity to do the same. She sends her letter to them open, as perhaps they may have received a command to give any letter from her to the Provincial. In that case, she asks the Prior to see that some one reads the letter to them. It might give them some relief to see a letter of hers. People at Avila thought that the Provincial might make them leave the convent, and that the novices would wish to go with them. She sees that the devil does not want any Discalced Carmelites, friars or nuns, at Seville, but she trusts to the Lord that Satan will gain nothing of what he wants. His Paternity must see that he has been all in all in keeping them there, and now, when the need is greater, let him help the glorious St. Joseph. May His Divine Majesty preserve his Paternity for the relief of the poor (for she knows the charity that he has shown to the Discalced Friars) for many years with an ever increasing sanctity, for which she constantly prays. She adds a postscript that he can read the letter to the nuns if it does not weary him.

We may now proceed to give the letter to the nuns which the Prior was to read to them, himself or by deputy.[1]

---

[1] Letter ccxxxiii.

JESÙS.

The grace of the Holy Spirit be with your charity, my daughters and sisters. You must know that I never loved you so much as now, and that you have never had so great opportunity of serving our Lord as now, when He has given you the great boon of being able to taste somewhat of His Cross, and with some of that great dereliction which His Majesty experienced therein. Blessed the day when you came to that place, since so great good fortune awaited you there. Great envy I bear you, and it is the truth that when I was told of all the changes that have been made, all of which were most accurately related to me, and they that wanted to drive you from the house, and certain other particulars, instead of its causing me pain, it gave me great interior joy to see that, without your having to pass across the sea, our Lord has been pleased to open to you His mines of eternal treasures, by which I trust in His Majesty you will gain great riches, and give some share of them to us who are here. I have great confidence in His mercy that He will grant you the favour to bear all without offending Him in anything. That it gives you so much pain must not afflict you, for our Lord may wish to make you understand that you were not so strong as you thought when you were so desirous of suffering.

Courage, courage, my children! Remember that God gives no one more trouble than he is able to suffer, and that His Majesty Himself is with those in tribulation. Since this is certain, we must not fear, we must trust in His mercy, which will bring to light the truth in all this matter, and we shall see discovered certain plots which the devil has kept hidden in order to upset everything. It is this which caused me more pain than what has passed. Prayer, prayer, my Sisters! And for the present let humility and obedience shine forth brightly, and in these let no one

surpass your charities in dealing with the Vicaress whom
they have appointed, and especially the former Mother
Prioress. Oh, what a good time you have now for gathering the
fruit of the resolutions which you have made of serving our
Lord! Remember that He often desires to test whether
our deeds are conformable to our intentions and our words.
Give a generous help to the daughters of the Virgin and
your own Sisters in this great persecution, and then, if you
help one another, the good Jesus will help also, for if He
now sleeps on the sea, when the tempest increases He will
make the winds to cease. He desires that we should pray
to Him, and He loves us so much that He is always
seeking in what He may profit us. Blessed be His Name
for ever. Amen, Amen, Amen.

In all these houses they are commending you much to
God, and so I hope in His goodness that He will soon
remedy everything. Be careful therefore always to be
cheerful and gay, and to reflect that, all things well considered, all is very little that we suffer for so good a God,
Who has suffered so much for us, and that as yet we have
not come to shedding our blood for Him. You are among
your Sisters, and not in Algiers. Leave your Spouse to act,
and you will see how before long the sea will swallow up
our enemies, as was the case with King Pharao, and leave
God's people free, and all desirous to suffer again, finding
that they have gained so much from the past. I received
your letter, and I wish you had not burnt what you had
written, for it might have been of use. You might have
excused yourselves from giving up my letters, as the learned
men here say, but there was little in them. Might it have
pleased His Divine Majesty that all the faults might have
been laid to me! But I have felt very much for the pain of
those who have had to suffer without any fault. What has
given me much pain has been that, in the Process of
Information made at Seville by the Father Provincial,

there were some things which I know were great falsehoods, because I was there at the time spoken of. For love of our Lord be very careful, lest out of fear or worry any one may have saïd it. For as long as there is no offence to God, the whole matter is nothing : but when there was a question of a lie, and especially in prejudice of another, it caused me great compassion, although I cannot believe it, for all know the purity and virtue with which Father Master Gratian behaved to all of us, and the great use and aid which he has been to us in advancing in the service of our Lord. And since this is so, even if the things be of light moment, it is a great fault to impute them to him. For charity's sake, admonish those Sisters of this, and now remain in peace, with the blessing of the Most Holy Trinity, and under His protection and guard. Amen.

All the Sisters here commend themselves to you very much. They hope that when all these clouds are passed, Sister St. Francis will be able to relate all that has happened. I commend myself to my good Gabriel, and I beg her to be content and happy. I have very present to me the affliction she must have been in at seeing Mother St. Joseph so treated. I have no compassion for Sister St. Jerome, if her desires of suffering are true—if not, I should pity her more than all.

To-morrow is Candlemas Eve. I would much rather talk than write to Señor Garcia Alvarez, and as I cannot say what I should like by letter, I do not write to his honour. Commend me to the other Sisters to whom you are not afraid to speak of this letter.

The unworthy servant of your charities,

TERESA DE JESUS.

St. Teresa speaks with her accustomed calm moderation of those of whom she has to complain. But it is clear that she was aware that some very

foul charges had been made against Gratian, and
though she does not mention it, it is clear that she
knew that she herself had been mixed up, as well
as Mary of St. Joseph. The next letter that we
shall 'quote is enough to show how very serious the
charges were. The two nuns, Beatrix and Margaret,
seem afterwards to have come to a better mind. It is
not quite clear at what time a change was made for
the better in the convent itself, by the substitution
of Isabella of St. Jerome, one of Teresa's companions
when she made the foundation, for the young nun
who had been appointed Vicaress. The affair was
evoked to the Royal Council, and a thorough investigation of the charges was made. Father Nicolas
Doria was the chief agent on the part of the nuns.
We shall speak of the result at the end of this
chapter.

We have another most interesting letter from
St. Teresa to the convent at Seville, written after the
cessation of the persecution, but before the final
sentence on the matter, of which we have spoken,
was given. It is addressed to Isabel of St. Jerome,
and Mary of St. Joseph. Isabel, as we have said, had
now been placed provisionally in the office of Prioress,
instead of the young Religious of whom so much use
had been made by the enemies of the Reform and
the lately deposed Prioress, who was not as yet
reinstated, and who, in fact, made great objections
to resuming her place. Things were safe in the hands
of the nuns from Malagon whom St. Teresa had
brought to Seville. The letter speaks in the singular
number, and seems to be chiefly addressed to Mary

of St. Joseph.   It is dated on the feast of the Invention of the Cross, the 3rd of May.[1]

The grace of the Holy Spirit be with your Reverence,
my dear daughter.   I received your letter and that of my
Sisters the day before yesterday.   Jesus ! what a consolation it would be to me to find myself in your house now !
and so it would also have been before, that I might have
a share in the treasures which our Lord has given you in
such abundance.   May He be blessed for ever.   Amen.

The love which I always had for you has been increased
and doubled, great as it was, and to your Reverence
especially, who has been the one to suffer the most.   But
be quite sure that when I heard that they had taken away
your vote and your office, I was particularly glad because,
although I know my child Joseph is a very poor creature,
I am convinced that she has the fear of God, and would
never have done anything to offend His Majesty, so as to
deserve such a punishment.

I wrote one letter to you through my Father the Prior
of Las Cuevas, that he might give orders that it might be
given to you.   I should like to know if his Paternity
received it.

Some of the sentences which follow are not
perfectly clear, because we do not know all that had
passed.   One letter had been torn up by Father
Nicolas (Doria), because, it appears, a letter of his
brother's had been intercepted.   Then Garcia Alvarez
is mentioned as having been much deceived.[2]   He
does not say Mass for the nuns any more, by the
Archbishop's command, who has refused to allow it
again, although the Prior of Las Cuevas and Father

---

[1] Letter ccxl.   [2] The word used is *engañado*.

Mariano had entreated it. Mariano also has given Teresa pain by " thinking that such things could be thought of in the convent, much more practised." If the charges made against Mary of St. Joseph were what they are stated to have been, St. Teresa may well have been annoyed that any one should think them even possible. However, the malice of the devil has been defeated, and our Lord is now, as she hopes, arranging that the truth may be known, which has not been the case hitherto. This has given her most pain, for when she saw the charges she knew they were false, having been herself on the spot at the time. But the two Sisters who had been led astray had said some very bad things, and she gives thanks to God that they had not said even worse.

The state of those two souls, she says, gives her great trouble, and she urges that a great many prayers should be made for them. She had feared something wrong since the time that Father Garcia Alvarez began doing as he did, and she had warned the Superior of it twice, mentioning the name of one of the nuns, as to whose spirit she had never felt satisfied, though she had been inclined to think it was a temptation on her own part that she had distrusted her. She had asked Gratian to take care about her, for he had a great deal to do with her.[1]

---

[1] Father Gratian had directed Beatrix to the Order. She had applied to him to hear her confession, but he only did so with difficulty, on account of her youth and beauty. He had told her that there would soon be Carmelite nuns in Seville, and that she should be received by them. It may be added, that she ended well, bitterly deploring the mischief she had caused.

She had considered her under illusion, and a person of weak imagination, just the sort of person for the devil to work upon, as he is very skilful in making his own profit out of the defects of our natural gifts and dispositions. He has succeeded, but we must not blame her so very much, but rather have great compassion upon her. She begs them therefore to have the charity to pay great attention to the directions she is about to give them, and also to give great thanks to God that He did not permit any one of themselves to be tempted in that violent manner. They are to think, as St. Augustine says, that we might all have done even worse things. They must take care not to lose the good opportunity which God has now given them, and remember what St. Catharine of Siena did when some one accused her of being a sinful woman.[1] " Let us fear, let us fear, my Sisters, if God takes away His protecting hand from us, what is the evil that we may not do?" The Sister of whom she speaks has not talent enough to invent all the things she has said, and so the devil managed to give her a companion to help and teach her. May God be with her!

Her first recommendation is that they will pray very earnestly and, if possible, continually—as the nuns who are with her at Avila will do—that God will grant them the favour that she may have light, and that the devil may let her wake up from the dream she is in. Teresa considers her out of herself.

---

[1] Teresa alludes to the calumny against St. Catharine by "Sister Andrea." See the excellent *History of St. Catharine of Siena*, by A. T. Drane, pp. 182, seq. (Edit. 1880).

There are many persons of weak imaginations,
though they are not found in her convents, who
think that they really see all that comes into their
minds, and the devil helps them to do this. This
poor Sister has been led to believe that she sees
everything that the devil thinks will bring destruction
on the convent. Thus she may not be so much to
blame as we suppose, any more than a mad person
is, when he takes it into his head that he is the
Eternal Father, and nothing can convince him to the
contrary. The Sisters must show their love to God
by their great compassion for her, as they would if
she were the own sister of each—and so she is, indeed,
for she is the child of the true Father of all, to Whom
they owe so much, and Whom this poor child had
desired to serve for all her life. Prayer, therefore,
my Sisters, prayer, my Sisters for her! Many saints
have fallen, and have recovered themselves again.
What has happened may have been necessary for her
humiliation, and if God gives her the grace to come
to a sane mind and retract what she has done, we
shall all have gained by the suffering, and she too,
perhaps, for God knows how to bring good out of
evil.

Her second advice is that they should not think
for the present of her leaving the convent. That
would be a great mistake, and by no means advisable.
While they were thinking of getting rid of danger,
they would be incurring it. Let some time pass, it is
not yet time for such a change, for many reasons, and
she wonders that the Superior does not see them. If
she reflects, God may show them to her. Let her

E 3

trust to God and those who have to think for the good of the house at leisure. For the present they should not speak of it or think of it, if they can help it. In the third place, let no sort of unkindness or want of affection be shown to her. Let the Superior especially be good to her, and let all treat her as Sisters and with affection. Each one is to think how she would wish to be treated if the case were her own. That soul must be in great suffering, though she does not show it, and the devil will pay her out for not having done more mischief. He may well make her do herself some harm so as to lose her senses or her soul, perhaps it has been near that already, and we must all think of that rather than of what she has done. Perhaps he made her think she was doing good to her own soul and serving God. Not a word is to be said about it before her mother, whom Teresa pities very much. She is surprised that no one has told her how she bears it all, what she says, and whether she knows what her daughter has been doing. She had desired to know this.[1] She fears lest the devil put new temptations into their minds, as that they are looked on hardly, or treated badly, and she would be much annoyed if there was any reason for it. She has been advised by the Fathers of the Society that it would seem bad to them if they were so treated. So let the Superior behave with the greatest prudence.

' The next thing she enjoins relates to the persons

---

[1] The nun who had helped her in spreading the calumny was Sister Margaret. The mother of Beatrix had also entered the convent, after the death of her husband. See vol. ii. p. 251.

with whom the nun is to talk and confess herself. A
third person is always to be present, who is to be on
her guard. No one is to hear her confession but a
Discalced Carmelite. The two are not to talk much
together. They are not to be treated severely, for
women are weak. They may be occupied in some
office which has nothing to do with people outside the
convent, for solitude, and to be left to their own
thoughts would be bad for them, and so the nuns
who can do good to them should be with them from
time to time.

The remainder of the letter is of less importance,
but it shows Teresa's extreme anxiety that all should
go well. She tells them that persons who love to
suffer must not be resentful with those by whom the
cross, which profits them so much, comes to them.
Their treatment of such persons is the proof of their
profiting or not. She hopes God will speedily remedy
everything and put the house into its former state, or
a better, for it is His way to repay a hundred-fold.
Again, she begs that they will not speak among themselves of what has passed, it can be of no advantage,
and may do great harm. Great care must be taken
for the future—she fears that the devil may tempt the
nun she speaks of to try to fly from the convent.
They must be careful, especially at night. The devil
will attempt anything for the sake of bringing dis-
credit on the convent! If the two can cease to be so
united some greater light about it all may be obtained
and they might more easily be undeceived, for the
more they cling together the more they help one
another in mischief. Prayer will do much, and so she

hopes that our Lord will give them light. The whole matter afflicts her much. If it is thought well that some account be written of what has taken place, it would be well to do it for the sake of the experience which would be gained, unfortunately not at the cost of others, but at their own, only if Sister Francisco is the historiographer, let there be no exaggeration or amplification, but a simple narrative of the facts.

The remainder of this letter consists chiefly of messages and personal remarks, but there is one passage which deserves to be given as throwing some light on this rather obscure history. There is a question among those who have written on the matter as to the complicity in the mischief of the priest Garcia Alvarez, who had been the chaplain to the convent from the beginning, and is said by some to have been implicated. It would seem beyond question that he was accustomed to spend long hours in the confessional with the two deluded nuns, that he was removed in consequence, and that he may have had to do with the reports spread against the convent afterwards. More than this it is difficult to believe of one of whom St. Teresa speaks so highly, and who was at one time undoubtedly of the greatest help to her and her nuns. It is certain, on the other hand, that several expressions of the Saint seem to favour the view that Garcia Alvarez had been to blame in some respects, and, human nature being what it is, it cannot be supposed impossible that a warm friend at the foundation of the convent should have become its enemy later on, after a slight had been put on himself. As has been said, we may believe that Garcia Alvarez made some mistakes, being misled by the two nuns who imposed on him, or flattered him, in the confessional. It may not be necessary to believe the whole story as to him.

The chief mischief consisted in the atrocious calumny of the worst kind against the Mother Superior, Mary of St. Joseph, with which the name of Father Gratian himself was connected, and it appears that even St. Teresa herself was not spared. Here again it is hardly possible to conceive that a man respected as Garcia Alvarez must have been could lend any countenance to such an invention, or that, if it had been so, Teresa could have wished him to continue to be chaplain to the convent. The evidence, such as it was, which was adduced in support of the charge, was that of the two poor nuns who were either simply deluded and out of their minds, or were induced to bear false witness against their Superior, most probably under the influence of the enemies of the Reform as such. Of Garcia Alvarez, St. Teresa speaks very moderately and kindly. She answers some remarks of Sister St. Jerome, who seems to have said that Garcia Alvarez would suffer in reputation from having to leave the convent. St. Teresa says that the convent will suffer much more than he, who was well known in Seville. "The poor strangers are those on whom all will fall." By strangers she means the nuns she had brought with her, who were looked on as foreigners in Andalusia. If some fault is attributed to Garcia, the nun will at all events not escape blame, and she is satisfied that it must be so, knowing his virtue. He is free from a great burthen in his connection with the convent, and they can never exaggerate what he has done for them, and what they owe him. She sends him a kind message, and says she would have written if her head could have borne it, nor could she say in writing what she wished. We may fairly suppose that she was not sorry to have an excuse.

She does not write, she says, for she might have some complaints to make. Other people were aware of the grievous charges which those poor nuns made against the convent, and it would not have cost much if she had been sometimes informed of them, especially as she had so much to suffer, and as "the matter had been left to be put right by people who loved us little, as all the world knows." It seems clear that the Friars of the Mitigation are the persons meant. Probably there was much imprudence to begin with on the part of Garcia, in his long interviews with the two nuns, and perhaps he resented the interruption of these interviews for their sake. But then came the order of the Nuncio, putting the convent under the Friars of the Mitigation. The gross and inconceivable charges against the character of Mary of St. Joseph, Gratian, and Teresa herself, came to light, most probably, after this change of government, after Mary of St. Joseph had been deposed, and in these we have no evidence that Garcia Alvarez was an agent. But when nuns become deluded, and when they communicate their delusions to a person who is himself deluded into trusting them, there is no amount of error that may not follow. Garcia was deceived, as St. Teresa says of him, and this prevented him from taking an active part in the defence of the accused, and not to take such a part was, under the circumstances, to foster the charge. We may add that the letter of which we are speaking has been thought of suspicious authority by some who cannot believe in the charge made against him. But, on the other hand, it is fully sanctioned as authentic by the latest and best Spanish Editor, who goes so far as to call it "one of the most interesting letters of the whole collection."[1]

It does not therefore seem impossible to acquit Garcia Alvarez of the most grievous part of the charge which has been brought against him, without going so far as to reject as spurious a letter of so much importance, in which St. Teresa seems to imply that he was to some extent to blame. It is one thing to be an imprudent confessor of one or two young nuns, and to get into some trouble in consequence of protracted interviews in the confessional, and another and a very different thing to be author of grave and most calumnious charges against persons of the highest reputation. There was undoubtedly a great deal of prejudice against the new convent in Seville, of which Garcia Alvarez had begun as an enthusiastic friend. This did not make him incapable of the imprudence alleged against him, nor perhaps incapable of resenting

[1] Don Vicente de la Fuente, *Obras de Santo Teresa*, t. v. p. 126. The original exists at Boadilla del Monte in the writing of the Saint. The Bollandists are for rejecting the letter as spurious, but they do not seem to have taken into account the evidence of the whole of St. Teresa's remarks—reserved as they are—in her letters, and again, her very great anxiety not to speak or write to others in disparagement of a benefactor.

the correction which he brought upon himself thereby. The two nuns were evidently deluded and weak-
headed—at least one of them was so, and she probably
influenced the other. If her influence extended so
far as to deceive the confessor also, we have enough
to account for his part in the business.

Thus it is probable that the true solution of the
difficulty may be found in considering the extreme
heat to which the animosity between the two branches
of Carmel had been fanned. We hear much less of the
very grave charges that were made on the authority of
the nuns, till after the time when the Discalced were
placed under the authority of the Friars of the Mitigation, the Prioress deposed, and the Religious subjected
to the most severe examination, hour after hour. If
they were not already the sort of persons of whom
St. Teresa speaks as believing they see whatever is put
into their head, and ready therefore to swear to it,
they were probably reduced to such a state of bewil-
derment by the interrogatories to which they were
subjected, as to say whatever was suggested to them.
This may account for the charges made by them, with
which it is not imperative to connect the name of
Garcia Alvarez. At the same time it is quite certain
that Teresa, all through, spared the name of Garcia
Alvarez to the utmost, and was extremely unwilling
to believe any evil of him. Gratitude, as she says,
was her weakness—and yet we have scattered sayings
of hers concerning his part of the business which
must have great weight in the formation of any
judgment. The proverb says, *Qui s'excuse, s'accuse,*
and St. Teresa's excuses for Garcia imply that he

had very great need of defence. The highest
authority on the spot, the Archbishop, the friend of
both, would not, she tells us, consent, though entreated, to allow him to return to the convent. As
to the two nuns, it is quite reasonable to attribute
their conduct to one of those diabolical illusions
which are more common in the history of spiritual
persons than is supposed.

The long letter which has occasioned these com-
ments was written and sent by Teresa before the
termination of the investigation to which the charges
made against the convent led. *En fin, en fin,* says
St. Teresa, *la verdad padece, pero no perece,* and
this she hopes will be the end of the business. The
affair was carried before the Royal Council, and
Father Nicolas Doria was of great use in urging the
cause of the accused. The result was that the inno-
cence of Father Gratian and of the accused Religious
was fully established, and, by order of the Nuncio,
Father Angelo de Salazar, who was then the Vicar
governing the Reform, declared this in a juridical
instrument. Mary of St. Joseph was reinstated in
her office, although after some resistance on her own
part. She had more to suffer afterwards in the
turbulent times which fell on the Reformed Carmel
after St. Teresa's death, but on this part of her
history we need not now enter.

NOTE TO CHAPTER II.

———

The letters belonging to this chapter are the following :

1. (ccxxxii.) *To the Reverend Don Hernando, Prior of the Carthusian Monastery of Las Cuevas, Seville.* From Avila, January 31, 1579.

An account of this letter is given at p. 38.

2. (ccxxxiii.) *To the Discalced Carmelite Nuns of the Convent at Seville.* Avila, same date as the preceding, in which the letter was enclosed to be read to them.

Translated, p. 42.

The following letters are not mentioned in the text of this chapter, but they belong to the same period.

3. (ccxxxiv.) *To Doña Inez Nieto, at Madrid.* From Avila, February 4, 1579.

The husband of Doña Inez had shared the disgrace and imprisonment of the Duke of Alva and his son, of whom he was one of the household, and St. Teresa wrote to her one of her beautiful letters of condolence.

4. (ccxxxv.) *To Father Jerome Gratian.* From Avila, February 20, 1579.

Remonstrating against the idea of his going himself to Rome, and suggesting the foundation of a house there. She says at the end, "What a letter for the poor old woman to write, full of advice." It is evident she did not expect her advice to be taken.

5. (ccxxxvi.) *To Father Jerome Gratian.* Beginning of April, 1579.

She expresses her gratitude for the change of affairs for better as to the Reform ; says she is content with the Nuncio's attitude, but hopes for a new Superior before long ; and speaks of the sending two Fathers to profess the obedience of the Reform to the Vicar-General at Rome.

6. (ccxxxvii.) *To Father Jerome Gratian.* From Avila, April, 1579.

A fragment on the persecution at Seville.

7. (ccxxxviii.) *To the same.* From Avila, April 21.

Mentioning the better news from Seville. The Discalced Friars go to hear the nuns' confessions, and Father Angelo promises that in a month's time Father Nicolas Doria will be sent there to restore Mary of St. Joseph to her place and vote, and that there shall be an election of Prioress. She speaks also of the profession of Gratian's sister at Valladolid.

8. (ccxxxix.) *To Roque de Huerta.* From Avila, May 2, 1579. Thanking him for his exertions for the Reform, and good news concerning it, and the journey of Father Juan de Jesus to Rome.

9. (ccxl.) *To Mother Isabel of St. Jerome and Mother Mary of St. Joseph, of the Convent of Seville.* Avila, May 3, 1579.

An account of this letter is given, p. 46.

CHAPTER III.

St. Teresa again at work.

ALTHOUGH some time was to elapse before the accomplishment of what St. Teresa had so long desired and laboured for, that is, the separation of her Reform from the Mitigated Carmel by its erection into a new Province, the decision which had been arrived at by the Nuncio and his four assessors, was the dawn of a new epoch in her life, from which she was enjoined by her Superior to begin once more the foundations which had been for so long interrupted. Fra Angelo de Salazar would not let her rest, and fresh work sprang up every day to her hands. Indeed, there seems to have been a similar burst of fresh life even among the still more oppressed friars as well as the nuns. There was some misgiving as to the prudence of doing much in the provisional state of things which was now established, and we gather from her letters that Fra Angelo did not, or could not, entirely satisfy the wants of the Reform. Teresa did not leave Avila till late in the June of this year (1579), and she tells us that it was before that time that she received a celebrated revelation which has been considered as a kind of charter to the Reform which she founded. She tells us that at Avila, on that feast of Pentecost, she was in deep seclusion in a little hermitage of "Nazareth," thinking of a great grace which our Lord had conferred upon her about twenty years before on the same day, when a powerful spiritual movement came over her, her mind was filled with fervour and caught up in a great recollection.

What I shall now relate I understood therein, namely, that I should tell the Discalced Fathers to be careful to observe four things, and that as long as they observed them, their Religious Order would always grow better and better. If they neglected them, it would fall off and decline from its first beginning.

The first of these conditions was, that all Superiors should be of one mind and in harmony among themselves.

The second, that t.. ᵗh they were to have many monasteries, the number of friars in each should be very small.

The third, that they should converse as rarely as possible with secular persons, and that only for the good and salvation of their souls.

The fourth, that they should teach more by deeds than by words.

These precious admonitions have always been cherished by the friars, as if the whole well-being and prosperity of the Order depended upon them. They were inserted in the Constitutions, and engraved in golden letters in the hermitage of "Nazareth."

. A little before this St. Teresa had written an urgent letter to the nuns of Valladolid, asking them to contribute liberally to the great expenses which the Reform was incurring at Rome, of which a little

has been said in the last chapter. The letter of
which we speak is in some respects unlike her usual
style.[1] There is a kind of formality about it, as well
as a tone of authority. The truth seems to be that
the Prioress, although St. Teresa's own dear niece,
Mary Baptist, was rather stiff, especially when the
interests of the convent were concerned. St. Teresa
mentions this in a letter about the application to
Father Gratian, and we shall see hereafter that it is
worth while to notice this point of character. The
letter is addressed to the Carmelites at Valladolid,
and seems to have been written that they might all
read it, at least those who had any voice in the
concerns of the house.

She begins by reminding them that she has never
yet asked them to take a novice free of dowry, or
indeed, anything else of much importance. Some
convents have taken as many as eleven. What she
now asks them, she takes to herself, as "done to me."
She sends them with her letter some letters from
Rome, from which they will see that there is an
immediate necessity for two hundred ducats. The
friars have no one at their head, and can send nothing.
She mentions that the convent at Veas has given one
hundred and fifty. It is a great mercy of our Lord
that there are some who can give. And it may be
said that after all, it is only once in a way. She then
says that Father Nicolas Doria has found a person
who will advance him two hundred ducats on the
dowry of Sister Mary of St. Joseph, one of their own
novices, if the convent will give him a receipt for the

[1] Letter ccxli.

sum. The money, of course, was to go to the expenses at Rome, and the convent would be, in fact, responsible for it. She tells them what formalities must be gone through, in order that there may be no delay.

They will say it is much, and why not try the other convents? But all the convents give what they can—Avila, where she is, has nothing to give. (The nuns had to sell their own work to get food.) We must all help one another, she says, *harto da el que do todo quanto puede.* The expenses at Rome are very great. She herself would work with her hands if she could—it is a great trouble to have to beg! Besides, she has promised the two hundred ducats to the Canon Montoya, who has given them life (*que nos ha dado la vida*), and it is very well indeed that there is not more to pay. This money, she says, is *necessary.*

But St. Teresa has further calls to make on the generosity of her Sisters. What follows is not necessary, but reasonable. She tells them that they had spoken of taking this Mary of St. Joseph—Gratian's sister—for nothing, but her mother had promised to pay four hundred ducats, and the delay had been in her making the arrangements, which were not easy to her. St. Teresa calmly suggests, first, that they should remit one hundred, and then two. Another of Gratian's sisters has been taken for nothing at Toledo. The girls have such good qualities, that they are worth taking free. Returning to the subject of the expenses for the Order, she says that when all the troubles are over, they must see what each house has paid, and divide the burthen fairly.

To St. Teresa's great delight, the quittance for the money was sent immediately and as she desired. She writes again on the 9th of June to return thanks: " May the Holy Spirit be with your Reverence and all your nuns, and repay you for the 'buenas Pascuas'[1] you gave me by sending the quittance so readily. The messenger had not gone, they had pressed me again. It was the greatest of boons, and if the money had wanted for me to eat, it could not have been more so! God will reward them." She had written at once to Madrid, to let the friars know what a treasure they had in their nuns. The Prioress is to take care of herself, as Teresa hopes to come soon, and to find her well. The Vicar (Fra Angelo) gave her some hopes, but only of seeing her in passing. She is to go to Malagon, to which place he is to send the patents for the foundation of Villa Nueva de la Jara, she is to be then on her way to Salamanca, where she is to get a new house for the nuns—this is the greatest of their needs now. " They say nothing, which obliges her the more to help them if she can."[2]

She is speaking of the silent endurance of the nuns at Salamanca of their most inconvenient lodging. Then she mentions the order which sends her again on her travels from place to place. " See what they are doing with this old woman!" and she adds a sly hint that the Friars of the Mitigation want

[1] Some readers may not be aware that in Spain and Italy—perhaps elsewhere—the word " Pasch " is used for any great feast, Pentecost, for example, and Christmas, as well as Easter. Pentecost in this year, 1579, fell on June 7.

[2] Letter ccxlii.

to get her away from Avila. In this letter she speaks of the foundation of Villanueva de la Jara as having been long resisted by her. We shall speak of this presently. She says that their old friend Pedro Hernandez (one of the four assessors of the Nuncio) had advised them to make no new foundations, even with leave, until the Province was granted them— "the Nuncio is so touchy."

St. Teresa wrote on the 10th of June to Father Gratian, partly on the same subject.[1] The letter is full of joy. Things are going on so well! The care that is being taken about the new Province is greater than has been taken about any in Spain. It shows God intends great good from the Discalced Carmel. She hopes "Paul" will be preserved many years to see it. As for herself, she will see it from Heaven if she gets there. She is very glad about the money that has been sent from Valladolid. Then she mentions the orders that have been given her. She does not like the office of Prioress at Malagon, which Father Angelo had told her to fill. (She could not follow the Rule as the others.) She feels very lonely without Gratian to speak to about her soul. The Sisters at Avila are much grieved at her departure. It is in this letter that she mentions the stiffness of character of the Prioress of Valladolid. "But I wrote her such a letter!" she says.

Another letter of this time is to Anne of the Incarnation, Prioress of Salamanca, announcing her visit. The letter is dated on the 18th of June.[2] She hopes the good Prioress has not "managed" the

[1] Letter ccxliii. [2] Letter ccxliv.

F 3

matter! Her coming must be kept secret from Pedro de la Vanda (the owner of their house), or "he will kill us with his contracts." *She writes also on the 21st of June to Mary Baptist, Prioress of Valladolid, in the same strain.[1] She has sent Mary Baptist's letter on to Fra Angelo Salazar, the Vicar. It seems to have been about the reception of a rich postulant. St. Teresa says she always fears these large fortunes, notwithstanding all the good she hears of the lady. She begs that there may be no "reception" on her arrival at Valladolid. Those things mortify her greatly. The Bishop and Doña Maria, her sister, have managed her going with Fra Angelo, who, to please them, has overcome all the obstacles. "Your Reverence also gets whatever you want, *Dios le perdone!*"

A few days after this we have another letter to Mary of St. Joseph, Prioress of Seville, who was holding out against her re-appointment to the office from which she had been deposed.[2] St. Teresa deals with her in a very summary way.

Pray leave off these booby bits of perfection! We have all been desiring this, and working for it, and here are you with all your nonsense—for it is nothing else. It is not your Reverence's concern, but the concern of all the Order. It is so good for the service of God that I greatly desire it, for the honour of the house and of Father Gratian. Even if you have no fitness for it, nothing is so desirable, and you know that when "good men are not to be had," &c.[3] If then God grant us this favour, hold your tongue

---

[1] Letter ccxlv.   [2] Letter ccxlvi.

[3] She alludes to the Spanish proverb, *A falta de hombres buenos, mi marido alcalde*—" Because good men are scarce, my husband mayor."

and obey, or else you will annoy me much. You have said quite enough to convince us of your unwillingness, but God will help you.

She asks after news of the nuns who have caused the trouble, and hopes the story of all that has passed may be written clearly and truly. Speaking of her journey, she says she is not needed much at Valladolid, but may find much to do at Salamanca, on account of the trouble about the house. They must pray that the nuns may get a good and cheap house, which she hopes to see before she dies.

After these letters, St. Teresa seems to have left Avila on the 25th of June. She spent a few days at Medina del Campo, and reached Valladolid on the 3rd of July, whence she wrote to announce her movements to Father Gratian. She stayed at Valladolid till the 30th of that month, and while there wrote some other letters of which we shall have to speak. The letter already mentioned is of considerable importance, as showing how early St. Teresa became aware of a possible antagonism between Gratian and Nicolas Doria. Father Nicolas was of a stern, uncompromising, determined character, by nature hard and austere. He had just the qualities which were wanting to Gratian, and he had not those in which Gratian excelled. He had visited St. Teresa, it seems for the first time, before she left Avila, and she had been much charmed with him. She tells Gratian that she was much consoled to see that he now had in the Order some one with whom he could treat of matters of business, and who could help him. She had suffered much from seeing how lonely he was.

Nicolas seemed to her discreet, a man of good counsel, and a servant of God. He had not "the grace and great gentleness which God has given to Paul "—that is, Gratian himself.

Few have it.   But he is certainly a man of substantial virtue, humble, penitent, a lover of truth, and one who knows how to gain people's wills.   He will soon know the worth of "Paul," and he is determined to follow him in everything, to my great contentment, and in many things— (if Paul gets on well with him, which I believe he will, if it is only to please me)—it will be a great help to both to be of one mind, and a great relief to me.   Whenever I think of what you have had to suffer from those who ought to have helped you, it has been one of my greatest pains. So, my Father, your Paternity must not keep him at a distance, for unless I am mistaken, he will be of great help in many ways.

These sentences show us two things.   First, how truly Gratian was isolated among the Discalced Friars, of which we shall see many proofs.   His training was utterly different from theirs, his sympathies and connections different, his very ideas of the end of the Carmelite Order were not the same. He came from outside, as it were, and then was put to govern them.   The second thing we see is St. Teresa's keen sense of the importance of his being thoroughly in harmony with a man like Nicolas Doria, a man already eminent, and one whose strong and active character would be invaluable to Gratian if they worked well together, and the cause of much misery if they did not.   Unfortunately, Doria could never abide Gratian's gentleness and softness, and the want of understanding between them cost the Reformed Carmel many a wound.

In the earlier part of the same letter Teresa speaks of a variety of matters. She has found Mary of St. Joseph, Gratian's sister, in good health and happy. They have a rich postulant, of whom we have already heard. But she will probably give most of her fortune to her sisters. The convent will get something, and the Prioress has laid by so much that they will soon be well founded. There was an idea of Gratian going himself to Rome, which she opposes strongly. He is not to think of it. At the end of her letter she speaks of a nun in the convent of Alba de Tormez who is quite insufferable, her head is gone. Her father, who was a benefactor of the Order, had asked that she might be kept a while, till some arrangement may be made for her. Salutations and messages occupy the rest of the letter. The letter is dated the 7th of July.[1]

There is another letter to Father Gratian from Valladolid, dated the 18th of July,[2] which we might pass over as of no great importance, were it not for a single passage which shows the simplicity with which St. Teresa dealt with him in telling him of his faults. " I should like to tell you a temptation which I had yesterday, and which still haunts me, about Eliseus," that is, about Gratian himself. " It seems to me that he is sometimes not careful enough to say the whole truth in certain matters. Although I see that it is in matters of little moment, yet I could wish that in this he would be very careful. For charity's sake let your

---

[1] Letter ccxlviii.   [2] Letter ccxlix.

Paternity ask him this very much on my part, for I do not consider that there is entire perfection without this diligence. See what things I meddle with, as if I had not other things to do!" Those who have carefully watched very perfect persons may have remarked how much they insist on this point.

On the 22nd of the same July,[1] St. Teresa writes to Mary of St. Joseph, lately mentioned. The letter is full of affection and joy at seeing her in her post of Prioress. She exhorts her not to choose her own crosses, but to imitate our Lord in the Garden, Who said, " Thy will be done." She gives various directions about the convent, and speaks highly of the state in which she finds that of Valladolid. She asks her to pray for that of Malagon, and for the wants of that of Salamanca. She is very busy. Mary of St. Joseph is to write for her to Father Gregorio.

On the 29th of July she writes to Don Teutonio de Braganza, Archbishop of Evora. The letter is partly about two books, which Don Teutonio was to get printed for her. One was her *Path of Perfection*, and the other a *Life of St. Albert*. It is strange to find her meddling, as we should say now, with politics. But the succession to the crown of Portugal was in dispute, since the death of the Cardinal Henry, who had succeeded the unfortunate Don Sebastian. Philip II. himself was one of the claimants, who had the advantage also of the support of the Pope and of a very powerful army under the Duke of Alva. St. Teresa believed that the claims of Philip were legitimate, but she is chiefly anxious for peace. Don

[1] Letter ccl.

Teutonio was a near kinsman of the Duke of Braganza, one of the claimants for the throne, and she urges Don Teutonio to do what he can in the matter. The immediate result of the dispute was the victory of Philip II., and Portugal was for sixty years under the Spanish crown.

We pass over some unimportant letters or fragments,[1] and come next to a letter to Don Lorenzo de Cepeda, her brother, of whom we have not heard for some time. It is dated the 27th of July, and she speaks of herself as still so much occupied at Valladolid that she has not yet had time to talk to the Sisters who wished to see her in private. She has been greatly bored by the visit of a relation whom she could not get rid of. *Asi se ha de pasar la vida.* She has been buying a silver chalice for Lorenzo, with which she hopes he will be pleased. She scolds him gently for having found something hard to bear —he who has so great a desire to serve God. He will say, perhaps, it was the service of God that he wished it otherwise. "O brother, how little we understand ourselves! it all comes from a little self-love." She tells him that Fra Juan de Jesus has got to Rome, and that things are going well. She had perhaps heard that letters from the King had been sent to Rome, in favour of the suit of the Reform. She tells him also of the restoration of the Prioress of Seville, and that she has not forgotten to remind her of the debt of her convent to him. She sometimes wishes for Teresita, "especially when in the garden."

[1] Letters cclii. ccliii. ccliv. cclv.

These exhaust the letters which remain to us of this short stay of St. Teresa at Valladolid. She reached Salamanca about the Assumption of our Lady, the 15th of August. It was at this time that her companion, Anne of St. Bartholomew, was the subject of more than one miracle. One day she had a severe neuralgic or rheumatic pain, which Teresa cured by blessing her with her hand. When the day came for the journey towards Salamanca, Anne was seized with fever and vomiting, and could not leave her bed. St. Teresa was anxious to get on her way, and came to her at midnight, saying, "Daughter, are you asleep?" She replied that she had slept. "Get up and see how you are!" She was quite well, and without any fever. St. Teresa told her to bless God, Whom she had prayed to restore her to health, and the next morning they set out. Anne also tells us that it was on this visit to Salamanca that St. Teresa was in a great strait because she had more letters to answer than she could manage, and said to her, "Now if you knew how to write, you might help me." Anne said, "Let your Reverence give me something to learn from." Teresa gave her a very well written letter of a Religious, and told her to take that and learn from it, but Anne objected that Teresa's own handwriting would be the best for her to learn from. Teresa gave her two letters, from which she wrote that same evening a letter to St. Joseph's at Avila, and was able to write ever afterwards, no one having taught her, whereas before she could not even read except from print, and that with difficulty. "From this she knew that it was the work of God, that she might help the Mother in these difficulties and straits, which she underwent for His love with so much joy and merriment."

It appears that St. Teresa's visit to Salamanca on this occasion was fruitless, except in the annoyances and sufferings which it brought to her and her nuns. In a letter to Father Gratian, of the 4th of October,[1] she tells him that all was arranged for an excellent house, the fittest for the nuns in Salamanca, the vendor an honourable gentleman, who had not only given his word, but had signed a contract before witnesses—and then suddenly all was broken off. The nuns had to remain for some years more in their uncomfortable lodgings. She complains very much, in the same letter, of Mary of St. Joseph, the Prioress of Seville, who had set her heart on changing the house which they had in that city, which, St. Teresa says, would seem a Paradise to the nuns at Salamanca. Teresa says that Mary of St. Joseph is too clever by half, she fears she has never been open with her, though she had written very strong letters to her, and hoped she had amended. She had put it into the heads of the nuns that the house was a bad one: quite enough to make them ill! We may remember how beautiful the house seemed to be when it was first taken. But it appears that in the end Mary of St. Joseph had her way.

Only one more letter strictly belongs to this time, although Teresa seems to have stayed at Salamanca till November, when she returned for a very short

[1] Letter cclvii.

time to Avila. The letter we speak of is to a lady named Isabel Osorio, who had a sister in the community at Salamanca, and who was desirous of joining the same convent. St. Teresa had spoken on the matter to the nuns, and Isabel had been accepted by them. But Nicolas Doria, who seems to have known her, had suggested that she should wait a while, in order to be of more use for the then contemplated foundation of Madrid, and Teresa wrote twice to her on the subject,[1] once before leaving Salamanca, and again on her arrival at Malagon, a little later. The letters are full of the grace and courtesy which marks all that comes from her pen. It seems that at the time she was in hopes that the difficulties about the foundation at Madrid—which were caused by the opposition of the Ordinary—might be overcome. As a matter of fact, the foundation was delayed till after St. Teresa's death. It is not certain that Isabel Osorio was able to carry out her desire of becoming a Religious. Teresa took from Salamanca Sister Geronima of the Holy Ghost to be Prioress of Malagon, Father Angelo de Salazar having given up the idea of making her remain herself in that office. He still insisted on her visiting the convent, which had got into a very relaxed and disordered state.

The journey to Malagon had been very tedious, and in very bad weather, but it did not damp St. Teresa's energy. She found the workmen saying that they could not finish the house in less than six months. But she determined to give them a fortnight, and on the feast of the Immaculate Conception of

[1] Letters cclix. cclx.

our Lady, the nuns actually ent'red it. She had
arrived on the feast of St. Catharine,. the 25th of
November.[1] She writes not long after this to Father
Gratian, to give him an account of what had passed.
She speaks of the nuns as being like little lizards, who
come out into the sun to bask.[2] There were worse
evils at Malagon than the inconvenience of the former
house. We have seen something of the state of things
from the letters in the last volume.[3] The community
was thoroughly out of hand. The " President," who
had been put in the place of Mother Brianda, had
not the gift of government, and Teresa now acknow-
ledges that she had been mistaken in blaming the
chaplain so much. She says that Paul, that is, Gratian
himself, had been to blame too. She has made it a
matter of confession, and let him do the same. They
ought not to have trusted so much to a young
Religious, holy indeed, but without experience. Now
things are in better train. "The evil that a Superior
can do in one of our houses is terrible." The Sisters
see things that scandalize them, and think it is
against obedience to notice them. She tells him that
any one who has to visit them must act with a great
deal of prudence—perhaps a gentle hint to Gratian
himself. They had had a confessor of the Order—
who seems to have died lately—who had no great
idea of perfection, and she herself had brought in
another, who may have made some mistakes also.

[1] See vol. i. p. 303, where this change of habitation on the part of the
nuns is spoken of in the future.

[2] Letter cclxi.

[3] See vol. ii. pp. 352—355.

A little later, on the 2nd of December,[1] she writes
again, and mentions the state of the convent as much
improved.   There is a strong passage about any
great intercourse between the nuns and clerics.   She
does not encourage this, although the person she
mentions was a good man, and has preached them a
very good sermon, and could never do any harm
intentionally, "but I am well assured that, though
they be saints, it is better in our convents to have
little intercourse and conversation with them—God
will teach them Himself.   If it be Paul himself
(Gratian), it is better to have little of it, except in the
pulpit ; much does harm, and takes away from the
credit that such a person ought to have."   The last
Spanish Editor justly remarks that St. Teresa could
not have said much more.

We next have a fragment, written to an unknown
person, in which she expresses her annoyance at the
manner in which people speak of her as a saint, and
says that she has long desired what she now finds, to
be at rest, although she has no one to give comfort
to her soul.   She has desired "that no one should
think of Teresa of Jesus any more than if she was
out of the world."   It does not seem clear where or
when this was written.[2]

The next letter[3] in order is to Father Nicolas
Doria (December 21st), who had been sent to Seville
by the Vicar, about the state of the convent at
Malagon.   It repeats a good many facts which are
already contained in a letter, a little earlier, to Father
Gratian.   She speaks strongly of the mischief done

[1] Letter cclxiii.   [2] Letter cclxiv.   [3] Letter cclxv.

by bad government. We must be very careful whom we place in these offices. The nuns are so submissive that their greatest discomfort is when they have the scruple of thinking that what their Superior does is not well, when it is not well actually. Now they are as content as possible with their Superior, and she regrets that she and others were mistaken at a distance, and arranged things rather inadvisedly. Another misery is that they have many debts.

She begs him to insist with the Prioress at Seville, now she is beginning again, to be very strict in taking care that the Constitutions are observed, and all matters of Rule, in doing which they cannot go wrong: if they do otherwise, please God even their best friends may become their accusers, and do not let them think that they can do and undo at will like married people: and "let your Reverence show them this letter." She renews her complaint that the Prioress had not been open with her, at a time when many things had not come about which passed later.

She has been told that some of the nuns at Seville had written to those at Malagon (where she was), urging them to be firm in asking for Brianda (the late Prioress) back. She begs that he will give the Prioress a good penance for it, and speaks strongly about the interference from a distance with what she is doing.

She mentions also the affair of Isabel Osorio, of whom we have heard. She had kept her back to see if she could help the foundation of Madrid, and now she hears from Doña Luisa de la Cerda (the foundress of Malagon) that the Archbishop will not give her leave unless the convent there is founded with an income, and she does not see her way out of the difficulty. There are several other matters touched in this long letter, which is useful also in showing that St. Teresa made great use of Father Nicolas as soon as he became known to her.

Some other fragments[1] to Gratian and Roque Huerta follow, which need not detain us, as well as a note to an unknown person, a graceful note to some one whom she had wished to speak with. One of the fragments to Gratian speaks of a girl of Antonio Gaytan's,[2] whom we are already acquainted with. The girl was apparently not old enough to enter as a nun —about as old as "la mi Isabelita," Gratian's young sister. Her father offers to support her, and give her by-and-bye all he has that is not entailed, six or seven hundred ducats or more. "What he has done for that house, and the labour he has gone through for our Order, is beyond price." So she asks his Paternity to send her the leave quickly, for charity's sake. "I tell you that these little angels edify us and give us recreation, and I see no inconvenience, but the reverse, in our having one in every house." It is not quite certain to what convent the application was made, and it must have been made at a time when Gratian was Provincial, which he was not at the time of which we write. The habit of admitting girls to live in the community does not seem to have been continued.

Early in January of the new year, 1580, we have

---

[1] Letters cclxvi. cclxvii. cclxviii. cclxix. cclxx.
[2] See vol. ii. p. 140.

St. Teresa writing to the convent at Seville,[1] apparently in answer to a number of notes which the nuns
had sent her as felicitations for the new year, as well
as on account of the re-election of Prioress. She says
these lines have consoled her much, and she would
gladly write to each one in particular, but want of
time and her many occupations prevent her. She
has a word or two for many of them, however. She
would gladly make acquaintance with the newly
professed or clothed among them, and wishes them
joy of their espousals. Sister Geronima signs herself
a "Dunghill." Teresa hopes her humility is not all
in word. "Gabriele" had sent her a picture of
St. Paul, which was very pretty, as it was like her
in being small, and Teresa was pleased. May God
make her tall in His sight! In truth, His Majesty
seems to wish to make them great, as He has given
them such great troubles. May they not lose the
fruit by their own fault! May He be praised for all,
and she is greatly consoled. She says a few words
about the gifts God gives to the first Superior in a
house, and says she is not to be changed unless there
is some grave reason, and that there are many causes
for this.

Sisters Beatrix and Margaret, the sources of the
late mischief, she begs, as she has the others, that they
will leave off talking of the past, except it be to our
Lord or their confessor, if in any matter they have
been mistaken, especially in a lack of the simplicity
and charity which our Lord requires of us, and for
the future take great pains to be open and true as to

[1] Letter cclxxi.

all. Any satisfaction that may be well, let it be done, for they will be uncomfortable without it, and the devil will be always tempting them. Now that our Lord is content, no account of what is past need be made. The devil has indeed endeavoured to hinder the holy beginnings that had been made, and the only thing to wonder at is the mischief he has done and the worse that he might have done. Our Lord often permits a fall that the soul may be more humble, and persons who return to Him rightly and ingenuously often advance much in His service, as we see in many saints. " My daughters, we are all children of the Virgin, and sisters. Love one another very much, and let all the past be as if it had not been." She assures those who seem to have given her most pain, that she has prayed for them particularly, and concludes by loving messages, especially to Sister Juan of the Cross. This shows us that things were now in a better state as to the two deluded nuns.

The next of these letters[1] from Malagon is of about the same date, and addressed to Father Nicolas Doria. Teresa was just now leaning on him a good deal. He seems to have delighted her by a plan for getting Gratian named Vicar-General of the Reform in Spain. This was a matter in which Gratian himself could not appear. He was at Alcala de Henares, living in a grotto, for which reason she often calls him "el de la Cúeva." This letter begins by an enumeration of several letters which she had sent for Doria to Seville, which had not reached him.

[1] Letter cclxxii.

Malagon was an out of the way place, she tells him, with little means of communication, not like Seville or Toledo. She wished Doria to come to see her at Malagon, but she tells him that she may soon have to leave it. There is the foundation of Villanueva de la Jara to be made, on which Antonio of Jesus and the Prior of the Roda had set their hearts, and she might have to go. We shall hear more of this foundation presently. The Mother Prioress of Seville, to whose letters Doria refers her, tells her nothing of the things she wishes to know. The affair on which she had written, is to be connected with a certain Velasco, and there is a good deal about it in the letter, though it would take too long to explain it all here. She proposes that all doubt about Gratian's power as Visitor, which some supposed to continue, should be set at rest, and that, if he was made Vicar, Antonio of Jesus should be named Provincial. We know that St. Teresa did not think Antonio fit to be Superior, but she wisely supposed that, with Gratian over him, he might succeed, and that thus the little division that there was in the Reform, as to his personal pretensions, might be set at rest. We shall see how nearly Antonio came to being elected in the place of Gratian, when the Provincial was at last to be chosen by the friars themselves.

Another letter[1] is addressed to Mary of St. Joseph, Prioress of Seville. It is very long, and apparently the first which St. Teresa wrote to her after the severe complaints she had made of her to Nicolas Doria. She says she had mentioned several things

[1] Letter cclxxiii.

G 3

which were meant for her to read in her letter to
Fàther Nicolas.   Mary's own letter had been long
and humble, and deserved a long answer, but she had
desired that Teresa should write to Father Rodrigo
Alvarez, and she had done so, and had not head
for more writing.   Serrano, a friend of the convent,
had undertaken to deliver hers, and his presence
had been a great comfort.   She hoped to send him
back, as it was a great thing to have some one to
rely on.

"Gabriela" had given her a bad account of the
Prioress's health, for which she guesses her heart
must have been of stone, if she had not felt all the
trouble she had gone through.   She must forgive
Teresa's severe letters.   When she loved some one
much, she became intolerable, she could not bear
their going wrong in any way.   It had been the same
with Brianda of St. Joseph, the Prioress of Malagon.
She had taken to writing her terrible letters, but had
not got much by them.   Then she complains very
much of the mischief that had been done at Malagon,
which she thinks almost worse than that at Seville.
Beatrix of Jesus, her cousin, who had been made
Superior there, had hurt her most by not speaking
to her at all about the troubles that were going on.
She enlarges upon the matter for some lines.   This is
probably one of the occasions on which St. Teresa
mentions a fault in a third person, for the benefit of
one to whom she was writing, who was inclined to
the same.   She bids the Prioress take great care not
to allow anything that might give scandal, if known,
and to beware of "good intentions" as an excuse.

She mentions a slight infraction of a rule which had been reported at Rome.

We need not go into all particulars, but it is evident Mary of St. Joseph had been defending herself too much. Teresa loved her too sincerely to spare her. A nun has been received beyond the number, and she is alarmed. There are several directions or bits of advice as to the Subprioress and the Mistress of Novices. She does not forget to remind Mary of St. Joseph of her debt to her brother Laurence, who really is in need of the money. Mention is made of the project of a foundation in Portugal, of which Don Teutonio was the promoter. Beatrix—this is the nun at Seville, not her own cousin at Malagon—has come to her senses, but Teresa would have her retract what she said to Garcia Alvarez, as a matter of conscience. This refers, of course, to the charges lately made, and may perhaps support the theory that Garcia Alvarez was misled by the two nuns, not they by him. She renews her caution against "good intentions," and also what she had said in the letter to Doria about the correspondence between the nuns at Seville— some of whom had come from Malagon—and the community there. She tells Mary of St. Joseph roundly that she has been astonished at what she has found out about her letters and those of Sister St. Francis. "Heavens! the stupidities that there were in that letter, for the sake of gaining her end! The Lord give us light, for without that even virtue and cleverness are of no use except for evil! I am glad your Reverence is now so completely undeceived, it will help you for many things. To have made a mistake is a great help towards being right another time, because experience has been gained." We see from letters like this that St. Teresa had great troubles with her best spiritual daughters, for Mary of St. Joseph was certainly one of these, and we see also how gracefully Teresa managed her corrections.

There is another letter[1] of nearly the same date (January 14) to Father Gratian, chiefly on the subject of the proposed Provincialate (or rather Vicariate) for him, and saying very much what she had said to Father Nicolas Doria, considering the difference of the person she was addressing in each case. At that time the great Duke of Alva was in disgrace with the King, for having married his son without the royal leave. Gratian had been in communication with him, and he had been reading St. Teresa's Life of herself in the confinement to which he was sentenced. She speaks of him in this letter, and of some letters of the Duchess. In this letter she mentions her book on the *Interior Castle* (*Las Moradas*), which she considers her "great" work.

The next letter[2] is also to Father Gratian, written the day after the other. She mentions her difficulty in finding a Prioress for the proposed foundation of Villanueva de la Jara, and says that "The Fleming" (Anne of St. Peter) has very good qualities. For Madrid—a convent there being then a favourite project, as we have seen—she mentions Inez of Jesus.

On February the 1st, she writes again to Mary of St. Joseph at Seville,[3] evidently after having received

---

[1] Letter cclxxiv.   [2] Letter cclxxv.   [3] Letter cclxxvi.

some penitent letters from that convent. She is easily appeased. "I don't know how it is, with all the trouble that your Reverence gives me, I can't help loving you much. All is soon over." She is glad all has passed so well at the election (this has been already mentioned), and she encourages the Prioress not to let the devil make her discontented with her office. There are some hints of complaints made against Nicolas Doria. Teresa knew all would not be quite well done by him, *Dios lo ha hecho como quien es!* She mentions that she has just received the letters patent for the foundation of Villanueva, which we have already heard. She saw many reasons against it, but Antonio of Jesus and the Prior of La Roda, Gabriel, have carried the day. She has to be back again before Easter.

This letter is full of the same matters as others to the same convent. There are questions about the appointment of the Subprioress, and other affairs, not omitting the old trouble with Garcia Alvarez. She had laid aside her displeasure with Sister Francis, who had made a mess of it also at Paterna, whither she had been sent, as has been said, as a "Reformer." She wishes her head would let her write at length about things that had passed in the convent at Malagon, in order that Mary of St. Joseph might gain experience, and also asks God to forgive Mary for not telling her—for it seems she had been present sometimes—of things which she ventures to wager had not passed in the whole of Spain in convents the most relaxed. Good intentions would save some—they would not be enough for all. Let her Reverence take

warning and be exact in following the Constitutions
which she was so fond of, if she does not wish to gain
a little with the world and lose with God. She blames
Beatrix of Jesus for not having told her, the others
did not know all that was going on.   There is a
good deal more of complaint. She remarks she had
no "carols" sent her on occasion of the election at
Seville.   She likes the nuns to have a moderate
amount of fun at such a time, but she seems to have
forbidden them at some other time—probably in her
own honour—and blames "mi Gabriela" for this.
The rest of this letter does not call for remark.

Teresa writes to Father Gratian, at the beginning
of this month (February), a short letter [1] which does
not contain much to our purpose. The plan for the
government of the Reform seems to be still going on.
Ambrose of Mariano is there waiting to see Father
Gabriel, who is to come to fetch the nuns for the
new foundation, and she has a good word to speak
for him to Gratian.   She is sure that Father John of
the Cross has "never even thought of it"—perhaps of
being Superior himself.   Then she mentions Gratian's
sister, "mi Isabel"—she is getting quite plump and
rosy.   She hears, too, good accounts of his family at
Madrid.   She mentions again the licence for the
admission of Antonio Gaytan's little girl, which it
seems Gratian had no power to grant.

The next note is an affectionate complaint to Mary
of Jesus,[2] the foundress of Veas, for not writing to her.
She mentions the new foundation of Villanueva de la
Jara to which she is going, which, she says, she has

---

[1] Letter cclxxvii.   [2] Letter cclxxviii.

fought off for years, but they have persevered so well that she thinks it must be greatly for the service of our Lord. She has no time or head to write more, but, "let your charity not be short in writing to me, and don't be surprised if I don't answer directly."

In February she writes again from Malagon to the Prioress at Seville.[1] She has heard with great grief of the serious illness of the holy Prior of the Carthusians. He had lately had a great fall. She owes him very much for all he has done for them—if he dies, there will be a saint taken from the earth, while those who do nothing but offend God live on. She excuses the Castilian convents, of which the Prioress seems to have complained that they have not written to congratulate that at Seville. She knows they have pitied the nuns much and prayed for them much, in fact, their prayers have helped to set things right. The new Subprioress is ill, for which Teresa is grieved. There is a good deal about the purchase of a new house, for, it seems, Mary of St. Joseph was bent upon it. Teresa is against it, but does not forbid it. She mentions the example of some Discalced Franciscanesses at Valladolid: now they are inconsolable, shut up as in a cavern, not able to make a noise without being heard by their neighbours, and dreadfully in debt. Teresa complains that there are great charges already on the income of the convent at Seville. She warns the Prioress not to trust the good friars of the Reform to get her a house. The Superior will give leave for her to go out herself for such a purpose. She thanks her for the liberal aid she has

[1] Letter cclxxix.

contributed towards the expenses at Rome. No convent, except that at Valladolid, had done so much.[1]

St. Teresa's next letter is to Father Gratian, announcing the arrival of Fathers Antonio and Gabriel to take her and her companions to Villanueva. She mentions also the convent at Madrid, for which she hopes to be able to satisfy the requirements of the Archbishop. It was not, however, to be founded till after her death. Another letter of the same date is to her good brother Lorenzo.[2] It contains little of interest to us.

NOTE TO CHAPTER III.

The letters which belong to this chapter are as follows :

1. (ccxli.) *To the Mother Prioress and Sisters and my daughters of Mount Carmel in the Convent of Valladolid.* From Avila, end of May, 1579.

A full account of this letter is given at pp. 62, 63.

2. (ccxlii.) *To Mother Mary Baptist, at Valladolid.* From Avila, June 9, 1579.

An account of this letter is given at p. 64.

3. (ccxliii.) *To Father Jerome Gratian.* From Avila, June 10, 1579.

An account of this letter is given at p. 65.

4. (ccxliv.) *To Anne of the Incarnation, Prioress of Salamanca.* From Avila, June 18, 1579.

An account of this letter is given at p. 65.

5. (ccxlv.) *To Mary Baptist, Prioress of Valladolid.* From Avila, June 21, 1579.

An account of this letter is given at p. 66.

---

[1] Letter cclxxx.   [2] Letter cclxxxi.

6. (ccxlvi.) *To Mary of St. Joseph, at Seville.* June 24, 1579.
A full account of this letter is given at p. 66.

7. (ccxlvii.) *To the same.* Date uncertain.
A mere fragment. St. Teresa says that she is much ashamed at hearing what certain people say of her nuns and herself, and that they are under a great obligation of being really what they have been described to be, that they may not make their friends liars.

8. (ccxlviii.) *To Father Jerome Gratian.* From Valladolid, July 7, 1579.
An account of this letter is given at p. 67.

9. (ccxlix.) *To the same.* From Valladolid, July 18, 1579.
This letter is mentioned and quoted at p. 69.

10. (ccl.) *To Mary of St. Joseph.* From Valladolid, July 22, 1579.
An account of this letter is given at p. 70.

11. (ccli.) *To the most illustrious Lord Don Teutonio de Braganza, Archbishop of Evora.* July 22, 1579.
An account of this letter is given at p. 70.

12. (cclii.) *To Roque Huerta.* From Valladolid, July 23.

13. (ccliii.) *To Father Jerome Gratian.* Same date.

14. (ccliv.) *To the same.* Date uncertain.

15. (cclv.) *To Roque Huerta.* From Valladolid, July 26, 1579.
These four fragments are mentioned at p. 71.

16. (cclvi.) *To Lorenzo de Cepeda, her brother.* From Valladolid, July 27, 1579.
An account of this letter is given at p. 71.

17. (cclvii.) *To Father Jerome Gratian.* From Salamanca, October 4, 1579.
This letter is mentioned at p. 73.

18. (cclviii.) *To Doña Inez Nieto.* From Salamanca, October 31, 1579.
A graceful letter of recommendation in favour of her cousin, Gonzalo de Ovalle.

19. (cclix.) *To Doña Isabel Osorio.* From Malagon, November 19, 1579.
Mentioned at p. 74.

20. (cclx.) *To the same.* From Malagon, December 3, 1579.
Mentioned at p. 74.

21. (cclxi.) *To Father Jerome Gratian.* From Malagon, December, 1579.

An account of this letter is given at p. 75.

22. (cclxii.) *To the same.* From Malagon, December 12, 1579.

A fragmentary letter on various subjects.

23. (cclxiii.) *To the same.* From Malagon, December 18, 1579.

Mentioned at p. 76.

24. (cclxiv.) *To a person unknown.* No date.

A few lines expressing her weariness at the way in which people talk of her as a saint.

Mentioned at p. 76.

25. (cclxv.) *To Father Nicolas of Jesu Maria, Doria.* From Malagon, December 21, 1579.

An account of this letter is given at p. 76.

26. (cclxvi.) *To Father Jerome Gratian.* Date uncertain.

27. (cclxvii.) *To Roque Huerta.* Date uncertain.

28. (cclxviii.) *To the same, or some person unknown.* Date uncertain.

29. (cclxix.) *To a person unknown.*

30. (cclxx.) *To Father Jerome Gratian.* Date unknown.

These five letters are mere fragments. See p. 78.

31. (cclxxi.) *To the Prioress and Discalced Carmelite Nuns at Seville.* From Malagon, beginning of January, 1580.

A full account of this letter is given at p. 79.

32. (cclxxii.) *To Father Nicolas Doria, at Seville.* From Malagon, January 13, 1580.

An account of this letter is given at p. 80.

33. (cclxxiii.) *To Mary of St. Joseph, Prioress of Seville.* From Malagon, January, 1580.

A full account of this letter is given at p. 81.

34. (cclxxiv.) *To Father Jerome Gratian.* From Malagon, February 14, 1580.

An account of this letter is given at p. 84.

35. (cclxxv.) *To the same.* From Malagon, January 14, 1580.

Mentioned at p. 84.

36. (cclxxvi.) *To Mary of St. Joseph, Prioress of Seville.* February 1, 1580.

Mentioned at p. 84.

37. (cclxxvii.) *To Father Jerome Gratian.* From Malagon February, 1580.

Mentioned at p. 86.

38. (cclxxviii.) *To the Ven. Mother Mary of Jesus, Foundress at Veas.* From Malagon, February, 1580.

Mentioned at p. 86.

39. (cclxxix.) *To Mary of St. Joseph, at Seville.* From Malagon, February 8, 1580.

An account of this letter is given, p. 87.

40. (cclxxx.) *To Father Jerome Gratian.* From Malagon, February 12, 1580.

41. (cclxxxi.) *To Lorenzo de Cepeda, her brother.* From Malagon, February, 1580.

These two letters are mentioned at p. 88.

CHAPTER IV.

Villanueva de la Jara.

ST. TERESA had been fully occupied during her stay at Malagon, as we see from her letters, in endeavouring to set right the very considerable evils which had disturbed the peace of the convent, and cooled the ardour of the Religious in the pursuit of perfection. The very strong language which she uses about the state of the community, where we have seen that she considered greater harm had been done than at Seville, shows us the depth of the mischief, though we are not perhaps able to understand all the details of the case. She had also a special desire to examine the spirit of one of the nuns, Anne of St. Augustine, whom she afterwards took with her to the foundation which she was to make at Villanueva de la Jara. We see from the last letters of which we have to give an account, that when the time came for the foundation she was somewhat pressed for time, as she was ordered to finish her work at Villanueva before the feast of St. Joseph, March 19th.

We shall presently give St. Teresa's own account of this foundation, which has a kind of idyllic beauty of its own, and was free from the troubles and difficulties that so often met her on such occasions.

She says truly that the nuns themselves, or rather those who were to become nuns, had had a full share of suffering before their wishes could be accomplished. For a long time Teresa herself had been very averse to making the foundation. The place was small, and not able to support by its charities a convent living upon alms, the house was small, and the prospects altogether discouraging. Probably the worst feature in the case, in her eyes, was the fact that the ladies on the spot, who had been living together for some years in the hope of being received as Carmelites, were nine in number, and would thus form a large majority of the inmates of the new convent. It would be difficult to train them, under the circumstances, in new ways, and their own, however good and holy, could not be the same as if they had been formed young and fresh in Carmelite convents. Any one at all acquainted with religious life would have felt the same objections as Teresa. But it was the will of our Lord to grant the prayer of these pious souls, as He so often shows His power by over-riding the most formidable difficulties and dispensing, as it seems, with the usual conditions under which enterprises begun for His honour are made prosperous and permanent.

The chapter in the *Book of the Foundations* in which St. Teresa gives an account of this foundation, is one of the most beautiful of all.

There lived [she tells us] in Villanueva de la Jara an ecclesiastic, born in Zamora, who had been a friar of Our Lady of Mount Carmel. His name was Diego de Guadalajara. He had a devotion to the glorious

St. Anne, and so he made a hermitage close to his house and thereby had an opportunity of hearing Mass. He went to Rome, out of this great devotion, and obtained a Bull for many Indulgences in this church and hermitage. He was a pious and interior man. He made a will when he was dying, and gave the house and all that belongs to it to a convent of nuns of Our Lady of Mount Carmel, and if that could not be done, then for a chaplain, who was to say certain Masses every week, but that, as soon and whenever the convent should be founded, there should be no more any obligation to say the Masses. For more than twenty years the hermitage belonged to the chaplain, and the property fell to ruin, and when the women, who afterwards became the nuns, took possession of the house, they had nothing else. The chaplain lived in another belonging to the chapel.[1]

This then was the first chapter in the history of the foundation.

After this the famous recluse, Catalina de Cardona, came to live in a cave in a sort of desert, and St. Teresa tells us a great deal about her life and marvellous austerities. For the present it is only necessary to mention that her example so moved certain young ladies of Villanueva de la Jara, that they wished to follow the same rule of life, and put themselves under the direction of the parish priest of Villanueva, who gave them a rule which was more adapted to their strength. They lived together as Religious, and were soon after joined in their life by a widow with four daughters, and obtained the hermitage of St. Anne from the municipality. They sent word of what they

[1] This passage is found at the *end* of the account of this foundation in the *Book of the Foundations*, ccxxviii.

were doing to Catalina de Cardona in her desert, and she told them that they were to be the beginning of a house of the Reform of Mount Carmel. This went on for between four and five years, and when St. Teresa was sent to Toledo in consequence of the Decree of Reclusion in 1576, an ecclesiastic from Villanueva brought her a letter from the municipality, telling her that it was the desire of the whole population that she would receive these ladies and found a convent of her Order in the hermitage by the side of which they lived. "I also received," she says, "a letter from a doctor, the parish priest of the place, Augustin de Ervias, a learned and a good man, and it was his great goodness that made him help as far as he could in this holy work."

St. Teresa goes on to speak of the objections which presented themselves to her at once :

As for myself, I thought it was wholly out of the question, that I should accept the convent, for these reasons, 1. Because they whom I was to accept were so many, and because I considered it would be a very difficult thing to train in our way those who had been accustomed to live in their own. 2. Because they had scarcely any means of subsistence, and the place had hardly more than a thousand inhabitants, which would furnish but scanty help to those who had to live on alms, and though the municipality did offer to maintain them, I did not think that was to be relied on. 3. They had no house. 4. They were far away from the other convents. And though I was told they were very good, yet as I had not seen them I could not tell whether they had those gifts which we require for our convents, and so I made up my mind to a thorough refusal. To do this I must first speak to my confessor, the Dr. Velasquez, Canon and Professor in Toledo, a most excellent and learned man, now Bishop of Osma, for I am in the habit of never doing anything of my own will, but only at the will of persons such as he is. When he saw the letters and understood the matter, he bade me not refuse, but to answer kindly, for if God made so many hearts agree together for a thing, it was plain He intended to be served thereby. I did so, for I neither accepted nor yet refused absolutely. Time passed on in their importuning me and in searching out persons who might persuade me to accept till this year, 1580, I all the while thinking it folly to do so. When I made any reply I never could reply altogether unfavourably.

The Father Fra Antonio of Jesus happened to come to the Monastery of Our Lady of Succour, which lies three leagues from the town of Villanueva, there to finish the term of his punishment.

St. Teresa here refers to the punishment which the Nuncio Sega had inflicted on him for the part he had taken in the unfortunate Chapter of Almodovar. He was first confined in a monastery of Franciscans in Madrid, and ther: allowed to accompany Fra Gabriel of the Assumption to Roda.

He used to go and preach at Villanueva, and the Prior of the monastery, who at this time is the Father Fra Gabriel of the Assumption, a most prudent man and a servant of God, went also frequently to the same place, for they were friends of Dr. Ervias, and began an acquaintance with those saintly Sisters. Attracted by their goodness and persuaded by the people and the Doctor, they took up the matter as if it was their own, and began to try to persuade me, writing very earnest letters, and when I was in St. Joseph's at Malagon, which is twenty-six leagues and further from Villanueva, the Father Prior himself came to speak to me on the matter. He told me how it could be done, and that the convent once founded, the Doctor Ervias would endow it with three hundred ducats a year out of the revenues of the living he held, that leave could be had from Rome to do so.

Teresa still resisted. In fact, it appears she had a great repugnance to such a foundation. It may have seemed to her like sewing a piece of new cloth on to an old garment. She gave her reasons to the Fathers, and left it on their conscience, thinking that what she had said was enough to stop them. In fear also that they would write to the then Superior of the Reform, Fra Angelo de Salazar, she wrote herself to him, entreating him not to give the permission. But the will of Providence was too strong for her. After some weeks, when she thought the affair was finally settled in the negative, she received another messenger, bringing her letters from the municipality as well as the two friars. They bound themselves to furnish all that was necessary, and Dr. Ervias again renewed his promise of the endowment.

My dread [she says] of receiving those Sisters was very great. I thought they would be a faction banded together against the Sisters whom I might take thither, as it usually happens, and also because I saw no certain means of maintenance for them, for that which was offered was not such as to make me accept it, so I was in great doubt. Afterwards I saw it was the work of Satan, for, though our Lord had given me courage, I was then so faint of heart that I seemed to have no trust in God at all. The prayers, however, of those blessed souls prevailed. One day, after Communion, as I was commending the matter to God, as I was often doing, for the reason why I had

H 3

answered favourably before was the fear lest I might
be hindering the progress of some souls, for my desire
ever is to help in any way to advance the glory of God
and to increase the number of His servants, His Majesty
rebuked me severely, saying : " Where was the treasury that
supplied the means for the foundations already made ? " I
was to accept the house without misgiving. It would be
greatly to His honour and the progress of souls. So
mighty are the words of God : they not only enter the
understanding, but also enlighten it to see the truth and
make the will ready to act. So it was with me, for I was
not only glad to accept the convent, but felt that I had
been to blame for holding back so long and clinging so
much to human considerations, seeing that His Majesty
had done so much for our holy Order in ways undiscover-
able to reason.

Having resolved to accept the foundation, I thought it
right to go thither myself, with the nuns who were to remain
there, and that for many reasons which suggested themselves,
though very much against my inclination, for I was very
ill when I came to Malagon, and was so still. But thinking
I should please our Lord by going, I wrote to the Superior,
in order that he might command as he should judge best.
He sent the licence for the foundation, with an order for
me to go there myself, and to take with me the nuns whom
I preferred, about which I was very anxious, because they
would have to live with those who were there already.
Earnestly commending the matter to our Lord, I took
two nuns out of the Convent of St. Joseph in Toledo,
one of whom was to be Prioress, and two out of that at
Malagon, one to be Subprioress, and as we had prayed
much to our Lord, the choice could not have been better,
which gave me no slight pleasure, for in the foundations
begun with nuns only from our own convents everything
falls happily into its own place.

The nuns whom she took from Toledo were Mary of the Martyrs and Constance of the Cross, and the two taken from Malagon were Elvira of Sant' Angelo and Anne of St. Augustine. There were nine in the convent already who were to receive the habit, so that the entire number was thirteen, a favourite number with St. Teresa. Fra Antonio and Fra Gabriel came to fetch Teresa and her companions, and they left Malagon on the 13th of February, the Saturday before Quinquagesima, 1580. St. Teresa found herself unusually well.

It was the pleasure of God to send us such fine weather, and to me such health that I seemed as if I had never been ill. I was amazed, and considered how important it is for us never to think of our own infirmities when we are employed in the service of our Lord, whatever the difficulties before us may be, seeing that He is able to make the weak strong and the sickly healthy, and should He not do so, it will be better for our soul, if we suffer and forget ourselves, with our eyes fixed on His honour and glory. Believe me, my Sisters, no harm will ever befall you if you travel on this road. I confess myself that my wickedness and weakness have put me very often in fear and doubt, but I cannot call to mind any occasion since our Lord gave me the habit of a Barefooted Carmelite, nor for some years before, in which of His mere compassion He did not enable me by His grace to overcome these temptations, and to venture upon that, however difficult it might be, which I understood to be for His greater glory. I see clearly that what I did myself was very little, but God asks no more than a resolution of this kind to do everything Himself. May He be blessed and praised for ever. Amen.

It seemed as if all was too smiling, even externally, in the beginnings of this foundation. Teresa found herself in unusually good health. The weather was beautiful. She was not quite so pleased with the devotion of the people as she passed from village to village over the plain, for her humility was pained. The news fled from place to place that she was coming. At the end of the first stage she took refuge in a labourer's hut, but hardly had she reached it before it was surrounded by the villagers. Each one offered his best. The room which served as refectory for herself and her companions was soon invaded. She was too charitable to repulse them rudely, and too humble to accept their homage. She left at three in the morning to escape their importunities. Further on, a rich farmer had assembled his family and even his stock to receive her. His house was decorated as for a festival, and a good dinner provided. She would not, however, enter the village. He went with all his family to a place by which she was certain to pass, and she could not refuse to bless him and his.

St. Teresa goes on to speak of her arrival at the monastery already mentioned, of Our Lady of Succour, three leagues from Villanueva, where they were to halt and give notice of their presence in the neighbourhood. This church there had been built over the cave in which the saintly Catalina had lived as a hermit, before receiving the habit of Mount Carmel, and adjoining the monastery of which she had obtained the foundation. St. Teresa breaks out into a long account of this holy woman and her extraordinary vocation, but this we must perforce omit. Then follows the continuation of the account of the foundation on which we are engaged.

They arrived, St. Teresa tells us, on the first Sunday in Lent. They alighted in the house of a certain Michael de Mondojar. He had three daughters, who had never thought of entering Religion, and, indeed, were averse to the very idea. But Teresa told them that they were to be nuns by-and-bye in the convent she was come there to found. The prediction was fulfilled, and one of them, who became Josepha of the Incarnation, swore to the fact of the prophecy in the process for St. Teresa's canonization. She also bore witness that whereas there had been a drought for five months before that day, the rain fell copiously and most refreshingly then, a grace which Teresa attributes to the goodness of the people, they to the power of her prayers.

On that same day the Blessed Sacrament was brought into the church of the glorious St. Anne, at the time of High Mass. The whole municipality and certain others, with Dr. Ervias, came forth to receive us, and we alighted at the church of the town, which is somewhat distant from that of St. Anne. The joy of the people was so great, that it filled me with consolation at beholding their pleasure in receiving the Order of the most holy Virgin our Lady. When we were yet far away we heard the ringing of the bells, and on our entering the church they began the *Te Deum*, one verse sung by the choristers, the other played on the organ. That done, they carried the Most Holy Sacrament on a bier, and on another our Lady, with crosses and banners. The procession moved on with great pomp, we in our white mantles and faces veiled, were in the middle, near the Most Holy Sacrament, and close to us our Barefooted Friars, who had come in great numbers from their monastery, the Franciscans—for there is a monastery of St. Francis there—walked also, and a Dominican, who was in the place, and though he was alone, it gave me great pleasure to see the habit there. As the distance was great, there were many altars raised. The procession halted at times, when something was sung about the coming of our Order which moved me to great devotion, so also to see that it was all in praise of the great God there present, and that so much was done for seven poor nuns who were there.

She then says that she usually had greater hopes. and joy when a foundation was made under persecution and with trouble. However, she corrects. herself by recollecting that the nuns for whom they came had really suffered very much.

They had been in trouble for nearly six years, at least for more than the five years which had gone by since they went into this house of the glorious St. Anne. I do not speak of their poverty and toil in earning their food, for they never would ask alms. The reason for that was that they would not have their neighbours think they were there to be supported by them. Neither do I speak of their long fasts, their scanty food, of their hard beds, and of the small house, which, with the strict enclosure they always observed,. was hard enough to bear. What was hardest to bear, they told me, was the earnest longing they had to put on the habit, and this was a most grievous torment to them, night and day, for they thought they were never to wear it, and accordingly their constant prayer, and that most frequently with tears, was that God would bestow that grace upon them. When they saw any difficulty arise, they were distressed beyond measure, and multiplied their penances.

They stinted themselves in their food, that out of their earnings they might have the means of paying the messengers who came to me, and of showing what gratitude they could in their poverty to those who were able to help them in any way. I see clearly myself, ever since I conversed with them, and saw how saintly they were, that they must have obtained their admission into the Order by their prayers and tears, and so I looked upon the possession of such souls as these as a much greater treasure than a rich endowment, and my hope is that the house will prosper greatly.

When we entered the house they were standing at the door within, each of them dressed as usual, for they were dressed as they were when they first came, and would never put on any religious dress, hoping for ours. What they wore, however, was most modest, and showed plainly how little thought they had taken for themselves. They were so poorly clad, and almost all of them so thin, as to show they had been living a most penitential life. They received us with tears of great joy, and those tears were certainly not feigned. Their great virtue shone forth in their joy, their humility, and their obedience to the Prioress, and to all those who came to make the foundation. They could not do enough to please them. All the fear they had was, lest the nuns should go back when they saw their poverty and the smallness of the house. Not one of them had ever exercised any authority over another, but each one had with great affection laboured to the utmost of her strength. Two of them, and they were the oldest, managed all their affairs when necessary, the rest never spoke to anybody, and would not do so. The door of the house had a bolt only, no lock, and the eldest answered it. None of the others ventured near it. They slept very little, that they might earn their bread and not miss their prayer, in which they spent many hours, on festivals the whole day.

They directed themselves by means of the books of Fra
Luis of Granada and of Fra Peter of Alcantara. Most
of the time was spent in saying the Divine Office—they
could hardly read it—one only could read well—and that
in breviaries that differed one from another, some of these
being the old Roman forms, which had been given to them
by certain ecclesiastics who used them no longer, others
they had got anyhow, and as they did not know how to
read, they spent many hours upon them. They did not
say the Office where strangers could hear them. God
accepted their intention and toil, but they must have said
very little that was correct. When the Father Fra Antonio
of Jesus began to know them he made them say the Office
of our Lady only. They had an oven in which they baked
their bread, and everything was as orderly as if they had
some one to give directions. The effect on me was to
make me give thanks to our Lord, and the more I conversed
with them the more glad I was that I had come. I believe
that whatever difficulties I might have had to undergo I
should not have shrunk from them to bring consolation to
these souls. Those of my companions who remained told
me that in the beginning, during the first few days, they
were conscious of a certain unwillingness to live with them,
but that when they came to know them and saw how good
they were, they were very glad to stay, and conceived a
great affection for them. Sanctity and goodness can do
great things. The truth is, they who came with me were so
good, that even if they had met with many difficulties and
trials, they would have borne all nobly by the grace of our
Lord, for they desire to suffer in His service, and that Sister
who does not feel this desire, must not look upon herself as
a true Carmelite nun, because the aim of our desire must be,
not rest, but suffering, that we may in some measure be like
unto Him, our true Bridegroom. May it please His Majesty
to give us His grace for that end. Amen.

St. Teresa remained about a month at Villanueva de la Jara, and left it just after St. Joseph's day, which was a week before Palm Sunday. She had been occupied in putting the very poor and inconvenient house in order, as well as in helping on the spiritual formation of the nine novices, and watching over the anxious beginnings of their community, which was to be formed under what appeared at first sight rather difficult circumstances. One of the greatest inconveniences of the house was the depth of the well from which they had to draw their water. Teresa had a wheel put up as a remedy for this, but it was the occasion of a severe accident to herself. A workman having neglected to fasten the rope, the wheel in consequence struck violently against her arm, and broke it afresh. Anne of St. Bartholomew tells us that an abscess was formed, which put her in great danger, but was suddenly relieved by the bursting of the abscess.

Humanly speaking, the objections which St. Teresa had felt to the foundation of Villanueva de la Jara were well grounded. Some of them were overcome by the humility and devotion of the nine postulants, but there still remained the material difficulties which were inherent in the situation of a convent, now considerably augmented in numbers, which had to be maintained upon so little in the midst of a poor and scanty population. In truth, the existence of the convent was an instance of the loving care of God for those who throw themselves upon His providence. We are told that when the day came for the departure of Teresa and those of her companions whom she did not leave behind her, the courage of some failed, and she had to strengthen it by a promise, the fulfilment of which was always considered miraculous. She promised them in the name of our Lord that, if they lived as good Religious, nothing should be wanting to them. In the course of the next year she renewed her promise. Now the time came for the nine novices to be professed, and doubts were again raised, on account of the extreme poverty of the convent. Teresa was then at Palencia, occupied with the foundation in that city, of which we shall have to speak. She wrote to them on Trinity Sunday, saying again that nothing necessary should be 'wanting to them, if they lived up to their Rule. The novices, on the reception of this letter, made their profession with great fervour.

The promise sent by St. Teresa in this case was abundantly fulfilled. The convent was always supplied with food and other necessaries, gave largely to the poor, and soon had a fine church and an annual income of four hundred ducats. All this was testified by four of the nuns, thirty years after, in the process of canonization of St. Teresa, and three of those who gave evidence had heard her make the promise. In the first year after the foundation, a very great marvel happened. A great dearth fell upon the neighbourhood, there was no corn in the town, and for six months the nuns had no assistance and no alms to support them. At the time when the famine began, in February, 1581, they had a store of not more than eight or nine " measures " of meal, hardly a month's supply, and there were thirteen or fourteen nuns, two servants, and two friars with them nearly all the time. Yet all the while they lacked no food, and gave considerable quantities in alms to the poor. The meal seemed to grow as it was taken from the store, like the five or four loaves in the hands of our Lord. Five of the nuns who were eye-witnesses of the fact, gave testimony in the process, among whom was Anne of St. Augustine, who had the charge of the store, and who knew that there was no other supply for the whole of the six months mentioned.

This Anne of St. Augustine was afterwards famous among the Saints of the Order. She had a special devotion to the Holy Infancy, a devotion which has always been specially cultivated by the Carmelites. Her office in the new community was that of purveyor, portress, and procuratress, and her prayers enabled her to supply well the necessities of the convent. St. Teresa gave her a little statue of the Infant Jesus, to Whom she constantly had recourse in all emergencies, her faith being as constantly rewarded by prodigious assistance.

St. Teresa had taken with her six Religious to Villanueva, one of whom, Mary of the Martyrs, was made Prioress, Elvira of the Angel Subprioress. Mary of the Martyrs was from Toledo, the Subprioress from Malagon. Constantine of the Cross, from Toledo, and Anne of St. Augustine, from Malagon, were the other two who remained. The number of six was made up by those who were not intended to remain, that is, her constant companions, Anne of

St. Bartholomew, and her cousin, Beatrix of Jesus' whom she seems to have taken with her in order to win her from her reserve—and, perhaps, to keep her away from Malagon—and these two went away with her.

Her accident was not allowed to prevent her departure, as the time prescribed by Father Angelo had nearly expired. She arrived at Toledo the day before Palm Sunday, where she was immediately prostrated by a paralytic attack which seemed at one time likely to end her days suddenly.

————

CHAPTER V.

A Chapter of Letters.

WHEN St. Teresa arrived at Toledo for Palm Sunday, 1580, as has been said at the close of the last chapter, she was unexpectedly struck down by a paralytic attack, which appeared likely to end her life. Though she recovered, she was not allowed to move till the beginning of June, when we find her at Segovia, on her way to Valladolid, with the object in view of undertaking immediately the foundation of Palencia. We have heard of the translation of her earliest friend, Don Alvaro de Mendoza, from the see of Avila to that of Palencia. Always devoted to the Reform, he was anxious to get a foundation of Teresian nuns in his new see. This could not be refused him, notwithstanding the many difficulties which, as usual, seemed to beset the plan. One great feature in all these histories, however, is that there never seemed to be lacking a supply of good and fervent postulants. There was little fear for the ultimate success of the Order as long as this feature existed. We have a series of letters written while Teresa was at Toledo, which will help us to follow the few incidents which belong to her history at this time.

The first letter[1] is dated the 3rd of April, that is Easter Day, and is addressed to Mary of St. Joseph at Seville. She speaks of her illness and the wretched state in which it has left her, and of a visit she has had from Father Nicolas Doria, who is wonderfully enchanted with Mary of St. Joseph. The worst is that she herself has caught the infection from him. " May it please God, my daughter, that you do nothing to make me less proud of you, and may He hold you by the hand!" Mary has spoken of the new Sisters at Seville. Teresa would like to see them. Mary is to pray for the affairs of Portugal, the matter of the succession to the kingdom—claimed by Philip II.— and the troubles of Doña Guiomar Pardo, daughter of her old friend, Doña Luisa de la Cerda, who is afflicted at having no children. Teresa has been taken aback by some of the things Father Doria has told her —apparently about the state of things with regard to one of the nuns who had lately given so much trouble. Father Gratian is to be at Seville, and the Prioress is warned about letting there be any occasion of tattling about his eating at the convent. She thanks the Prioress again for her generous contri-

[1] Letter cclxxxii.

butions to the necessities of the Order. With regard to the new house, she rather comes round to Mary of St. Joseph's view, but warns her against trusting any one till she has seen it herself, and some nuns with her. She is particularly anxious that she should not trust the report of the Discalced Friars, from whose monastery it seems the house was inconveniently distant, as the confessors had to come from the former.

Teresa says she has asked some one to write to the Prioress an account of the late foundation at Villa-nueva de la Jara, and mentions the nuns she has left there, and her plans for Valladolid and Segovia. She complains much of the pains in her heart, and ends rather abruptly, leaving to her cousin Beatrix to write the postscript. Beatrix, who had lived at Malagon with Mary of St. Joseph, mentions that Brianda of St. Joseph had received Extreme Unction, and adds a few details as to the house and other matters. At the end, apparently by Teresa's injunction, she begs the Prioress to send and inquire after the ex-Prior of Las Cuevas, the Carthusian monastery, who is ill, that the Carmelites may not seem to forget him now that he is out of office.

A short note to Father Gratian about the chap-laincy to the nuns of Malagon, seems to belong to this time. The next is to Isabel Osorio, the lady on whom St. Teresa was looking to help in the foun-dation of Madrid. She has been ill. St. Teresa is glad that she is better, and that her illness has not put an end to her good desires, which she trusts to see accomplished. She hopes for certain to be at Madrid before long, though she wishes this to be kept secret.

If it comes about she will inform Isabel secretly, that they may meet. The new Provincial of the Society is to be there about this time—no other than Balthasar Alvarez, one of the greatest friends she has, who was her confessor for years. She sends a note to him to be given him by Isabel, if, as she hopes, she sees him. She cannot have a better guide. Unhappily, Father Balthasar Alvarez was not long to survive. He died on St. James' day this year, July 25, 1580. The letter ends with a good account of Isabel's sister, Inez of the Incarnation. She is well, a great servant of God, Who has her by the hand, she is great in obedience and in all virtues.[1]

There follow next two letters to Lorenzo de Cepeda, who was in trouble about their brother Pedro, a melancholy and, apparently, half imbecile person, extremely difficult to manage. Teresa writes with immense charity in his favour, for he seems to have had no support but from Lorenzo, and had made himself almost intolerable. She says she feels tempted to give him up, her charity is so small, but she looks upon the poor fellow as left to her by God, for Whose sake she would suffer anything for him. He had set off on a foolish journey to Toledo, which she dislikes. But she begs Lorenzo not to keep him in his own house. Pedro is half mad on that subject, though not on others, and she is told by learned men that this sort of madness is quite possible. The fault is in his extreme weakness of mind. She is much afraid of what may happen. Lorenzo may well be annoyed. Pedro talks of going to Seville, what for, no one knows,

[1] Letters cclxxxiii.

except to spend his money.   His head is so bad that
the heat may kill him in a day.   She had got him to
consent to stay yet a while at Toledo, till Lorenzo
answers the letter which she is writing, and she begs
the latter to answer her favourably as soon as possible.

Teresa speaks beautifully and strongly to induce
him to grant her request. When God has given any one
so many graces as He has to him, He expects great
things in return, and this is one.   The poor man is
out of his mind, and Lorenzo is bound, according to
the law of perfection, to assist him rather than others,
on account of his relationship.   Joseph was still less
obliged than he is to assist his brethren after what
they had done.   She is afraid Pedro may die in the
journey, and then Lorenzo will be always mourning,
and perhaps God will reproach him.   It is well to
consider before anything is done that cannot be
repaired.   Then she proposes the sum which she
thinks Lorenzo might give him, and it may be
arranged that he may live with Juana de Ahumada
and her husband.   It is very sad, but it is the best
that can be done.   Lorenzo is to think he gives the
money to her, and she wishes with all her heart
she could avoid being chargeable to him by giving
something to Pedro herself.[1]

This letter is dated the 10th of April. Teresa writes
again to Lorenzo five days later, to urge him to write
quickly.   The Prioress will forward the letter, as there
are at Avila many opportunities.   She repeats what
she has said about her sorrow not to be able in conscience to give anything herself.   She is better in

[1] Letter cclxxxv.

health. What has been proposed about Pedro lodging with the Carmelite Friars is impossible : they cannot take in seculars, and he could not abide the food. This melancholic humour is a terrible thing! bad for himself as well as others.[1] We need not stop more than to mention a short note to Mary of Christ, the Prioress of Avila, written at the same time with the letter just mentioned.[2] The next letter is to Father Gratian, and we gather from it that Father Angelo de Salazar had given him some delegated powers over the Reform, on which, however, it was thought prudent for him not to act, in view of the Brief which was expected from Rome, and which would give them entire liberty. The remainder of the letter is on matters relating to the foundation at Madrid, and the admission of a postulant at Segovia. She mentions in passing that in her late illness she had felt as ready to die as to live, whereas she used formerly to fear death. It would be a great joy to her to see Gratian, who had said that perhaps he might come to Toledo. But she does not wish to put him to trouble, and she is afraid the friars will talk of it.[3] This letter is dated May 5.

She mentions the good news they expect from Rome in another note of this date, the 5th of May, to Pedro Juan de Casademonte.[4] We next come to an interesting letter to the Duchess of Alva, which

---

[1] Letter cclxxxvi.
[2] Letter cclxxxvii.
[3] Letter cclxxxviii. "Temo lo notaran estos nuestros hermanos." She perhaps means the Calced Friars.
[4] Letter cclxxxix.

seems really to be written for the sake of inducing
her to exert her influence in protecting a house of
the Society which had recently been founded in
Pampeluna. The Duchess had lately been comforted
by the deliverance of the Duke from his "prison" in
Uzedon. The King had been displeased with him,
as has been said, for marrying his son without the
royal leave. But Philip now had need of him, as he
was sending an army into Portugal, which, in effect,
conquered the country to the Spanish crown in a few
weeks, under the command of the Duke, who was
sent, as was said, "from chains to conquer kingdoms."
Teresa tells the Duchess of her own bad health and
troubles. "May His Majesty too give them to me
alone, and not to such as it would pain me more to
see them suffer than to suffer myself." She speaks·
of the vanity of human things, and the wisdom of
putting ourselves entirely in the hands of God. She
hopes the Duchess will let her hear of her. Then
she makes her petition, which she says she should
have made to the Duke if he was not away. The
"Condestabile" of Navarre, who has been kind to
the Jesuits, might perhaps be got to assist the Fathers,
who are persecuted much in the same way that the
Carmelites are from time to time, people objecting
to the new foundation because it will have to be
supported by alms. Teresa explains that they spend
something in Pampeluna, that the house has been
moderately founded, and after all, it is want of faith
to think that so great a God cannot provide for His
servants. The letter to the Condestabile is not to
be a mere formal recommendation, but one which

shows that the Duchess has the affair at heart.[1] The date of this letter is May 8.

In a letter to Gratian, of the 30th of May, Teresa tells him that the admission of the postulant at Segovia is arranged, and that she herself is to take her. It has been rather difficult—" each Prioress looks to the good of her own house." She wants Gratian to come with her for Corpus Christi, and they may travel to Palencia together, as she hopes they may be able to talk over other things, which she therefore leaves.[2] But she writes again on the 3rd of June,[3] in some doubt. Father Antonio has been so ill, that Gratian might well have come to see him, but he has not—not even written that his recovery has been a consolation to him! She still hopes to start in a few days for Segovia.[4]

The journey to Segovia was accomplished in about a week, and was full of pain and discomfort to St. Teresa, who probably was utterly unfit to undertake it. Father Jerome apparently, accompanied her. She was now to receive a blow in her tenderest affections, by the sudden death of her much loved brother, Lorenzo de Cepeda. It is curious that her first letter from Segovia was to him, dated June 15, 1580. She complains that she has had no news from Avila, "since Pedro went back there," from which we learn that she gained her wish with Lorenzo as to the allowance to be made Pedro and the arrangements concerning him. She mentions that Gratian is with her, and that Father Antonio was taking her letter

---

[1] Letter ccxc.
[2] Letter ccxci.   [3] Letter ccxcii.   [4] Letter ccxcii.

to Avila. She had been two days at Segovia when she wrote. A letter from Lorenzo crossed hers on the road, or he answered it at once, for on the 19th she wrote to him again. This letter had spoken of great depression, and a strong presentiment of his coming death, as to which she encourages him. He ought to go out more, at least as far as St. Joseph's. She does not know why he thinks he is going to die. A few days later he was dead. Teresa was at recreation, with the nuns at Segovia, when she suddenly became pale, rose up, and went straight to the chapel. The nuns followed her, and joined her in prayer. They soon learnt that she had seen Don Lorenzo expire at La Serna, as if before her eyes. She had the consolation—which she did not speak of at the time—of seeing Lorenzo in glory. He had but just passed through Purgatory. A few days later, when about to receive Holy Communion, she saw St. Joseph on one side of the priest, and on the other her brother, beaming with joy. The letter in which she communicates this to Mary of St. Joseph is one of the most interesting of all.

JESUS.

The Holy Spirit be with your Reverence, my Mother. Our Lord does not seem to wish to let me pass much time without suffering. You must know that He has been pleased to take to Himself His good servant and friend, Lorenzo de Cepeda. A severe hæmorrhage came on him, which choked him, and he died in six hours. He had been to Communion two days before, and as he died was able to commend himself to our Lord. I hope in His mercy he was taken to enjoy God. He was in such dispositions that he could feel no interest but in what was for God's service. This was why he took so much delight in his property near Avila, he said he could not bear the complimentary nothings of society. His prayer was continual, for he always kept himself in the presence of God, and His Majesty bestowed on him favours which sometimes astonished me. He was much inclined to penance, and did more of it than I liked, for he told me about everything of the kind, and the regard he had for anything I said was extraordinary, and came from the great love he had for me. I repay him by rejoicing that he has passed out of this miserable life, and is now in safety. This is not a mere form of speech; it gives me joy when I think of it, I am full of pity for his children, but for the father I think God has had mercy.

I tell all this to your Reverence, for I know that his death has afflicted you, as it well may, and all my Sisters who are with you, and I say it to console you. The pain he felt at your trouble was wonderful, and the love that he bore you. Now is the time for repaying him, commending him to our Lord, with the condition, that if his soul does not require prayers—which I think it does not, and we may think so according to what our faith teaches—they may be applied to the souls that are in the greatest need, that the profit may be theirs. A little before he died he had written me a letter, here in St. Joseph's of Segovia, which is where I then was, eleven leagues from Avila, in which he said things to me he could not apparently have said, if he had not known how short a time he had to live, which astonished me. It seems to me, my daughter, that all passes so quickly, that we ought to make how to die more the matter of thought than how to live. May it please God that as long as I remain here it may be to do Him some service. I was four years older than he, and I go on living, indeed, I am well of the illness I had, though I still suffer as much, especially in my head.

She says she is to go on the morrow to Avila, to
look after the necessary steps to be taken for the
family, to see what Teresa—his child—will have.
She has an immense loss in her father, who loved
her much, and all the family will lose likewise. God
find a remedy!

She has already told Mary of St. Joseph that the
bills of exchange she has sent for the payment of
part of her debt to Lorenzo, are worth little or
nothing, and she says it is better to wait and not
pay quickly than to pay badly. This subject occupies
a few sentences. She remembers messages to her
friends; the good Prior of Las Cuevas, who is now
allowed to rest—he must have suffered much—also
Father Rodrigo Alvarez, who had written just at the
nick of time to teach her the full value of troubles.
It seems as if God worked miracles by him when
alive—what will it be when he dies? The change in
esa pobrecita—Beatrix, the nun who had caused so
much mischief—would be one, if she really came to
herself. She does not approve of the nuns con-
demning Garcia Alvarez, she does not believe much
of what is said about him, for she thinks he was
always in good faith. She always thought the
others had taken him in. She says that a great
many prayers have been made for Beatrix, perhaps
our Lord will have mercy on her. She strongly
reprimands the Prioress for having been too easy
in allowing her to go to Communion. "I tell
you, Mother," she says, "that it is not reasonable
that those who do such things should go un-
punished. The perpetual imprisonment which had

been determined for her was not too much for her deserts."

These sentences show that St. Teresa was still very loth to condemn Garcia Alvarez, but that it was on the ground of his having been deluded and having acted conscientiously. The remainder of the letter is less important. There is a passage in which she speaks of the report of an intended rising of the Moriscoes at Seville, which would have given the nuns a good opportunity of martyrdom. She wishes to hear all about it. She is also anxious for news from America, whether an old gentleman, who was at Lima, Don Diego Lopez de Zuniga, was alive or dead, as, if he is dead, the next heir will be able to sell the nuns at Salamanca a new house, which was so much and so long wanted.[1]

Next after this letter comes another, written we are not told to whom. It is on St. Teresa's favourite topic, as we may call it—the consolation of the afflicted after some great loss.

JESUS.

The grace of the Holy Spirit be with your honour, and give you strength both in spirit and in body to bear the great blow you have received by this trouble. If it were not inflicted by a Hand so full of tenderness and of justice, I should not know how to comfort your honour, for it has filled me with pity. Since I understand how truly this great God loves us, and as I know that your honour well understands the misery and instability of this wretched life, I hope His Majesty will give to your honour ever more and more light to understand the mercy that our Lord shows

---

[1] Letter ccxcv.

to one whom He takes out of it, with knowledge of this truth, all the more as we can be certain, as our faith teaches us, that that holy soul is where it will receive its reward, according to the many travails it has undergone in this life, bearing them with so much patience. I have begged our Lord very earnestly, and caused our Sisters here to pray also, that He will give your honour comfort and light to begin afresh the battles with this miserable world. Blessed are they who are in safety! It does not seem to me that it is now the time to dwell on this at large, except with our Lord, praying Him to console your honour, for creatures are of little worth when our pain is like yours, much more such poor creatures as I am. May His Majesty do this as His Power is able to do it, and be a companion to your honour henceforth, so that you may not miss the very good one whom you have lost.

The unworthy servant and subject of your honour,

TERESA DE JESUS.

Teresa left Segovia early in August, taking her nephew Francis with her on her way to Valladolid, where he and she had some papers to sign in execu- tion of his father's will. At that time Don Francis was thinking of becoming a Carmelite friar, but we shall see that his thoughts of a religious vocation soon evaporated, much to his own loss. Teresa writes again to Mary of St. Joseph on the 6th of August, before she knows whether her former letter had been received—a matter about which there seems to have been continual uncertainty in the Spain of those days.

She repeats, therefore, in a few lines the contents of her former letter: the death of Don Lorenzo, her journey to Avila to look after the young Teresa, and the like. She says that troubles will not be lacking to the young Francis, nor to her. He is not apt in business, and would have already "left all"—she means for Religion—as he is very virtuous. Her Reverence at Seville must help her, especially as to the news from America. She wishes to know whether any remittances have come for her brother—"may he have glory!"—or any papers, and also whether the Diego Lopez de Zuniga spoken of in her former letter is alive or dead. She mentions that Lorenzo has left money for a chapel at Avila, where he wished to be buried—apparently, as has been said before, the money which is owing to him from Seville. There is something more about the bills of exchange which the Prioress has sent, and which cannot be realized. Teresa as executrix has to look after the business.

This letter contains important news from Rome. "Father Jerome Gratian, who is here now and has accompanied my journey and been of great use in these business matters, has heard from Fra Juan de Jesus, in Rome. The Brief has already been given to the King's Ambassador to send it to Spain, the courier who brings Fra Juan's letter has it in charge, so we know for certain that the King now has it. Juan gives the substance of it, for it is of considerable length. God be praised for His mercy to us. We may well thank Him." She asks for news how the Prioress is, and all such matters. She is afraid of the great acts for her. She does not forget to ask how Beatrix is going on. The date of the letter is the feast of the Transfiguration, August 6th.

We next find a tender letter to the young

"Teresita," her niece, now an orphan. Her letter has delighted her. As to her aridities in prayer, our Lord seems to treat her as if she were strong, and He tests her love, whether it is as great in dryness as in delight. She is to consider it a great boon. Perfection lies not in devotion, but in virtue, devotion will come back when she does not expect it. Teresita has apparently some temptation—an aversion, perhaps —with regard to some one in the community. Let her not think about it. A thing coming into the mind is not at once evil, although the thought be of something bad, which this is not. When any evil thought comes, she should bless herself and recite the *Pater*, or strike her heart, and think of something else. Thus she will merit by resisting.

She sends loving messages to some nuns she cannot write to. Don Francis acts like an angel, and is well. Yesterday he went to Communion with his household. She will write from Valladolid, where they go to-morrow.[1]

A few days later, the 9th of August, she writes a line or two to her sister, Juana de Ahumada, full of sympathy and consolation. It is a great grace to have to suffer. All ends quickly, as we have seen. Let her take courage, the reward is endless. She is overwhelmed with fatigue and business, but it is for the service of God, and for his sake who He has taken to glory. She sends tender messages to her nephew and niece.[2]

There is next a very graceful letter of thanks for certain favours and kindnesses received by the com-

---

[1] Letter ccxcviii.   [2] Letter ccxcix.

munity at Valladolid from Don Diego de Mendoza, the brother, as it appears, of the good Bishop, Don Alvaro. She speaks of Gratian's great interest in him, and of prayers made for him. The letter is rather too long to translate, but it is thoroughly Teresian. Its date is the 21st of August, so we know that Teresa had by that time reached Valladolid.[1] In another, to our old friend Roque Huerta, of the 8th of September, a mere note, she mentions that she has not as yet heard any more details of the news from Rome.[2] The next letter is to Doña Inez Nieto, whose husband was in the service of the Duke of Alva. It speaks of the great troubles of Doña Inez, whose husband had shared, it is said,[3] the imprisonment of the Duke. Teresa assures her that she feels for her so much that if that was enough to make her troubles cease, they would be already at an end. She speaks in her usual manner on the value of sufferings and the joy which a knowledge of their value ought to bring to us.[4]

Teresa's next letter[5] is to Father Gratian, and

[1] Letter ccc.   [2] Letter ccci.

[3] The letter is fixed for this year, on account of the death of the Marchesa de Velada, which is mentioned. But at the time it was written the Duke had been set free for some months, and was entering on the short but brilliant campaign by which Portugal was conquered for Philip II. The Battle of Alcantara took place on August 25th, and on the same day the Spaniards also gained a naval victory, which placed Lisbon at their mercy. Don Antonio, the Grand Prior of Crate, who was at the head of the opposition, was defeated a second time off the Azores on September 22nd, and fled to France. The conquest of the kingdom was soon completed, and before the end of the year Philip was acknowledged King.

[4] Letter cccii.   [5] Letter ccciii.

almost entirely occupied with her family affairs. The
poor Pedro de Ahumada was already giving trouble
to the young Don Francisco, writing to him unreason-
able demands, and taking no part in business in
which he might have helped. Teresa begs that he
may be left to her, for whom he has some respect,
and that Don Francisco may be encouraged to hold
his own and be very stiff with his uncle. Pedro will
have all that he ought to have, and give no trouble
to a cousin, Peralvarez Cimbron, who had been left
guardian to the children. Francisco was at that time
bent on becoming a Religious, and it appears that this
news, which they had tried to keep secret, had got
out through the garrulity of a page. She does not
see why it should not be published. She evidently
quite expected at this time that he would persevere
in his intention.

On the 7th of October she writes to the Prioress
and nuns of St. Joseph of Avila about the testa-
mentary dispositions of Lorenzo (her brother). If
Don Francis makes his profession, they must see how
he disposes of his property, and he can leave by will
the income of the present year. After his profession,
the property is to be divided between "Teresita"
and her other brother, Lorenzo, then in Peru. The
"major-domo" will look after what is to be spent on
his part. There are arrangements for the chapel in
St. Joseph's, for which the deceased has left a legacy,
as has been said. If the younger Lorenzo dies
without issue, then the whole "Capella major" is to
be built, which is not her wish unless that happens.
They are cautioned not to place too much confidence

in the major-domo, one of the chaplains should from time to time be sent to see how things go on.

Oh, my children, what fatigue and trouble these temporal matters cause! I have always thought it, and now I have experience. All that I have had to go through in any foundations have not upset and wearied me like this. Perhaps my illness has had something to do with it, but the business has helped to wear me out. Pray to God that all may be for His service, for it has been in great measure for your sakes that I have taken it so much to heart, and recommend me much to His Majesty. I never seemed to love you so much. May He guide it all, as it may be for His greater glory and honour, and may temporal riches never take from us our poverty of spirit.

There is a note at the end of the letter directing this paper to be kept in the "chest with three keys."

A letter, dated the 25th of October, to Mary Joseph at Seville does not contain any matter of special importance to us. Teresa had not heard of the community at Seville for some time, and is glad to have the letters she is answering, though of rather old date, for she has been very ill, and they thought she would die. She does not know why God leaves her here, this year she has seen so many servants of God die, that it has pained her much. Beatrix is mentioned. If God in His mercy lets us see the new Province erected, they must settle what is to be done with her, for it is not well, as she has said before, that she should be left without punishment. There is still no news from America, at which she is much surprised. The rest of the letter is on various subjects. Father Nicolas Doria sends it on

with a postscript of his own, saying that what they
have heard about Don Francis, her nephew, will not
come about, he has already given up his ideas of
Religion. They are to pray much for Fra Pedro
Hernandez, who had been nominated Commissary
for the execution of the Brief about the Province, but
who was dangerously ill. We shall speak of this
Brief presently. The affair was much delayed by
Philip II.'s attention to the affairs of Portugal.[1]

St. Teresa tells Father Gratian what has taken
place as to her nephew in another letter of the 20th
of November. She does not write with her own
hand, as she has tired her head with writing a long
letter yesterday, to Father Gratian's mother, Doña
Juana Dantisco. Many letters seemed to have failed,
if Gratian has written any, but it is enough she has
heard he is well.

The letter of yesterday has told him all about
her nephew. All are astonished he has been "unmade
and made again," that he is quite changed. No
wonder, as he has been among his relations. She
does wonder how God has abandoned a soul that
desires to serve Him. Impenetrable are His judgments! She is full of compassion. He has become
devoted to the business of managing his property,
and very fond of it, and so afraid of speaking to
Discalced Carmelites, either friars or nuns, that she
thinks he does not wish to see them, and her first of
all. He is said to say that he is afraid his first
desire will come back again. This is the great temptation. She beseeches Gratian to pray much for him.

[1] Letter cccv.

He talks of marrying, but not out of Avila. He will
be very poor, and afflictions will not be wanting to
him. It seems that he has been sent to Pastrana,
and left there, by Gratian and Father Nicolas, and
the aspect of the house frightened him. At all events,
she is quit of a great charge, for he will have to
manage his affairs himself. The matter of the chapel
must now go on as if he was not to make profession.
Fra Angelo has written to her about it, and she is
very weary.

She mentions Fra Pedro Hernandez—he is not
dead, but very ill. All the nuns with her are very
well, long to hear about his Paternity, and ·the writer
of the letter and Inez of Jesus kiss his hand.

There is a piece added on to the letter, some of
which is by Anne of St. Bartholomew, but some may
be by Teresa herself. It says that " this Francis,"
her nephew, is very restless. She mentions she has
known him suffer much in his stomach, his head, and
from weakness of heart. She considers his not taking
the habit a great mercy. He told her at Avila that
no one was forcing him. " I tell you, my Father,"
Teresa's usual expression, " I always feared what has
happened." Somehow it has been a relief to her not
to have to look after him. Even in his marriage he
·says he will do as she wishes. She is afraid he will
not have much happiness, it is only not to seem
angry at what he has done that she continues her
care of him. If Gratian saw the letters she had had
from him from Avila and Pastrana, he would wonder
at the alacrity and content with which he sought to
have the habit. He had seen Teresa, apparently,

since the first part of her letter was written, and she says she had not said a word to him, and that he was silent because another relative was present. He was much ashamed of himself. May God make it all right! With the saints, she thinks, he would have been a saint. She hopes in God he will save his soul, for he is very much afraid of offending Him. She mentions Casilda of the Conception—Casilda de Padilla—as recommending herself to Gratian's prayers. This shows that Casilda was still at Valladolid at the time. The last part of her letter is signed by Anne of St. Bartholomew.

We may as well finish, as far as is necessary, the story of this poor nephew of St. Teresa, of whom she speaks so touchingly in the letter which has just been mentioned. He seems to have been a weak youth, who might have been kept perfectly right and happy by the assistance of religious discipline, but the Reform was as yet in its infancy, and there may have been many features in its scarcely regulated existence which might have been adverse to beginners of no very strong character. Gratian himself had passed a novitiate at Pastrana of which the details were terrible, his novice-master having been a person of no experience and very narrow mind. We are not told what sort of a friar he was who received the young Cepeda. Teresa informs us that he was left very suddenly there by Gratian and Father Nicolas. Perhaps they thought that it was enough to take him to the door and leave him there. Perhaps if he had been more judiciously handled, something might have been made of him, but his vocation was evidently not mature, and he gave it up at once. His stay at Avila may have affected him somewhat, for he could not help feeling that he was all of a sudden master of his own fortunes. The austerities frightened him, and he was ashamed of himself when he came to see or think of his aunt, and his bright, happy sister Teresita.

His project of marriage was soon carried out, and this perhaps shows that among his relations were many who did not wish to see him a friar. His bride was Orofrisia de Mendoza y Castillo, both her parents being of very noble families. She was not rich, but had a fortune of four thousand ducats. She was then a girl of fifteen, quite old enough to marry as things went in Spain, and St. Teresa speaks highly of her in all respects. She had but one brother, and if he died, she was to inherit his property. She had a clever, prudent mother, and Francis got on well with both. The marriage came about in the December of the year of which we are writing. It was the cause of much trial to Teresa, not on account of any disagreement or misconduct of the young couple, but because the family thought of trying to annul the provisions of Don Lorenzo's will, in which a certain legacy was reserved for the Convent of St. Joseph which Teresa could not conscientiously give up. There would have been a lawsuit, if she had been less firm, and we shall see hereafter the letter which she wrote to Doña Beatrix, the mother-in-law. Francis took the side which favoured his interests, and by the time the question was raised he was in difficulties, though he is still said to have led a pious life and to have been devoted to his aunt.

J 3

He sailed to America in hopes of bettering his
fortune, and died many years afterwards in Quito
without leaving any issue. St. Teresa was repaid for
her tender family affection by many consolations,
which the progress in grace of those dear to her must
have occasioned. But she had also much to suffer in
consequence of her family affairs, and we shall see
this trouble haunting her up to the very last. At the
time of which we write, she had little happiness from
her kinsfolk, except from " Teresita." Indeed, she
had not now much longer to live.

As we shall very soon have to mention the other
nephew, to whom St. Teresa wrote after the death of
his father, we may give a short account of him here.
Lorenzo was the second of the two sons. He went to
Peru during the lifetime of his father, to take an office
there which Don Lorenzo had held, and resigning
at the same time his portion of his father's fortune in
Spain to his younger brother. He prospered in the
New World. He married a lady of Hispaniola, Maria
de Hinejosa, and had a good income in 1581. His
father-in-law held a high position at Quito, so high,
that when the Viceroy died, he administered the
province as Vicar. Lorenzo filled a lucrative and
honourable post under the King. He followed his
father's example in largely helping his poor relations,
and in other good works. He had four sons and two
daughters, and his family took root and flourished in
Peru.

We have a letter on the 21st of November,[1] from
Valladolid, to Mary of St. Joseph at Seville, which

[1] Letter cccvii.

may pass without remark as we know already almost all that it contains. Father Gratian was at Seville— where, about this time, he was made Prior of the friars—and Teresa writes to give the Prioress joy. There is again mention of the unfortunate bills of exchange which are of no value. She asks that the money may be taken by the convent from the dowry of some nun whom they have received, as she cannot wait, for the chapel must be begun. She has no resources where she is, and she does not know where to turn. Father Gratian will tell her all about the affairs of the Order. She desires news of her health. She slips in a caution about behaviour, evidently with a view to her treatment of Father Gratian. "For charity's sake be very cautious, for you have in the house one to whom what is nothing seems a great deal. Tell me how the poor thing goes on, and how the Prior of Las Cuevas is." She of course alludes to the poor Sister Beatrix. The letter ends with kind messages, and an injunction to pray much for the affairs of the Order.

At the beginning of December, Teresa writes to the Prioress of Salamanca upon some business not quite intelligible to us, relating to the house and a contract with Pedro de la Vanda, the landlord who had given so much trouble. It is a note tacked on to a letter which is lost, and therefore short. Their friend Father Garcia Manrique, however, recommends them to do what is asked, and she sees no harm in it. Besides, it appears, the contract is made and that is enough. "We have not thought so well of the gentlemen of Salamanca for breaking their word to us, that we should imitate them and do the same."[1]

Our next letter is to the second son of Don Lorenzo de Cepeda, of the same name with her father, of whom we have lately spoken. He was, as has been said, settled in Peru. The letter is dated from Valladolid, in December, 1580.

JESUS.

The grace of the Holy Spirit be with your honour, my child. You may well believe that it gives me great pain to have to write to you the bad news which I now send. But considering that you will hear what I write of from others, who cannot tell you so much to console you under your great sorrow, I would rather that you heard of it from me. And if we consider well the miseries of this life, we have reason for rejoicing in the joy which those have who are already with God. His Majesty was pleased to take to Himself my good brother, Lorenzo de Cepeda, two days after St. John's feast. He was taken after a very short illness, a vomiting of blood, but he had been to Confession and Communion on the feast of St. John, and I believe, considering his state, it was a favour that he had not longer to suffer, for as to his soul, I know well that he was always well prepared. Only eight days before, he had written me a letter, telling me how short a time he had to live, though he did not know the exact day. He died recommending himself to God, like a saint, and so, according to our faith, we may believe that he staid a short time or not at all in Purgatory. As you know, he was always a servant of God, but of late he liked to have nothing to do with the world. If he was not with persons who conversed of God, everything wearied him so much that I had much to do to comfort

[1] Letter cccviii.

him. So he had gone to La Serna to be more alone, where he died, or rather, where he began to live. If I could write some particularities concerning his soul, your honour would understand. the great obligation to God under which you are, for having given you so good a father, an obligation also to live so as to appear his son. But on paper I cannot say more than I have. Let your honour take comfort, and believe that, where he now is, he is able to do you more good than when he was upon earth.

St. Teresa no doubt alludes in this sentence to the vision by which she was made to know the happy estate of her brother. She then speaks of the loss to herself and to Teresita, who is so intelligent and judicious that she bears "it like an angel as she is, and a very good nun, and very happy to be one." Teresa hopes she will be like her father. She herself has not lacked troubles, till she saw Don Francisco settled. She feels her loneliness much—"your honour sees how few relations I have left." So many persons in Avila had desired the alliance of Don Francisco that she had feared he would make an inconvenient choice. God has been pleased to arrange that he has been betrothed on the feast of our Lady's Conception to a lady of Madrid, whose father is dead and her mother alive. The mother desires it so much as to astonish her—being who she is, the girl could have made a much better marriage. Though her dowry is small, still no one in Avila whom they thought of could have had more.

She then speaks of the beauty and discretion of Doña Orofrisia de Mendoza y Castillo, and the noble families with whom she is connected. Francisco writes that he is well content. She herself is glad that the mother, Doña Beatrix, is so discreet and excellent in every way, able to guide them both, and, as is said, live economically. The only inconvenience she can see is that Don Francisco's estate is much burthened, and he may want ready money to live on, unless some comes to him from America. As to this, she urges Lorenzo to help. (Apparently there was some money owing to Don Lorenzo the father, which was expected, but had not arrived.) Francisco is very virtuous—a good Christian. Please God she may hear the same of Lorenzo! "You see, my child, how all passes, and the evil or the good we do in this life last for ever." She mentions her other relatives, Pedro de Ahumada, Juan de Ovalle, and his son.[1]

She also writes, nearly at the end of December, to Mary of St. Joseph at Seville.[2] She is soon to go to Palencia, and her occupations before that prevent her writing much. She gives her some strict injunctions as to diet, and mentions rhubarb as having been of use to some Sisters who had the same disease. She is very glad that Mary of St. Joseph has found out some one in Peru to interest himself as to the matter she has written so often about, and she gives very particular instructions as to what is to be done. As for the money for Don Lorenzo's chapel, she begs her not to put herself out to send it at once. But let her send it to Teresa herself, and not to Don Francisco, who is just married, and might spend it on other things. There are also directions for

---

[1] Letter cccix.　　[2] Letter cccx.

Lorenzo, the brother, who is to address his letters to Seville. The letter concludes with some messages and salutations, but before the end there is a severe sentence about "Beatrix," whose faults she does not think are made enough of by Mary of St. Joseph.

There are several short letters which are placed here by the last Editor, which have no dates, and so come in at the end of the year to which they seem to belong. As is often the case, some of them contain allusions to important matters, but they are not all very clear. The first is to Father Gratian about some troubles at Alba de Tormes, which were occasioned by the foundress. The most important paragraph is one in which Teresa insists on a clear explanation of the rule of the nuns being veiled when they talk with externs, and as it speaks of arrangements to be made in the Constitutions, it is perhaps put here before its date. She wishes it to be made clear who are the persons whom they may see unveiled. She is greatly afraid of their losing the great spirit of joy which our Lord gives them as to all these things. She knows what a discontented nun is, and as long as they give no more occasion for blame than hitherto, there is no reason for being more strict with them than what they have promised to God. Confessors are never to see them unveiled, nor any friars, much less is there to be general liberty to the Discalced. It might be said if there was an uncle of one who had no father, who took care of her as a father, or very near relations, that of itself would be a reason, or a great lady, "a duchess or countess," in short where there is no danger, but rather profit, the veil might be raised. In other cases of doubt, let them get leave from the Provincial—otherwise, never. She fears the Provincial may be too easy. She thinks matters of conscience may be discussed without lifting the veil. His Reverence will see. This can hardly have been written until the Constitutions were under revision.[1]

Our next letter is to a Religious of another Order, who wished to enter as a Discalced Carmelite. Teresa tells her it is impossible. The Carmelites have a Constitution, which she herself asked for, against it. The applications were and might be so many, that although they might have liked to have some of the nuns who applied, it was inconvenient to open the door to such, and she has only to say that she is sorry she cannot oblige her honour. She adds that, before their convents of the Reform were begun, she had lived twenty-five years in one in which there were eighty or a hundred nuns. She has only time to say that to a person who loves God as she is sure her correspondent does, these things will be a cross, and help to advance her soul, and not be able to cause its ruin. "If your honour lives with this desire, to look to God and yourself as the only beings in the house, and take no notice of things which some office does not oblige you to look after, to regard the virtue you may see in each, to love it in her and profit by it, and take no notice of any faults you may see in her, you will do very well. That helped me so much, that though the nuns with whom I lived were so many, it was

[1] Letter cccxi.

no more trial to me than if there had been none, rather a profit. *Senora mia!* after all, we are able to love this great God anywhere."[1]

Another letter consoles some ladies who wanted to be Religious, but were opposed in their desire by their families. She counsels patience, and leaving themselves in God's hands to bring about His own will in them. That is perfection—more might be temptation.[2] Then follows a graceful letter to a lady who asked leave to visit her,[3] another about a reliquary which Doña Maria wishes her to give to the lady to whom she writes,[4] and another to a confessor of one of her convents.[5] The two that remain at this point of the collection are to another confessor, and to Doña Juana Dantisco, Father Gratian's mother.[6]

[1] Letter cccxii. [2] Letter cccxiii.
[3] Letter cccxiv. [4] Letter cccxv.
[5] Letter cccxvi. [6] Letters cccxvii. cccxviii.

NOTE TO CHAPTER V.

The letters which belong to this chapter are the following :

1. (cclxxxii.) *To Mary of St. Joseph, Prioress of Seville.* From Toledo, April 3, 1580.

An account of this letter is given, p. 109.

2. (cclxxxiii.) *To Father Gratian.*   Date uncertain.

Mentioned at p. 110.

3. (cclxxxiv.) *To Doña Isabel Osorio.* From Toledo, April 8, 1580.

An account of this letter is given, p. 110.

4. (cclxxxv.) *To Lorenzo de Cepeda, her brother.*   From Toledo, April 10, 1580.

5. (cclxxxvi.) *To the same.*   April 15, 1580.

These two letters refer to the same subject, and an account of them is given, pp. 111—113.

6. (cclxxxvii.) *To Mary of Christ, Prioress of Avila.* From Toledo, April 16, 1580.

Mentioned at p. 113.

7. (cclxxxviii.) *To Father Jerome Gratian.*   From Toledo, May 5, 1580.

An account is given, p. 113.

8. (cclxxxix.) *To Pedro Juan de Casademonte, at Medina.* From Toledo, May 6, 1580.

Mentioned at p. 113.

9. (ccxc.) *To the most illustrious and excellent Doña Maria Henriquez, Duchess of Alva.*   From Toledo, May 8, 1580.

An account is given at pp. 113—115.

10. (ccxci.) *To Father Gratian.*   From Toledo, May 30, 1580.

An account is given at p. 115.

11. (ccxcii.) *To the same.*   From Toledo, June 3, 1580.

Mentioned at p. 115.

12. (ccxciii.) *To Lorenzo de Cepeda, her brother.* From Segovia, June 15, 1580.

Mentioned at p. 115.

13. (ccxciv.) *To the same.* From Segovia, June 19, 1580.

Mentioned at p. 116.

14. (ccxcv.) *To Mary of St. Joseph, Prioress of Seville.* From Segovia, July 4, 1580.

Translated at pp. 116, 117.

15. (ccxcvi.) *To a person unknown.* About August 5, 1580.

Translated at p. 119.

16. (ccxcvii.) *To Mary of St. Joseph, Prioress of Seville.* From Medina del Campo, August 6, 1580.

An account of this letter is given at p. 121.

17. (ccxcviii.) *To Sister Teresa of Jesus, her niece, a Carmelite at St. Joseph's at Avila.* From Medina del Campo, August 7, 1580.

Mentioned at p. 122.

18. (ccxcix.) *To Doña Juana de Ahumada, her sister.* From Valladolid, August 9, 1580.

Mentioned at p. 122.

19. (ccc.) *To the most illustrious Señor Don Diego de Mendoza.* From Valladolid, August 21, 1580.

Mentioned at p. 123.

20. (ccci.) *To Roque Huerta, or another friend of the Order.* From Valladolid, September 8, 1580.

Mentioned at p. 123.

21. (cccii.) *To Doña Inez Nieto.* From Valladolid, September 17, 1580.

Mentioned at p. 123.

22. (ccciii.) *To Father Jerome Gratian.* From Valladolid, October 4, 1580.

An account is given, p. 124.

23. (ccciv.) *To the Mother Prioress and Religious of St. Joseph's at Avila.* From Valladolid, September 7, 1580.

An account is given at p. 124.

24. (cccv.) *To Mary of St. Joseph, Prioress at Seville.* From Valladolid, October 25, 1580.

An account is given at p. 125.

25. (cccvi.) *To Father Jerome Gratian.* From Valladolid, November 20, 1580.

A full account is given of this letter at pp. 126, 127.

26. (cccvii.) *To Mary of St. Joseph, Prioress at Seville.* From Valladolid, November 21, 1580.

An account of this is given, p. 130.

27. (cccviii.) *To Anne of the Incarnation, Prioress at Salamanca.* From Valladolid, December, 1580.

An account is given at p. 131.

28. (cccix.) *To Don Lorenzo de Cepeda, her nephew, in Peru.* From Valladolid, December, 1580.

Translated at p. 132.

29. (cccx.) *To Mary of St. Joseph, Prioress at Seville.* From Valladolid, December 28, 1580.

An account of this is given at p. 134.

30. (cccxi.) *To Father Jerome Gratian.* End of 1580.

An account is given at p. 135.

31. (cccxii.) *To a Religious of another Order desirous of entering as a Carmelite.* Date uncertain.

An account of this is given, p. 136.

32. (cccxiii.) *To same ladies at Avila, desirous of entering as Carmelites.* Date uncertain.

Mentioned at p. 137.

33. (cccxiv.) *To a lady unknown.* Date uncertain.

34. (cccxv.) *To another lady.* Date uncertain.

35. (cccxvi.) *To a confessor of her nuns.* Date uncertain.

36. (cccxvii.) *To another confessor.* Date uncertain.

37. (cccxviii.) *To Doña Juana Dantisco.* Date uncertain.

These five are short fragments. See p. 137.

CHAPTER VI.

Palencia.

IT has been already mentioned that St. Teresa had left Villanueva de la Jara, the foundation which has been described in a preceding chapter, with the intention of proceeding at once to undertake another at Palencia. These were the orders under which she proceeded to Toledo, having left Villanueva sooner than was her custom after a new foundation, and in a state of suffering from her recent accident. That had been near the end of Lent, 1580, but on reaching Toledo on Palm Sunday she had, as we have said, a paralytic attack which endangered her life, and her convalescence from which was slow and painful. At midsummer she has lost her much-loved brother, Lorenzo de Cepeda, and her first journey from Toledo was to Medina del Campo and Avila directly after her loss, in order to look to the affairs of the deceased —of whom she was left the executrix—and his two children, Francis and Teresa, the latter of whom was in the convent at Avila. She soon returned so far on her way to Palencia as Valladolid, and it is from that city that her letters are dated until close on the end of the year. At last, on the feast of the Holy Innocents, 1580, she left Valladolid, escorted by

Father Jerome Gratian, and accompanied by four nuns, as well as by her inseparable companion, Anne of St. Bartholomew. The four nuns were Isabel of Jesus, Beatrix of Jesus, Inez of Jesus, cousin of St. Teresa, and Mary of the Holy Ghost. The two first named of these were nuns taken from the convent at Salamanca, and as they were very good Religious, taken from a small community, it is very natural that their removal cost the good Prioress of Salamanca a pang, which she appears to have expressed in a letter to St. Teresa. Affections of this kind are the natural growth of the life of a community devoted to God ; they give it a great part of its holy joy, as they furnish occasions for the most beautiful exercises of charity, and also of mortification.

A very few days after their arrival at Palencia, we find Teresa writing to the Prioress—Anne of the Incarnation—a pleasant letter of consolation which is quite characteristic of the Saint. His Majesty evidently chose that Anne of the Incarnation should have to suffer in every way. May He be praised for all. And may His Majesty also repay her for the limes she has sent her—so unwell she was the day before !—she was much pleased with them, and the veil too, for the one she had on was too high, and what her Reverence gives her is much nicer. "All the same, do me the charity not to send me anything till I ask for it. I had rather you spent it on yourself." Then she has fitted out the nuns from her convent so completely, she is so pleased ! Not all of the Prioresses do this, but it is reasonable,

especially for Isabel of Jesus, to whom they owe
so much. She seems quite happy.[1] St. Teresa's
letters abound in little touches of this kind, which her
historians do not mention.

We already know that it was at the urgent
request of Don Alvaro de Mendoza, Teresa's first
friend at Avila, when Bishop of that see, that the new
foundation of Palencia, to which he had been translated, was undertaken. The place was very poor,
and yet the convent was not to be endowed. She
was at first, therefore, very averse to this foundation,
as was also Father Jerome Gratian. Teresa was
urged to it by her niece, Mary Baptist, Prioress of
Valladolid, with whom she spent so much time this
summer. Mary Baptist was very naturally a strong
supporter of the Bishop, as her own convent had been
founded by his family, and they were in the closest
relations of friendship with the nuns therein. St.
Teresa puts down her own reluctance very much to
the great weakness of her health, which, in fact, was
very bad, and continually failing, from this time till
the end of her life. Probably, if she had been less
entirely on fire with the love of God and the zeal for
His service, she would have pleaded that she was
unfit for any exertion at all long before this. Let us
hear herself speak.

I know not whether this came from my illness and the
weakness it left me in, or from the devil, who wanted to
hide the good that was afterwards done. In truth, I am lost
in amazement and grief—and I have often complained of it

[1] Letter cccxix.

to our Lord—at the great share which the poor soul has in the weakness of the body, for it seems to have nothing to do but to observe its laws according to its needs, and anything else which makes it suffer.

One of the greatest trials and miseries of this life seems to me to be the absence of a great spirit to keep the body under control. Illnesses, and grievous afflictions, though they are a trial, I think nothing of if the soul is strong, for it praises God, ánd sees that everything comes from His hands. But to be on the one hand suffering, and on the other doing nothing, is to be in a fearful state, especially for a soul that has had earnest desires never to rest, inwardly or outwardly, but to spend itself wholly in the service of its great God; there is no help for it but in patience and confessing its wretchedness, and in being resigned to the will of God, so that He may use it for what purpose He pleases, and as He pleases. This was the state I was in then : though my strength had begun to come back, yet such was my weakness that I lost that confidence I usually had when I had to begin any of these foundations. I thought everything impossible, and it would have been of great service to me if I could have found any one to encourage me, but, as it was, some helped me to be afraid, others, though they made me hope a little, could not overcome my faint-heartedness.

At that time came thither a Father of the Society, the Doctor Ripalda, a great servant of God, who at one time used to hear my confession. I told him the state I was in, and that I looked upon him as standing to me in the place of God. He must tell me what he thought of it. He began by rousing my courage, and told me that my cowardice was the effect of old age; but I saw well enough it was not, for I am older to-day and I feel none of it, and he too must have known it was not, and therefore rebuked me in that way that I might not think it came from God.

She mentions after this that she had been encouraged also by her old friend, Father Balthasar Alvarez, who was now near the end of his course. He was made Provincial in 1580, and was mentioned by Teresa in her letter to Doña Isabel Osorio,[1] as being in Madrid in the spring. She entreated Isabel to make his acquaintance, and take him for her guide. Notwithstanding all this encouragement, she was still averse to the foundation.

One day, being in doubt, and not determined on making either of the foundations,[2] I implored our Lord, when I had just received Communion, to give me light, that I might in all things do His will, and my lukewarmness was even such as to make me falter for a moment in that desire. Our Lord said to me, as it were reproaching me, "What art thou afraid of? When did I ever fail thee? I am to-day what I have always been. Do not give up these two foundations." O Thou great God, how different are Thy words from the words of men! So my courage and resolution came, the whole world was not strong enough to oppose me, and I began at once to make my preparations, and our Lord to furnish the means.

I received two nuns, that we might have wherewithal to buy a house, and though they told me it was not possible to live by alms in Palencia, it was as if they said nothing, for as to founding it with an endowment I saw it could not be done then, and as God commanded it to be made, His Majesty would see to that.

[1] Letter cclxxxiv. p. 110.

[2] The other foundation which was in contemplation at this time was that at Burgos—the last which St. Teresa made. The Archbishop of Burgos had given leave (by word of mouth, not in writing) for the foundation, when he was passing by Valladolid, and received the pallium from the Bishop of Palencia, who was commissioned to deliver it to him. We shall hear more of this in due time.

K 3

Teresa then relates how she set out on the Holy
Innocents' day, 1580. Father Gratian had been to
look at Palencia, and had come back adverse to the
undertaking. But his mind had afterwards changed.
A gentleman of the place had offered to lend them
a house till midsummer, and it was on the strength
of that that they went. She wrote to a Canon
Reinoso, whom she only knew by reputation, hearing
"that he was a servant of God," to get the house
ready for them, and he did his work so well that they
were most abundantly supplied with all wants. With
her usual quickness, she had Mass said the first
morning after their arrival. The foundation was
made on the day on which King David, to whom
she had a devotion, is commemorated. It was the
feast of St. Thomas of Canterbury. The Bishop was
informed, and came at once with great joy, promising
to supply them with bread, and the people shared
the joy of their prelate. Their good friends, Reinoso
and another canon, helped them in everything. The
idea was that they should have a church given them,
a much frequented hermitage dedicated to "Our Lady
of the Street." There was a great devotion to the
spot. There were two small houses adjoining, which
it was proposed that they should buy for the convent.
The Chapter gave them leave to put up a "grille" so
as to hear Mass in the church, and the confraternity to
which the hermitage belonged, consented to make it
over to them.

The house to which they first went was of
course the house lent them till midsummer. We
have already mentioned the nuns who accompanied

:St. Teresa on her journey. So far, the first beginnings
were prosperous, and everything seemed going well
for the acquisition of the house adjoining the shrine
of "Our Lady of the Street." Soon after, they began
to doubt whether the place would suit them. Let us
have St. Teresa's account.

When the owners of the houses saw that we wished to
get them they raised the price, and very reasonably so. I
would go and see them, but they seemed to me and to those
who went with us so poor that I would not have them on
any account. Later on I saw clearly that Satan, on his
part, exerted himself because it vexed him that we were
come. The two canons who helped us thought we should
be there at too great a distance from the Cathedral Church,
yet it was the most thickly peopled part of the town. In a
word, we all made up our minds, as that house would not
suit, to look for another. This the two canons began to do
with such care and diligence that I gave thanks to our Lord,
and neglected nothing they thought to the purpose. They
were satisfied at last with a house belonging to a person
they called Tamayo. Some parts of it were very well
arranged, so that it was exceedingly convenient for us, and
it stood near the house of a great nobleman, Suero de Vega,
who was a good friend of ours, and who, with others living
in that part of the town, was very much pleased at our
going to live there. The house was not large enough, but
another would be given us with it, which, however, was not
so placed that we could well join the one to the other.
  In short, they gave such an account of the matter that I
wished the purchase to be made, but the two canons would
not settle anything before I saw the place myself. I felt
the going out among people very keenly, and I had so
much confidence in them as to make it unnecessary. At last

I went, and also to see the houses by the Church of our
Lady, though not with the intention of taking them, but to
hinder the owner of the other house from thinking that we
could not help taking his.   To me, and to those who went
with me to see them, they looked so wretched, as I said
before, but we are now astonished that we could have thought
so badly of them.   In this mind we went to the other house,
being fully determined to take it and none other, and
though we found many difficulties, we made light of them,
notwithstanding the great trouble we should have in over-
coming them, for all that part of it which was fitted for our
living in would have to be pulled down in order to build
the church, and after all an inconvenient one.   A strange
thing this predetermination to do a particular thing!   In
truth, it taught me to have little confidence in myself,
though I was not alone in my then delusion.   In a word,
we went away fully resolved that no other would do for us,
and to give the money asked, which was too much, and to
write to the owner, for he was not in the town.   He was,
however, not far off.

This long account of the purchase of a house will seem
foolish until we consider the object which Satan must have
had, that we should not go to that of our Lady, and I
tremble whenever I think of it.   All having made up their
minds, as I said before, to take no other house but that,
the next morning during Mass I began to be very anxious,
doubting if we had done right, and ill at ease, so that I had
hardly any peace during the whole of Mass.   I went to
receive the Most Holy Sacrament, and at the moment of
Communion I heard these words, "This is the house for
thee," in such a way that I made up my mind at once not
to take the other house at all of which I was thinking, but
that of our Lady.   I began to consider the difficulties of
withdrawing from a bargain which had been carried so far,
and which they who had so carefully considered it wished

so much to see settled, and our Lord answered me, "They do not know how much I am offended in that place, and this will be a great reparation." The thought came, Was it a delusion? but not to believe that it was—for I knew well, by the effect it had upon me, that it was the Spirit of God. He said to me at once, "It is I."

I became perfectly calm, delivered from my former uneasiness, though I did not know how to undo what had been done, and to remove the evil impression given to my Sisters of that house, for I had spoken strongly of the unfitness of it, and that I would not have them go there without seeing it for anything in the world. However, I did not think so much about this, for I was well aware that they would take in good part whatever I did. But my doubts were about my friends who wished to have the other house. They would look on me, I thought, as capricious and uncertain, seeing that I changed so quickly—what I hate exceedingly. All this thinking had no influence whatever, much or little, to make me give up the house of our Lady, neither did I remember that it was not a good house, —for if the nuns could hinder but one venial sin, everything else was of no moment, and every one of them, if they only knew what I knew, would have been, I believe, of the same mind.

I had recourse to this. I used to go to confession to the Canon Reinoso, who was one of those who befriended me, though I had never told him anything of the kind before, because nothing had happened to make it necessary for me to do so, and, as I have been accustomed when these spiritual visitations occur always to do that which my confessor may advise, in order that I might travel on the safe road, I determined to tell him all as a great secret, though my mind was not inclined to leave undone what I had been told to do, without a feeling of great pain. I would have ended, however, by doing what he told me, for

I trusted in our Lord that He would do again what I have known Him do at other times, for His Majesty changes the confessor's mind, though of another opinion, so that he shall do what our Lord wills.

I spoke to him first of the many times that our Lord was wont to show me in this way what to do, and that before now many things had happened whereby I knew it to be the work of His Spirit, and then told him what had taken place, but still I would do what he desired, though it might be painful. He is a most prudent and saintly man, and endowed with the gift of good counsel in everything, though he is young, and though he saw that this change would be talked about, his decision was not that I should refrain from acting according to what I had learnt. I told him we would wait for the return of the messenger, and he thought so too, for I was now confident that God would find a way out of it ; and so it came to pass, for the owner of the house, though we had given him what he wanted and had asked for, now asked three hundred ducats more, which seemed absurd, for the sum to be paid was more than the house was worth. Herein we saw the hand of God, for the sale of the house was very serviceable to its owner, and to ask for more when the bargain had been made was not reasonable. This helped us exceedingly, and we said we could never agree with him ; but it was not enough to excuse us, because it was plain that for the sake of three hundred ducats we ought not to give up a house that seemed fit for a monastery. I told my confessor not to trouble himself about my good name, now that he thought I ought to do it, but merely to say to his friend that I was bent on buying the house of our Lady, whether it might be dear or cheap, in good or in bad repair. His friend has a singularly quick understanding, and though nothing was said to him, I believe he grasped the reason when he saw so sudden a change, and accordingly he never pressed me further in the matter.

The progress of the business was slow, and it seems that, if it had been quicker, the nuns might have made the mistake of going to the house of Tamayo. They arrived, as has been said, on the feast of the Holy Innocents. In a letter of the 17th of February to Father Gratian, Teresa speaks of the objections which they felt to the houses at "Our Lady of the Street," and says that they did not mean to take them. On the 27th of the same month, she mentions, in a letter to Gratian, "a good house" as in prospect, meaning that of Tamayo. On the 4th of March she writes to a noble lady, Doña Anna de Enriquez, to thank her for a present of a handsome picture, and then there is still a difficulty about the house, but they are still in treaty for it. In Holy Week, that is, on Good Friday, she writes to Gratian that she thinks they will go to the house of our Lady, showing thereby that their minds are at last made up.

We all saw afterwards the mistake we might have made in buying that house, for we are now amazed when we consider how much better is the one we have, to say nothing of the chief thing of all, and which everybody sees, the service of our Lord and of His glorious Mother therein, and the removal of occasions of sin, for nightly vigils were kept there, and therefore as it was only a hermitage, many things might have been done there, the hindering of which was a vexation to Satan, and we ourselves are glad to be able to serve our Mother, our Lady, and our Protectress in anything. It was very ill done on our part not to have gone there sooner, for we ought never to have looked at any other house. It is plain enough that the devil makes us blind to many things, for there are many conveniences in the house which we should not have found elsewhere. The people, too, wished us to take it, and their joy is exceedingly great, and even those who would have us go to the other house afterwards looked on this as much the best.

Blessed be He for ever and ever Who gave me light herein !—and He does so whenever I happen to do anything well, for every day I am amazed at the little ability I have for anything. This must not be understood as humility, for I see it to be so more clearly day by day. It seems to be our Lord's good pleasure that I and everybody else shall learn that it is His Majesty alone Who makes these foundations, and that, as He by means of clay gave sight to the blind, so He will make one blind, as I am, not to act blindly. Certainly we showed great blindness in this matter, as I said before, and whenever I think of it I give thanks anew to our Lord, only even to do this I am not able, and I do not know how He can bear me. Blessed be His compassion for ever ! Amen.

Those saintly friends of the Virgin then made haste at once to purchase the houses, and they had them cheap in my opinion. They laboured hard, for in every one of these foundations, God would have those who helped us to gain merit, and I am the one who does nothing, as I have elsewhere said, and wish never to refrain from saying, because it is true. Then the help they gave us in arranging the house, and also in paying the money for it, and in becoming our sureties also, as I had no money myself, was very great, for before I found any to be sureties for us in other places, and that for not so large a sum, I was put to great trouble ; and they were right, for if they did not trust in our Lord they would not have done so, because I have no means. But His Majesty has been always so gracious unto me that nobody lost anything by doing me that kindness at any time, nor have I ever failed to repay them fully, and I look upon that as a very great grace.

As the owners of the houses were not satisfied with the two canons as sureties, these went in search of the steward, whose name was Prudencio; but I do not know that my recollection of his name is exact—so they called him then—for as he was called the steward I did not learn his name. He was so charitable to us that our debt to him was and is great. He asked them whither they were going; they answered, to find him that he might sign the bond. He laughed and said, "So this is the way you ask me to become security for so much money?" And thereupon, without dismounting from his mule, he signed, which is a wonderful thing for these times. I should like to speak much in praise of the charity of the people of Palencia, of all together and each in particular: the truth is, it seemed to me like that of the Primitive Church—at least it is not very common in the world now; they knew we had no revenue, and that they would have to find us food, and yet they not only did not forbid us to come to them, but declared our coming to be a very great grace which God gave them; and if it be looked at in the true light, they spoke truly, for, if it did no more than give them another church, wherein the Most Holy Sacrament had another house, that is a great thing.

May He be blessed for ever! Amen. For it is plain enough that He is pleased to be here, and something wrong that must have been done in the place is done no longer—for as much people kept vigil here formerly, and as the hermitage was lonely, some of those that came did not come out of devotion—that is a change for the better. The image of our Lady was in a most unseemly place. The Bishop, Don Alvaro de Mendoza, built a chapel for it, and by degrees much was done for the honour and glory of the glorious Virgin and of her Son. Praise Him for ever! Amen, amen.

At last, when the house was fully prepared for the nuns
to go into it, the Bishop would have them go with great
solemnity, and accordingly it was done one day within the
octave of Corpus Christi ; he came himself from Valladolid,
and was attended by the Chapter, the Religious Orders, and
almost the whole population of the place, to the sound of
music.   We went from the house in which we were staying,
all of us in procession, in our white mantles, with veiled
faces, to the parish church close to the house of our Lady.
Her image had come for us, and we took the Most Holy
Sacrament thence and carried It into our church in great
pomp and order, which stirred up much devotion.   There
were more nuns, for those who were going, to make the
foundation in Soria were there ; and we all had candles in
our hands.   I believe our Lord was greatly honoured that
day in that place.   May He grant it may be always so of
all creatures !   Amen.

It is remarkable that although the house which
thus became a convent of Carmelite nuns was so
especially selected at the time by St. Teresa, it did
not continue to be the home of her spiritual children
for more than ten years.   No doubt the establishment
of the nuns on the spot was of great temporary
advantage to religion, but, when the work which was
immediately required was done, the great inconveniences which were inseparable from the situation
remained.   The church was always frequented by
crowds, and was often filled up to midnight.   Probably
there were numbers of conversions and confessions,
but it was not the place where the nuns could say
their Office undisturbed and pour out their souls in
devotion to the Blessed Sacrament, even though their
grilles protected them from the gaze of the public.

After ten years it was necessary to remove to another place.

After having given this account of the foundation of Palencia, we may supplement it by a brief summary of the letters written from that place. On the 4th of January, Teresa writes to Father Juan de Jesus Roca, then at Pastrana. The first part of the letter refers to some request he wishes her to make to the Cardinal Archbishop of Toledo. Teresa gracefully excuses herself. The Archbishop does not count her letters for much, as Fra Juan knows, and besides, she is going soon to make a petition for the foundation of Madrid, the difficulties that beset which came, as we shall see, from a personal dislike of the Archbishop to something in which Teresa was supposed by him to have a hand with regard to a niece of his own. Then she speaks of the Constitutions which are so soon to be revised, as to which she has very few changes to make, but there must be a conference with the friars, she does not trust her own judgment. She is glad to hear that Tostado is ordered not to meddle with the Discalced.[1] There are also a few words about a postulant whom he wished to have received at Villanueva, but Teresa declines, as the number there is fuller than she wishes. She gives an account of their good reception at Palencia—all on account of the Bishop! Things go so well that she should think it a bad sign, if there had not been contradictions before. The Archbishop of Burgos has

---

[1] After the promulgation of the "Brief of Separation," the Discalced were under the General of the Order, but not any vicar of his, unless taken from their own body.

given her leave to found in his city. Of this leave we shall hear more later on. She mentions that she thinks of going there before Madrid, and she wishes to wait for the arrival of the Brief of Separation, so as not to have to ask the present Vicar. The letter was written just about the date of the arrival of the Brief appointing the Commissary, but St. Teresa did not know it yet. In the rest of the letter she enlarges on the kindness they have received at Palencia, and their good prospects there.[1]

In her next letter, to Mary of St. Joseph, she speaks with delight of the report Mary has sent her of Father Gratian's sermons. Still there is the saving clause, from the anxiety she feels lest he should over-work himself.[2] She makes an arrangement about the money that is to be sent from Seville to Avila to repay the debt to her brother Lorenzo, and begs that it may not be sent to Pedro Casademonte or to Father Doria, "otherwise it would be paid to his brother—this is for your Reverence only." The reason for this was that the brother in question was a creditor of the convent. We are told that the mistake was made, and the nuns did not get the money after all. She writes to Gratian the reason for her wish that it should be paid straight to her. Mary of St. Joseph is still unwell, and Teresa thinks that the air of Seville does not suit her.[3]

---

[1] Letter cccxx.

[2] "Tiene razon en decir es menester se modere en los sermones, que podria ser hacerle daño, siendo tantos." When Father Gratian was elected Provincial, and had the whole of the affairs of the Order to look after, he seems to have gone on preaching Lents and Advents, besides occasional sermons, continually, as if preaching was his chief duty.

[3] Letter cccxxi.

We have next an affectionate letter to her sister, Juana de Ahumada, written as her greeting for Christmas and the New Year. It is a long time since she has thought so much of those that remain to her of her family. Their troubles pain her. May He be praised, Who came at this time only to suffer. Those who imitate Him well in this, will have the more glory. She would gladly suffer in their place, and give them the merit, or, at all events, be where she was able to be with them more! The letter consists chiefly of news of her new foundation and of her family. Francisco has been bled twice. He is very happy with his new home. Pedro is the only uncomfortable one of them all. The more she knows of them all at Madrid the more delighted she is, especially with the discretion and character of Doña Orofrisia. God bless them, and give them grace to serve Him, for all earthly happiness soon comes to end! She urges Juana to write often.[1]

The next letter[2] is rather obscure, but it shows the courtesy and amiability of St. Teresa so strongly, that it is worth mentioning. It is addressed to Canon Reinoso, of Palencia, who had been so kind and useful to Teresa and her nuns, and it seems to have been written on the morning of the day after he had taken her to see the two houses which were then under discussion, the house by "Our Lady of the Street," and the house of Tamayo. She begs that he will tell the bearer how he finds himself, the morning after a day of so much exertion, and she says she has had a good night, and finds herself very

---

[1] Letter cccxxii.　　[2] Letter cccxxiii.

well. Then she mentions the advantage of the house on which they are bent, but it does not seem clear that it is not written before she changed her mind, as is mentioned in the *Book of the Foundations*, that is, after our Lord's injunction that they were to go to "Our Lady of the Street." The value of this letter lies in the charming air of courtesy and gaiety which runs through it.

We next come upon a series of letters which are addressed to Father Gratian during the sitting of the Chapter of Alcara, and contain the views of St. Teresa on some of the points in the Constitutions that required clearing up, and on other matters relating to the Order. The first[1] is mutilated, and begins in the middle of a sentence referring to Father Antonio of Jesus, whom she was very anxious not to see elected as Provincial. There was evidently a strong party for him, as has been said, partly, it may be supposed, on account of his being the oldest friar of the Reform, and partly because his was the only alternative to the election of Gratian that seemed possible. She goes on to say that Father Gabriel ought to be Prior of La Roda, for the sake of the nuns of Villanueva. She is also anxious, if Gratian is Provincial, he will have as his Socius, or companion, Father Nicolas Doria. We have already said something of this favourite plan of St. Teresa, which came to nothing. Gratian's late assistant, Fra Bartolomeo de Jesus, was, like himself, a bland and indulgent character, and she probably wished that Gratian should correct himself by having at hand a stern,

---

[1] Letter cccxxiv.

strong man like Doria. She says Fra Bartolomeo is so delicate, that he cannot do without meat, and this has been remarked by some people. Doria will not give Gratian so much to suffer as others have. In this prophecy we know that she was quite mistaken. She adds a sentence which looks very like a silent reproof of his excessive love for external activity, commends herself to Fra Bartolomeo, "he must be very much fatigued, considering his state of health and your Reverence's way of never resting. It is the way to kill yourself, and your companion as well." She remembers how ill he looked in Holy Week a year ago, and she begs him not to be so much in a hurry about preaching this Lent, and also not to eat so much bad fish. "It does harm and causes temptations." Gratian was gentle to others, and hard on himself. His defect may have been that kind of softness which arises from a want of appreciation of the duty of a Superior to enforce observance, and he seems also, as has been said, to have differed from St. John of the Cross as to his estimate of the mission of the Carmelites "to preach"—in the words of the revelation to St. Teresa—" more by their example than by words."

She speaks in this letter of the building of a chapel at Avila—not that for which Lorenzo had left the money—which was likely to make a quarrel. She is getting on well at Palencia, thanks be to God. Father Bartholomew says that, however much Gratian may shrink from the labours—of being Provincial— the prayers of the nuns will force him into the seat. Mariano had written to her about what she calls his temptation—the idea of voting for Father Antonio. She does not understand him at all. No one will do but Gratian. What she has said on the matter must be kept secret, and the friars of the Chapter must not think that Gratian wants the post for himself. She thinks they cannot in conscience vote but for one of the two.

The next letter[1] to Father Gratian is dated the 21st of February. It is mainly concerned with the points which she wishes insisted upon in the Chapter. One of them is the liberty of the nuns to have preachers freely. She tells Gratian that provision must be made for the future. Persons may some day come to be the Superiors who will interfere in that or other things—and in this she may well have instinctively prophesied. If the Commissary's power does not extend to the limiting of such liberty, it must be asked at Rome. It is of great importance for the comfort of the souls of the Religious, and she sees them in other convents too much tied up in spiritual matters. "A soul under constraint cannot serve God well, it is a cause of temptation, whereas when they are free they very often require nothing more." If the Commissary has power to amend their Constitutions, she wishes that the nuns should be attended to in what is done, whether in the way of taking out what is already there, or in inserting new regulations. She wishes too that Gratian himself and Nicolas should be the persons consulted, and not the rest of the friars. Father Fra Hernandez never consulted them. Everything passed between himself

[1] Letter cccxxv.

and herself, and he put in nothing without telling her.

St. Teresa then goes into much detail on certain minute prescriptions as to the clothes and other such matter. Fra Hernandez had forbidden them to eat eggs in Lent, and to have bread at collation. She wishes this abolished. What the Church allows and what she forbids is enough, without anything added. To require more causes scruples, and does harm, for some think they have no need to get dispensed, when they really have. She has heard that the Chapter has made many regulations about the Office, and ordered two ferial Offices every week. She does not want so many changes, and asks that they may say their Office as they do now. Again, where there are monasteries of the (Mitigated) Order, the Discalced on their journeys are to be obliged to lodge with them. It ought rather to be, that they may be free to go to other lodgings, provided it can be done with edification. Again, the Constitutions require that the convents should be founded in poverty, and not have incomes. But she sees that all are on the way to have foundations, and so this ought to be altered, in order that the Constitutions may not contain anything which has been at once relaxed. It may be said, as the Council at Trent allows foundations, let them have them. She asks also that the Constitutions may be printed, for there are different versions of them. Some Prioresses think nothing of leaving out or inserting what they like. She wishes a strict precept to be made, that no one may do this. In all these matters she looks to Gratian to act for the nuns—Father Nicolas, too, and

L 3

Juan of Jesus. She concludes with an affectionate outburst, because Gratian had said that he would be all on their side. The nuns will never be happy unless he is made Provincial.

She continues the same subject in the next letter,[1] dated the 27th of February. She sends some memorials which were lacking before. It is well that Gratian has ordered them to be sent to her from the convents. If the things which were asked for by St. Joseph's at Avila were granted, they would come to be the same as the nuns of the Incarnation! She lays the blame on the good Julian of Avila, who was their too indulgent confessor. One of the requests was that all might eat meat! She is grieved indeed at seeing the decadence of that house. The nuns are very good, also, yet they ask Father Angelo, the Provincial, that some of those in bad health may keep something in their cells to eat. She should not be surprised if he granted it. A fine request to come from such a place to Fra Angelo! This is the way everything is gradually destroyed. She asks that the Superiors may not give leave for their having anything of their own. When they are sick the Infirmarian is to leave them what they may want during the night, and this is the charitable practice that is observed in the convents if sickness requires it.

She asks that the Constitutions may determine the prayers and suffrages to be said for any one who dies, and that the enclosure be enforced, so that the nuns may not go into the church or to the " porteria."

[1] Letter cccxxvi.

This is enjoined by the Pope, and would be the best
thing, even if it were not enjoined. The convents that
cannot observe it, at the beginning of things, must do
it as soon as they can. It has been done already at
Toledo and Segovia, without telling her, and she
takes it as a spur to herself for her want of zeal.
She had asked that the Religious who are sent to
make foundations should stay there, unless they are
elected as Prioresses in their first convents. She
asks that it may be added, "or unless there is some
grave necessity on other accounts." She wishes all
the Constitutions and Acts of the Apostolic Visitors
should be collected and made into one body, for as there
is sometimes a contradiction in them, the ignorant are
puzzled. Although Gratian has so much to do, he
should take care that all these things are plain and
clear, for the love of God. She is afraid she has
written so much that he will forget the best part
of it.

She tells him that she finds some of the friars
inclined to vote for "Macario," that is, Antonio of
Jesus. She speaks also of Father Nicolas. She
prays that God might guide it all. After the signa-
ture comes a postscript, asking him to take notes of
what she has written, and then burn it. It may do
harm among some if they know it. At the end of
the letter she speaks in favour of a projected College
of the friars in Valladolid, which is a little out of the
town, not too far, she thinks. A poor woman who
had the charge of this "Hermitage of St. Alexis,"
had, she says, bought it with her tears. She is eager
about it.

In another letter [1] of this time Teresa repeats
what she has said before as to the person to be
elected Provincial. But the letter is only a fragment.
She considers that it will be well if either himself,
Gratian, or Nicolas Doria be chosen, provided one is
the companion of the other, but it will be best, this
first time, that Gratian be chosen. He has experience, and this is wanting in " Macario "—Antonio of
Jesus. She is speaking of a *terna*, or list of three,
she has made for the Commissary, and says she has
made Juan de Jesus the third, although she does not
think he has the gift of government. Still, if he has
one of the other two for Socius, he will do.

Gratian seems to have been reluctant to urge the
point which St. Teresa thought of so much importance, the liberty of the nuns as to their confessors.
She urges it again in another letter.[2] She does not
understand why he should not speak for it. She
has written to the Commissary strongly about the
good to the nuns which resulted from Gratian's
visitation. He owes it to them to take up a course
that has cost them many tears. She again repeats
that the Constitutions of the nuns ought not to be
treated in the General Chapter. As she has said
before, Father Pedro Hernandez (may he have glory!)
always dealt with her alone, and although Gratian
may think the " eight points " she has put forward in
her memorial to be of slight importance, she tells him
he is wrong in this. They are of great importance.
And she has seen many things that appeared of
little moment become the seeds of great ruin. She

[1] Letter cccxxvii.   [2] Letter cccxxix.

wants the Prior—the Commissary was Prior of Talavera—to give some degrees to some of the friars, to
save them having recourse to the General, but that
she gives up, as Gratian says the Commissary has no
power. She does not wish them to have to go to
Rome often. They should write to the General,
giving him an account of what they are doing, a very
humble letter, offering themselves as his subjects,
which is reasonable. Also let Gratian write to
Father Angelo, thanking him for all the good he
has done, and begging him always to consider him
as a son.

We pass over a graceful letter of thanks and compliments to Señor Pedro Casademonte, a benefactor
who had taken much interest in the affairs of the
Separation, and sent Teresa constant information
about it.[1] There is also another of the same sort,[2]
written just at the time of the opening of the Chapter
at Alcala, to Doña Anna Enriquez, of Valladolid.
She rejoices over the Separation with Doña Anna,
speaks tenderly and feelingly of the lady's sufferings
in health, and of the goodness of the people of
Palencia, whence she writes. She thanks her also
for a large and beautiful picture she has sent her,
which is placed over the high altar, and is quite
enough, without more. The Prioress is a good one,
and so are some of the nuns, and the foundation
seems already to have been made some time ago,
things have settled down so well. They are much
in want of the spiritual help of the Fathers of the
Society. As long as Balthasar Alvarez was alive—

---

[1] Letter cccxxx.   [2] Letter cccxxxi.

he had died the year before—she always felt less
lonely, although he was at a distance. Doña Anna
was probably a friend of his. She speaks joyfully of
the honourable Chair of Theology that Fra Domingo
Bañez had lately obtained at Salamanca. She says
they are not yet at the end of the business of buying
their house at Palencia, which she regrets, as she had
hoped to go to Burgos before long, and to pass by
Valladolid to see her friend afterwards.

The next letter[1] is written to Gratian, soon after
his election. It begins abruptly, some lines having
been torn off. The chief matter of interest for us is
that she begs him if possible to see her nephew
Francis and his young wife—they are spending too
much money, and his mother-in-law has been told
that his income is larger than it is. He is shy, and
must not be allowed to suppose that Gratian will
have nothing to do with him because he gave up his
idea of becoming a friar. The mother-in-law has
taken a great affection to Teresa, and she is rather
put out by it all. She mentions that she has had a
visit from Fra Angelo, without her having asked it,
and she thinks he has no grudge against Gratian.
She wants to know how " Macario," that is, Father
Antonio, is, probably after the election, and Gratian
is to tear up the letter.

Teresa writes again from Palencia, the 23rd of
March, Holy Thursday.[2] She is delighted that the
Brief of Separation has been printed, and that there

---

[1] Letter cccxxxii.

[2] Letter cccxxxiii. The letter was begun on Holy Thursday and
finished on Good Friday.

is a hope that the Constitutions will be so also. She has not been able to read all, the *Tenebræ* had taken up much time, and her head must not be overtaxed. When this holy time is over, and she has some one to explain to her the Latin, she will read all he has sent. She wishes to know when he goes to Madrid. She tells him they have not been able to get a house at Palencia, and think of taking to the " Hermitage of our Lady" again, as in effect they did, though after some years they had to change. She playfully asks Gratian, who has now again become her Superior, to give her an Easter egg.[1] It is, that she had been one day comforting St. John of the Cross, who had said how much he suffered in Andalusia— *que non puede sufrir aquella gente*—and she had told him that when they got their own Province, she would try and get him moved into Castile. He made her promise, for he was afraid of being elected at Baeza. She asks Gratian not to confirm the election. If it can be done, it is reasonable to console him, for he has much to suffer. She desires they may have few houses in Andalusia—they will hurt the other houses. It is curious to see how strongly provincial characteristics were felt as annoyances by saints like St. John and St. Teresa. She had certainly suffered enough herself in consequence of her obedience to Gratian in going to Seville.

Our next letter is written to Antonio Gaytan,[2] the gentleman of Alba de Tormes of whom we have already heard as the companion of St. Teresa in the

---

[1] *I.e.*, a present for Easter—*una cosa en hornazo*—eggs baked in dough.
[2] Letter cccxxxiv.

journeys to some of her foundations, especially that of Seville.[1] We have mentioned more than once his application to Teresa to admit his little girl into one of her convents to be brought up there, an application which Teresa out of gratitude to him wished to be able to favour, although she had not herself the power to give leave. He seems to have written to her now to complain of her having changed towards him, and she takes the opportunity to express her feeling about some evil reports that had been spread at Alba concerning her niece, Beatriz de Ahumada, of which she thinks she ought to have been informed sooner.

After her usual salutation, she says she has received his honour's letter, and would have written to him many times if it had depended on her, but of late years she has been too busy for any but necessary correspondence. Antonio had lately married a second time, and this probably was the reason for his anxiety about the home of his little daughter. Teresa tells him there have been saints in all states of life, and that it will be his own fault if he misses the blessing attached to his. The complaint she might, amid all these affairs, have to make against his honour, is the not having told her as soon as he knew it himself of some evil doings or reports which affected the reputation of her niece, Doña Beatriz de Ahumada, who resided with her parents at Alba.

The story seems to have been this. Beatriz, whose life has been told at great length, and very interestingly, by the chronicler of the Reform,[2] was

[1] Vol. ii. ch. vi.   [2] *Reforma de los Discalços,* vol. v. l. 21.

now in the prime of youth. It is said that she had been born ugly, at a time when her parents hoped for a boy, and was neglected in consequence, but that she became suddenly beautiful when she was baptized. There are stories of her youth which imply that she was high-spirited, rather proud, and given to the vanities of the world. St. Teresa loved her with a peculiar affection, partly because she was like her grandmother, Beatriz Davila y Ahumada, Teresa's own mother, who as a girl had been famous for her beauty. The little family at Alba de Tormes were not rich, but noble, and proud of their birth, with a pride which in Spain seems to have been

> That last infirmity of noble mind,

—and of many minds that were not noble. A married gentleman, much older than herself, used frequently to visit her father, with whom he was very intimate, and it seems that Beatriz had once been reproved, when she was about fifteen, for not withdrawing from the company when he entered. She was a handsome girl, and the gentleman's wife took occasion to be jealous. The consequence was that a number of reports were spread about injurious to the good fame of Beatriz. The author of the scandal, later on, repaired matters fully, as far as she could, by acknowledging the calumny—but the reputation of a young Spanish lady was easily tarnished. At the time of which we speak, Beatriz was twenty or twenty-one, and the gentleman had become a widower, still keeping up his intimacy with her father. It seems that an attempt was made to induce her to marry

him, but she refused, as she also refused several other
advantageous offers. St. Teresa was no advocate for
"living down" scandalous reports, as long as any
unnecessary intercourse was allowed, and she wished
Beatriz to leave Alba, although it might seem like
an acknowledgment of the story. She complains
strongly of the great freedom which the good lady
had allowed to her tongue.

"When God judges all, we shall understand what
we cannot now judge of without great offence to
Him." The friendship between the families was so
great, and of such long standing, that there must have
been some malice to see in it so great a harm. "My
sister's character is so gentle to all, that she seemed
unable to be hard to any one, if she wished it. It is
her nature; and I never heard of any such disorder
in her daughter as to make it necessary. On the
contrary, she is a very quiet girl. It is true, I have
not seen much of her. But I know that I have been
grievously pained, for the offence against God which
the person must have committed who has done her
so much harm. It is denied strongly on oath, and I
believe it, because my sister would never lie, nor had
any one in that place a right to use her so. Only her
poverty gives occasion for people to treat her so, and
God allows it that she may have all sorts of suffering,
for she is truly a martyr in this life. God give her
patience!"

Teresa says that if she had her way, she would
remove the occasion, even though it were all false,
but she can help them only by her prayers. She
complains of Antonio, however, that it has been of no

use her being his friend, since he had not told her of this business when it began. He says that she is not to him as she used to be. She sees no reason for his so judging. What affects him, affects her, as ever, and she serves him in words when she cannot in deeds, by saying what his deserts are. This is the simple truth. It is he that is so greatly changed towards her, that she is astonished. Truly she deserves no more. She seems to refer to her former letter to Father Gratian, where she had pleaded his cause out of simple gratitude.

The Prioress had said that he had fixed the dowry of the "little angel" with Teresa. What she remembers is, that he means for her all that he had, and could give her outright seven hundred ducats, and she remembers it because, besides the advantage of doing him a service, she was glad of so good a dower, so that the Father Visitor—she seems to mean Gratian—might willingly give the permission required, and she had said this in her letter to the Visitor, and insisted on it as much as she could. No one had entered as a child in any of the houses except Casilda and Teresita, her own niece, and another, a young sister of Father Gratian. She would not consent to more. She has now less power than before, but in the new Constitutions these things go by the votes of the nuns. They cannot have the habit till they are twelve, nor profession till sixteen. So it is not time yet to talk of that. She concludes by some requirements as to the support of the girl. If she could, she would not give him so much trouble about it.

Our next letter[1] is a fragment which does not explain itself, about the new foundation of Soria, to the Bishop of Osma, Dr. Velasquez, who had been for some time St. Teresa's confessor. There follows a long and most beautiful letter to the same prelate,[2] in which she gives an account of the state of her soul, as it appears, for the last time before her death, which ought to be read by the side of the later chapters of the *Interior Castle.* The only fact which concerns her external history is the warning which our Lord gave her in prayer about the house which she had thought of declining in Palencia, but to which she afterwards reverted, as has been already said. But the letter is so important on account of her spiritual state that it must be inserted entire.

JESUS.

Would that I could convey to your lordship the quiet and consolation which my soul possesses! It has such certainty that it is to possess God, that it seems as if He had already given it that possession, though not the enjoyment thereof; as if some one had given to another a great income by very secure deeds, to enjoy it after a certain time and gather its fruits; though for the present he was to possess only the property, which had been given him, from which he was to receive the income, and the other was to be so grateful for it as not to wish to enjoy it, because he does not think he has deserved it; but instead of that, he desires to serve him, although it be at the cost of much suffering—and sometimes it even seems that from now to the end of the world would be a short time, in which to serve him who has given him this possession, for, in truth, the soul is already not subject to the miseries of this world, as it was wont to be, because, although

[1] Letter cccxxxv.   [2] Letter cccxxxvi.

there is more suffering, it seems to be only like a blow over the clothes, and the soul is, as it were, in a castle of which it is the lord, and so never loses its peace. Nevertheless this security does not take from it great fear of offending, nor great care of avoiding all that may hinder his service, rather, the soul proceeds with greater care than ever as to that. But it proceeds with such a forgetfulness of its own advantage, that it seems to have lost a part of its being, in its oblivion of itself—all is for the honour of God, and how to do His will more perfectly and that He may be ever more glorified.

With all this, it seems, as for one's own health and body, one has less care of it, less mortification in eating, and less practice of penance, and, it seems, less desires than before. Its whole end is to be able to serve God in other things, and often it offers to Him, as a sacrifice, the care that is required of the body, and it is a great fatigue, and the soul tries to do something of penance sometimes. But to the best of its understanding, it cannot do this without injury to its health, and passing over what its Superiors command. In this, and in the matter of desires for its own health, there may no doubt be much self-love. But to the best of my understanding, to be able to do a great deal of penance would give me more pleasure, as it did give, when I could do it. I thought at least I was doing something, and giving good example, and had not the pain which comes from not doing anything in the service of God. Your lordship has to see what I had better do.

The imaginary visions have ceased, but it seems that the intellectual vision of the Three Persons and of the Sacred Humanity continues, which in my opinion is very sublime, and then I think I understand that the other visions I had were from God, to prepare the soul for the state in which it now is, only, that as I was so miserable and wanting in strength, God thus led me on as was fitting for me; though as far as it seems to me, such things are highly to be valued when they come from Him. The interior locutions have not ceased, and our Lord gives me some communications when it is necessary—if it had not been for this, just now in Palencia, we should have made a great blunder. The acts and desires of virtues do not seem to have the force they used to have, for although they are great, the wish that the will of God may be done, as well as that which may be more for His glory, is greater; and as the soul clearly understands that His Majesty knows well what is thereto convenient, and as it is so separate from all interests of its own, these desires and acts soon cease, and as I think, lack force. From this comes a fear which I have sometimes, although without any disquiet and pain, as it used to be, lest the soul should be as it were agape and inactive, doing nothing at all—for penance I cannot do, the acts of desire of sufferings, martyrdom, and the sight of God have no force, and ordinarily I cannot make them. I seem to live only to eat and to sleep, and trouble about nothing, and although this does not trouble me, except now and then, yet as I say, I fear sometimes it may be a delusion—but I cannot think it, because to the best of my judgment no attachment to any creature has any powerful dominion over me, not even all the glory of Heaven, but only to love this my God, and this does not diminish, but rather, as I think, increases, and the desire that all may serve Him. One thing that surprises me is that I no longer now feel so much those excessive and piercing pains which used to torment me at seeing souls lost, and at the thought whether any offence was being given to God, although as far as I can judge, my desire that He be not offended is not less than it was.

Your lordship must remark that, in all this, whether as to the state in which I am now or in the past, I can have no power to do more than I do, nor is it in my power to serve Him better. I might indeed if I were not so worthless! but I mean that if I were to take great pains, for instance, to desire to die, I could not, nor make the acts of desire as I used, not feeling the pain at the offence against God, nor the fears as great as they were, that I had for many years, when I thought I might be under delusion. So too I have no need of communicating with learned men, nor talk about these things with any one. I only want to be satisfied that I am going on rightly now, and if I can do anything for God. I have talked of this with some of those whom I have consulted on other matters, that is Fra Domingo,[1] and Master Medina, and some of the Society. I shall be satisfied with what your lordship tells me now, for the great opinion that I have of your lordship.

Consider it much, for the love of God. I have also not lost the intelligence which I have that certain souls of those who were near to me are in Heaven—others not. This interior peace neither pleasures nor pains are able to disturb, so that the presence I have spoken of, the Three Persons, cannot be doubted of, and the soul seems clearly to experience that which St. John mentions, of their "making their abode in the soul," not only by grace, but by the intelligence that they are there. This brings with it blessings which cannot be told in particular, and the soul has no need of seeking for considerations to make it know that God is there. This is, as it were, ordinary, except in the case of great illness. Sometimes it seems that God wills I should suffer without interior consolation, but never even in its first movements, is the will that God's will may be done in it disturbed in the soul. The surrender of itself to His will is so fixed, that it desires neither life nor death, except for a short time, when it desires to see God— and then the representation of the presence of the Three Persons is so forcible, that it heals at once the pain occasioned by its absence from Him, and the desire to live remains, if it be pleasing to Him, for the sake of serving

[1] Bañez.

Him more, and if it might be that perhaps a single soul might love Him more, or praise Him more, even for a short time, through my intercession, that would seem a more important thing than to be in glory.

The unworthy servant and daughter of your lordship,

TERESA DE JESUS.

There is another affectionate letter to Mother Anne of St. Augustine, whom she had taken with her as foundress to the Convent of Villanueva de la Jara, in which she speaks of the value she attaches to her prayers, the love which she bears to her, and the high esteem in which she holds Fra Gabriel of the Assumption, who has been fixed, according to her wish, at La Roda, in order that he may be of use to the nuns at the new convent.[1]

The letters from Palencia end with one of some importance to Father Jerome Gratian, which is the expression of her great disappointment in not, as she had expected, having him as her companion on her journey to Soria.[2] "Please God that he who was the occasion of taking his Reverence away may manage matters better than she thinks." The bulk of the letter is devoted to the case of Juan Diaz, a good priest of Almodovar del Campo, a relative and disciple of the famous Master John of Avila. He was now desirous of entering the Order of Mount Carmel, or the Society of Jesus, and Teresa has much to say in his praise, but does not feel certain about his vocation. It is in this letter that St. Teresa uses the expression *Sancta Sanctorum*, as applied to Gratian. Indeed, it is full to overflowing of affection, forced

[1] Letter cccxxxvii.   [2] Letter cccxxxviii.

from her by her sudden disappointment. She speaks of Nicolas Doria, who has been sent to take his place. Gratian was apparently occupied with the foundation of the College at Valladolid.

We shall speak 'presently of the foundation of Soria, which was almost singular among the foundations for the smoothness and easiness with which all was conducted to a happy end. There is a short note to Father Gratian, written from Palencia before leaving, in which Teresa gives an account of the preparation made for taking possession of their new house on the following day.[1] On the 16th of June she wrote to Cardinal Quiroga,[2] the Archbishop of Toledo, in whose diocese Madrid is situated, to ask him to grant leave for the foundation of a convent in the last-named city. This had long been a special desire of Teresa, as it was natural she should expect great fruits from the introduction of the Reformed Carmel into the capital of Spain and the seat of government. Our readers may remember St. Teresa's visit to Madrid in 1567, when she was on her way to the convent of Alcala, founded by Maria of Jesus. The fine ladies of Madrid, who did their best to make a "lion" of her, and her other visit shortly after, when she was on her way to Pastrana, did not give her a great attraction for the place, and she laid aside the plan, if she had already entertained it. In the course of the year 1579, however, we find her writing to Doña Isabel Osorio on the subject, and she says she had come to the conclusion that it would be well to have a foundation in Madrid. It was even suggested that

---

[1] Letter cccxxxix.   [2] Letter cccxl.

M 3

Isabel herself should delay her entrance—she had been admitted at Salamanca—in order that she might be of use in helping to found the convent at Madrid. The Archbishop had given as a reason for refusing his permission, that he could not allow any more convents which were without income, and Isabel and others had been thought of as able to supply the endowment required. After this time, we find Madrid mentioned from time to time as a place in which the foundation was contemplated, and the objection made by the Archbishop was to be met by having the endowment ready.

The truth, however, was that the Cardinal Archbishop was much set against St. Teresa by what had taken place in his own family. We have mentioned[1] Doña Elena Quiroga, the munificent and pious lady who gave so much help to the first foundation of the Reform after St. Joseph's at Avila, which was made at Medina del Campo. She was the niece of the Cardinal. At that time, 1567, she had given the most substantial help to the first venture of Teresa in the way of a new convent, having furnished all the means by which the house was furnished for enclosure and the chapel built. One of her daughters had entered the convent, and Doña Elena had already determined to follow the example when she was free from the care of educating and settling her family. Now, after so many years, her children were all either dead or provided for, two daughters married, two sons priests, and two others in the next world. But the Cardinal was still opposed to her entrance, and

[1] Vol. i. p. 288.

seems to have shown his dislike to her project by opposition to the extension of the Reform of Mount Carmel in his diocese. This will explain the letter now before us, as well as others which follow, more or less on the same subject.

St. Teresa wrote to his Eminence on June 16, 1581. She begins her letter in her usual way. She had already written to him some time since, and was expecting a reply from his illustrious lordship. Her letter, she is told, was delivered in Holy Week, or soon after. She had asked for leave to found a convent in Madrid. His lordship had said he was pleased with the project, but delayed to give leave on account of a certain obstacle which our Lord had now removed. (That is, the Cardinal could not allow of the foundation unless an endowment was provided for the convent, and this had been provided for by the dowries of some ladies who had been admitted.) Perhaps his illustrious lordship will remember having said that when this obstacle was removed he would grant the leave? She has taken it for granted, and arranged everything for the foundation, which she desires to make with greater convenience before King Philip returns to Madrid, as the house will be cheaper. She is now at Soria (though the letter is written at Palencia, she will leave that place before it arrived), and will not leave her present place till she has this favour from his illustrious lordship, as it will save a long journey, and, as she told his lordship, there are some persons in Madrid who are waiting for the foundation, and delay is a loss to them. His illustrious lordship always helps those who desire to serve God, and this work will certainly be to His service, and a great advance to her Order, and so she entreats his lordship to be so kind as not to delay any longer the granting of this favour, if he so will.

She then passes to the dangerous subject of his niece. Doña Elena remains firm in her purpose, but can do little or nothing till she has his lordship's leave. She is so holy, and so detached, that Teresa is told that she would be glad to enter the convent at Madrid (rather than elsewhere), hoping, in truth, to see his lordship sometimes. This does not surprise Teresa. She herself desires this, and takes care every day to recommend him to our Lord, and to get the other nuns to do the same. May He be pleased to hear them, and preserve his illustrious lordship for many years, with that increase of sanctity which she begs for him ! Amen.

This letter did not immediately melt the Cardinal, and the foundation of Madrid did not take place within the short space that remained of the life of St. Teresa. There was still some delay, also, about the fulfilment of Doña Elena's vocation, which, however, was at last won by her own persever-ance.

We pass over a few letters of minor importance for the present, in order to finish the history, so to speak, of Doña Elena's vocation. At the end of June we find Teresa writing to the confessor of the Cardinal Archbishop, Dionysio Ruiz de la Peña, a letter which is meant to defend herself against the charge of disobedience to his Eminence's wishes with regard to his niece.[1] Peña had evidently written to her intimating the displeasure of the Cardinal, who believed that she was at the bottom of her niece's resolution to enter the Order of Mount Carmel. Teresa tells the Canon that she had received the letter just too late to send an answer by a returning messenger who had brought a letter from Doña Luisa de la Cerda. She is very sorry for this, as they have no regular post where she is, and she wishes him to know as soon as possible. She says she has no fault to accuse herself of in the matter. So true is this, that it is only on account of the near relationship between the Cardinal and the lady in question that she has not put before his Eminence what she has done to prevent her entering one of her houses. If Father Balthasar Alvarez were alive, who had had the greatest influence with Doña Elena, he would bear witness to the truth of what she says. She had entreated him to make her put away the thought, and he had promised her to do so. Teresa had opposed it for some years, not on account of thinking that his illustrious lordship did not wish it, but in order that her nuns might not have to suffer what had happened in consequence of the admission of another lady who left daughters behind her. (This lady seems to have been the "Fleming," Anne Wasteel, already mentioned, who had been received in Avila when Teresa was at a distance.) They had had ten years of trial in consequence. The lady was a good servant of God herself, but God seems to have permitted that there should be suffering for herself

---

[1] Letter cccxlv.

and the nuns, because the order of charity had not been observed. That is the rule she insists on in her convents, and she is certain that the Prioress at Medina del Campo has been strongly opposed to Doña Elena's entrance whenever there has been question of it. This is the truth, and the contrary is the invention of the devil.

She generally has the grace to be strong when suffering false accusations,[1] of which she has had not a few in the course of her life. This one occasion pains her on account of the obligations she is under to his Eminence, who was so kind to her at Toledo, and to whom she owes many more kindnesses which he, perhaps, does not think she knows of. She should be out of her senses to consent to Doña Elena's entrance, knowing, as she does, his will in the matter. It is true that the lady sometimes weeps much about it, when she gives reasons against her wish. She has seen good to give her some hope for the future, which may have made her think that it was her wish—but of this she has no particular recollection. She loves Doña Elena, certainly, and owes her much. (She had, in fact, helped most effectively to the first foundation at Medina del Campo, as has been said.) Thus apart from all that touches the Order, she earnestly desires that she may succeed in everything. The Prioress of Soria, who is taken from the community of Medina, and had been on very intimate terms with Doña Elena, says that the vow of Religion she has made is under the condition that she cannot serve God better by

---

[1] *Testimonios.* In Spanish the word seems often to be used without the adjective *falsos*, but in the sense of calumny.

remaining in the world, and that if she is told that she cannot, she will give it up. Teresa thinks that having children still young enough to require her help, and her daughter-in-law so young also, she cannot enter yet. If the priest to whom she is writing thinks the same, let him tell his Eminence, that he may understand what the vow really is. Some learned men whom she has talked with tell her the contrary, and that is enough for her.

Doña Luisa's letter had come to her hand before the chaplain's, and she is glad to learn from it that his Eminence had been disabused, and no longer thinks her in fault in the matter. Blessed be God, Who has done her this favour without her having to defend herself. All her life she has never thought herself wrong in this regard. She thanks him very much for having told her. As to the leave to found at Madrid, she has already begged it of his illustrious lordship, both because she thinks our Lord will be served in such a house, and it will be of use to the whole Order to have it there. As his Eminence is in the place of God, if he does not think it well that it should be founded, it will give her no pain. She thinks it well for the greater service of God, and so she would not have it be hindered by her own refusal of the labour, of which there is plenty for her in each foundation. Her great pain would be if his Eminence were dissatisfied with her on account of what had been said of her, for she loves his illustrious lordship tenderly in the Lord, and whatever comes of it, she is glad he is under no misconception. The rest of the letter is in the same affectionate strain.

The matter, however, did not end here. In another letter[1] to the same chaplain, written a few days later, the 8th of July, Teresa tells him that she has spoken to the Dominican Prior of Soria, Fra Diego de Alderete, a man of great holiness and reputation, about the case of Doña Elena, and that he has come to the same conclusion with herself. It seems that Doña Elena's vow could only bind her to seek admission, and came to nothing if she was refused. The Prior had always thought she had better stay to manage her family, but he had been influenced by the opinion of a very learned man which inclined to the contrary decision. He thinks that she should be told that she will never be admitted. This Teresa undertakes to do, and to inform the Provincial. So his illustrious lordship is to be without further trouble in the matter.

On the 13th of September, she writes to the same priest again from Avila, to which place she was sent from Soria, as we shall hear, by order of the Provincial. She urges in her letter the oft-repeated request about the foundation of Madrid.[2] She says she has also written to the Cardinal about the affairs of Doña Elena, who has written to say that if the Carmelites reject her, she will apply to the Franciscans. This would pain Teresa very much, for she knows that her spirit is more that of Mount Carmel, and she has her daughter there already. She describes Doña Elena as in the greatest affliction. She loves her much, and she does not know how to console her. This, she says, is for himself alone. In the gentlest

---

[1] Letter cccxlvi.   [2] Letter cccxlvii.

way, therefore, she really asks the Cardinal to yield
to his niece's wish. The end of the story, as far as
the admission of Doña Elena is concerned, is told
us by another letter of St. Teresa, dated the 30th of
October.[1] It is to the Cardinal himself. She has
received two letters from his illustrious lordship, and
kisses his hands many times. She has obeyed his
commands by giving the habit to " our dearest Sister,
Elena de Jesus," as his illustrious lordship will see
by the letter from her which is enclosed. She hopes
that what has been done may be for His glory and
for the good of the Order of His glorious Mother,
and that she will be able to serve his illustrious
lordship better with her prayers, for the more she
increases in holiness, the more acceptable will they
be before God. She thanks His Majesty much for
what she has heard about the good health of his
Eminence, which she hopes may be for many years,
as all those Sisters his subjects pray. She has
more confidence in their prayers than in her own,
for they are good souls, and she is a poor thing,
although she remembers his Eminence especially
before God every day, when she is in His Presence.
She mentions that the Father Provincial has come
himself to give the habit to Doña Elena, and has
written to say how happy he has been to do this.

In the beginning of the next year (1582) Teresa
was at Medina del Campo, on her way to Burgos ;
and she writes again to Peña to tell him, and the
Cardinal through him, how well Doña Elena is
getting on,[2] as well as her daughter, niece, and

[1] Letter ccclvi. [2] Letter ccclxxiii.

cousin, who were all in the same convent. These were Geronima of the Incarnation, her daughter, professed in 1577, Anne of the Trinity, her niece, professed in 1575, and Mary Evangelist, her cousin, professed in 1581, whose dowry Doña Elena had paid, and who entered, out of humility, as a lay-sister, though she was obliged afterwards by her Superiors to take the black veil. Teresa speaks of Doña Elena as exceedingly happy, and as growing stouter. She says she is as much at home in Religion as if she had been in the convent many years. We are told of her that she was always remarkable for her love of obedience and the practice of poverty. Her reputation reached Toledo, where the nuns elected her Prioress in 1586. After eight years she returned to Medina del Campo. One day the bell rang for some public duty, and she did not appear at the first stroke. Her punctuality was so well known, that the nuns ran at once to her cell, thinking something must have happened, and found her in her last sickness.

NOTE TO CHAPTER VI.

—

The letters mentioned in this chapter are the following :

1. (cccxix.) *To Anne of the Incarnation, Prioress of Salamanca.* From Palencia, January, 1581.

An account is given, p. 142.

2. (cccxx.) *To Father Fra Juan de Jesus Roca at Pastrana.* From Palencia, January 4, 1581.

An account is given at p. 155.

3. (cccxxi.) *To Mary of St. Joseph, Prioress at Seville.* From Palencia, January 6, 1581.

An account is given, p. 156.

4. (cccxxii.) *To Juana de Ahumada, her sister.* From Palencia, January 13, 1581.

An account is given, p. 157.

5. (cccxxiii.) *To Don Geronimo Reinoso, Canon of Palencia.* From Palencia, January, 1581.

An account is given, p. 157.

6. (cccxxiv.) *To Father Jerome Gratian.* From Palencia, February, 17, 1581.

An account is given, p. 156.

7. (cccxxv.) *To the same.* From Palencia, February 21, 1581.
An account is given, p. 160.

8. (cccxxvi.) *To the same.* From Palencia, February 27, 1581.
An account is given, p. 162.

9. (cccxxvii.) *To the same.* From Palencia, February, 1581.
10. (cccxxviii.) *To the same.* From Palencia, February, 1581.
These are both fragmentary. See p. 164.

11. (cccxxix.) *To the same.* Same date.
An account is given, p. 164.

12. (cccxxx.) *To Pedro Casademonte.* From Palencia, February or March, 1581.

Mentioned at p. 165.

13. (cccxxxi.) *To Doña Anna Enriquez.* From Palencia, March 4, 1582.

Mentioned at p. 165.

14. (cccxxxii.) *To Father Jerome Gratian.*   From Palencia, after March 12, 1581.

An account is given at p. 166.

15. (cccxxxiii.) *To the same.* From Palencia, March 24, 1581.

An account is given at p. 166.

16. (cccxxxiv.) *To Antonio Gaytan, at Alba de Tormes.* From Palencia, March 28, 1581.

An account is given, p. 167.

17. (cccxxxv.) *To his Lordship Alonzo Velasquez, Bishop of Osma.*   From Palencia, March 28, 1581.

Mentioned at p. 172.

18. (cccxxxvi.) *To the same.*   From Palencia, May, 1581.

Translated at p. 172.

19. (cccxxxvii.) *To Anne of St. Augustine, Foundress at Villanueva de la Jara.*   From Palencia, May 28, 1581.

Mentioned at p. 176.

20. (cccxxxviii.) *To Father Jerome Gratian.* From Palencia, May 24, 1581.

Mentioned at p. 176.

21. (cccxxxix.)   *To the same.*   From Palencia, May 29, 1581.

An account is given at p. 177.

22. (cccxl.)   *To his illustrious Lordship Don Gaspar de Quiroga, Cardinal Archbishop of Toledo.*   June 16, 1581.

An account is given at p. 179.

23. (cccxlv.)   *To Dionysio Ruiz de la Peña, Almoner and Confessor to his Eminence Cardinal Quiroga.*   From Soria, June 30, 1581.

An account is given at p. 180.

24. (cccxlvi.) *To the same.*   Soria, July 8, 1581.

An account is given at p. 183.

25. (cccxlvii.)   *To the same.*   From Avila, September 13, 1581.

An account is given at p. 184.

26. (ccclvi.)   *To the Cardinal Archbishop of Toledo, Don Gaspar de Quiroga.*   From Avila, October 30, 1581.

27. (ccclxxiii.)   *To Dionysio Ruiz de la Peña, at Toledo.* From Medina del Campo, January 8, 1582.

An account is given at p. 186.

CHAPTER VII.

The Brief of Separation.

SOME of the letters mentioned in the last chapter are of a date that carries us to a time which we have not yet reached in the course of our direct narrative. It has been necessary to keep the history of events, to some extent, apart from the series of letters, and one of the two has sometimes outstripped the other. The present chapter will be devoted to the history of the Reform, which, as will have been gathered from many of the letters last quoted, had now entered on a new phase, to the great delight of Teresa and her friends. There was still much to be done, but affairs had already made a wonderful advance from the state in which the first steps of Mgr. Sega as Nuncio had placed them. We must, therefore, go back somewhat in the historical order for the purpose of making the course of events as clear as possible.

The decision of the Nuncio Sega and his assessors that the Reform was in future to be a Province by itself, and be thus separated from the " Mitigation," was laid, as has been said, before Philip II., on July 16, 1579. The decision arrived at could not, apparently, be carried out at once without the authority of the Holy See, even by the Nuncio, for it involved the erection of a new Province of the Order of Mount Carmel, which was to be dependent upon no authority inferior to that of the General. The King was to write to Rome, and ask the Pope to arrange the matter. The King's part was done, but it was impossible for the Pope to understand the matter completely without hearing or seeing some deputies from the Reform, especially as the other parties in the question thus raised had abundant means of laying their own view of the case before Rome. We have mentioned another incident which was likely to cause trouble. The death of Rossi, and the assemblage in Rome of the chief men of the Order for the election of his successor, in a General Chapter of the Order, would give the Pope an opportunity of consulting its chief authorities, and it might well be expected that the majority of these could not be very favourable to the cause of the Reform.

It was, therefore, as has been said, a dangerous mission which was undertaken by the two friars, Juan of Jesus Roca and Diego of the Most Holy Trinity. They would find Rome full of their enemies, and they had no official position to protect them. They might at any moment be seized as apostates and severely punished. The friars therefore travelled with as much secrecy as possible, and when they arrived at Rome, concealed their character until it was safe to declare themselves. The letters from the King did not arrive till they had been some time in Rome. Philip wrote to the Pope, to some of the Cardinals, and to his own Ambassador, Luis de Requesens. There seems also to have been some delay, while the Report of the Commissaries who had been assessors to the Nuncio was waited for, in order that the Holy See might have the whole case before it. It appears that the affairs of Portugal, not to say the usual dilatoriness of Philip, kept things back for some time. In the meanwhile, the deputies of the Reform had to proceed slowly and with caution. It ultimately became known that they represented the cause which had the approval both of the King and the Nuncio, and the time of danger passed away. Even then they could only act privately, and with the persons known to favour their project.

Gregory XIII. laid the matter before a Congregation of Cardinals, among whom Cardinal Montalto, afterwards Sixtus V., was conspicuous. He took up the cause of the Teresian Reform warmly, and induced his colleagues to adopt his opinions. Everything seemed to promise well, when Gregory XIII. expressed a wish that the General Chapter of the Carmelites should be consulted, and the Chapter delegated the matter to the new General, Caffardi, the same who, as Vicar of the Order before his election, had so cleverly put an end to the first deputation sent by the Teresian Friars to Rome. Seeing the cause of the Reform so much in favour, Caffardi did not attempt openly to oppose the proposals which were supported by King Philip, the Nuncio Sega, the Cardinal Archbishop of Toledo, and many other Spanish Bishops. But he hit upon a middle course, which certainly seems likely, if it had been adopted, to destroy all the good that was nearly being secured. This course was that the Provinces should not be divided, but the Calced and Discalced governed by the same Provincial, who was to be chosen from each section in turns. How this could have worked it seems difficult to understand. The Reform was already in existence in two Provinces in Spain, and if it spread to others, each Province in which it existed would be liable to this alternation of Superiors. Caffardi had recourse to Cardinal Buoncompagni, the Protector of the Order, and a near relative of the Pope. The Cardinal approved of the plan, and it seemed almost certain, after all, that the General would carry his point. The Spanish Ambassador happened to die just during this crisis, and the Abate Briceno, who took his place for the time on necessary business, had not courage enough to make a stir under the circumstances.

The two deputed friars gave the matter up, when one of those providential changes took place, of which the history of affairs at Rome is more full than is commonly supposed. The friars went to pay farewell visits to some of the friends who had helped them. Among these friends was Mgr. Spinola, a chamberlain of the Pope, who recommended them to apply to Cardinal Sforza, the Protector of Spain, a man of much weight and influence with the Holy. Father. This Cardinal saw the danger into which the friends of the Reform were being led, and was able to bring the Pope to see it also. After Cardinal Sforza's interference, Gregory made up his mind to recur to more decided measures.

The matter was once more debated before the Cardinals, among whom Montalto and Massei distinguished themselves for the energy with which they maintained the Teresian cause. The result was a final victory for the Reform, and the Pope acted as he had been asked to do by the King. The Letters Apostolic were dated June 22, 1580. The Reformed friars and nuns who observed the Primitive Rule—with the few additions which have been made to it—were entirely and for ever separated from the Provinces of the Observants of the Mitigated Rule of Eugenius IV. The new Province was to be formed of all the monasteries and convents of the Discalced, and to remain under the obedience and government of the Prior-General. He was himself, or by means of some fit person taken from among the Discalced themselves, to visit, reform, correct, or punish those of that Province, according to their Primitive Rule and Constitutions, and they were not to be sent to other houses or provinces by him. The Provincial of the Discalced had full powers to exercise his office, as soon as he was elected, without any confirmation, which he was, however, to ask at once from the General. The Discalced were to enjoy all the privileges, favours, and the like, which the Mitigated had, so long as these were not contrary to the Decrees of the Council of Trent, Apostolical Constitutions, and their own Primitive Rule. The Discalced were not to pass either to the Mitigated Rule of Carmel or to any other Order, except the Carthusians, unless by leave of the Holy See, without incurring the guilt of apostacy, and the Superiors and other officials of the Miti-

N 3

gation were forbidden, under pain of excommunication, to molest, vex, or disturb any of the Discalced
as to their concerns ; and any authority of governing,
visiting, or punishing them, which might have been
granted to any of the Mitigation, was entirely revoked,
quashed, and annulled..

The Letters Apostolic, as has been said, were
issued on the 22nd of June, but there was a good
deal of delay as to their promulgation. Briceno, as
already stated, sent them to the King, who received
them at Badajoz, where he was arranging the in-
vasion of Portugal of which we have previously spoken.
The letters reached him on the 15th of August.
They contained ample powers to all patriarchs, archbishops, and bishops for their publication, and the
two Archbishops of Seville and Toledo, and the
Bishop of Palencia, were particularly named, probably
as being friends of Teresa and her friars. The Archbishop of Seville died at this time. The King, for
some reason or other, asked the Pope to commit the
execution of the Letters to Teresa's old friend, Fra
Pedro Hernandez, but, when the Pope's assent came,
Pedro was on his death-bed. Another name had to
be sent to Rome and back to Spain, and the answer
reached Spain on the 4th of January, appointing
Fra Juan de las Cuevas, the Dominican Prior of
Talavera, who was able to carry out the commission.
A Chapter of the Discalced Priors and others was
summoned by him to meet at Alcala on the fourth
Sunday in Lent, March 12, 1581. Thus an end was at
last put to the danger which threatened the Reform of
St. Teresa in its birth. It had much to suffer, almost

immediately after, from internal dissensions, but she
did not live to see many of the troubles to which the
work which she had founded was exposed, and which
would certainly have given her a very peculiar pain,
as they fell most heavily on the persons among her
friars and nuns whom she esteemed the most highly
and regarded with the greatest affection.

We shall now briefly continue the history of this
celebrated Chapter of Alcala, the starting-point of a
new life to the Teresian Reform. As we have said,
the Pope, at the request of the King, nominated Fra
Juan de las Cuevas, the Dominican Prior of Talavera,
to be the Commissary for the holding the Chapter.
Though the Brief appointing him arrived in Spain on
the 4th of January, it had of course to be sent to the
King, who had gone to Elvas to receive the homage
of the nobles of Portugal. Philip wrote on the 24th
of January to thank Fra Juan for accepting the
commission, and it is worthy of notice that in his letter
he desires him to get the information he may want
about the affairs of the Carmelites from Father
Jerome Gratian, whom he recommends strongly, and
who, as well as Nicolas Doria, seems to have accompanied the Commissary in his journey to Alcala.
This recommendation of Father Gratian is signifi-
cant, and we shall see how much influence had to be
exerted to induce the Priors to elect him Provincial.
Philip also tells the Commissary to pay a visit to the
Nuncio on his way, and to act in concert with him
and with the President of the Royal Council, who is
to see the original Brief. The Rector of the University of Alcala is also to be informed of all, and of the

King's orders that all should be done in due form. Philip also gave orders that everything required for the Chapter should be defrayed at his expense, including the entertainment of the friars and others during the whole of the time.

Fra Nicolas de Jesu Maria (Doria) was then sent to Fra Angelo de Salazar to inform him that the powers committed to him on the government of the Reform were now at an end, at which he greatly rejoiced. Invitations were then sent to all the Priors, each of whom was to be accompanied by another Father elected by the community which he governed. The convents of nuns were also written to, as one of the matters on which the Chapter was to be occupied was the examination and revision of their Constitutions. They were to pray fervently for the good issue of the Chapter during the whole of the sittings. Teresa wrote chiefly to Father Gratian, as was natural, but also to Fathers Nicolas Doria, Mariano, and Juan de Jesus, as we shall see. Her greatest anxiety was that nothing new in the way of severity should be added to her Constitutions. It was the most delicate and difficult part of her great work for her Order, to prevent the inevitable mischief which must have followed if the worthy friars, such as Antonio of Jesus, Ambrose Mariano, and others, had been allowed *carte blanche* to "reform" the Reformed nuns whom she had founded and whom she so admirably governed. In fact, the liberty of the nuns was in the greatest danger, though Teresa was able to prevent any grave infringement on it, as long as she lived.

The Commissary arrived at Alcala with Father Jerome Gratian and Nicolas Doria in his company. They were both Priors, Gratian of Seville, and Doria of Pastrana. Fra Elias of San Martino, the Rector of the Carmelite College of Alcala, was also one of those who arranged the subjects to be considered by the Chapter. Antonio of Jesus and St. John of the Cross, Priors of Mancera and Baeza, had not yet arrived. The Conde de Tendiglia had just succeeded his father as Marquis of Mondejar, and, being a great friend of the Reform, was present at the Chapter as well as his brother, and the head of the Collegiate Church.

On the 3rd of March, the third Friday in Lent, the assembly met. The Priors that came, each with his "Socius," were from the following monasteries: Mancera, Pastrana, the College of Alcala, Altomira, La Roda, Granada, La Penuela, Seville, Almodovar, "Calvary," and Baeza. Thus the "vocals," or voters, were twenty-two in number, two for each monastery or college. The same day the Commissary Apostolic, in their presence and that of the noblemen mentioned, of the authorities of the University or Collegiate Church, as well of all the Carmelite friars who were in Alcala, promulgated the Brief of Separation, which he prefaced by a grave and learned harangue, declaring that a separation made between brethren, for the sake of greater peace and union, did not deserve the name of division, but rather conformation.[1] The next day all the "vocals" were to meet for the election of a Provincial.

---

[1] "Una platica muy docta y grave, probando con autoridades de la

On that Saturday, May 4, the Father Commissary sang the Mass of the Holy Ghost, and Brother Diego Evangelista, who afterwards was a famous preacher, recited a Latin oration, written by Father Mariano. "The elegant Latinity, the gracefulness of the delivery, and the gravity of the discourse," we are told, pleased the whole University which came to listen. The first thing after Mass was to elect four Definitors, who are in some other orders called Assistants or Consultors to the Provincial. The first named was Father Nicolas Doria, who had been but a short time professed, but was already very highly thought of. The next was Antonio of Jesus, the first friar of the Reform. The third chosen was St. John of the Cross, and the fourth, Gabriel of the Assumption, "socius" of the Prior of La Roda. Ambrose Mariano, who was a good Latinist, was named Secretary.

It is at once a matter of remark that there was no mention of Jerome Gratian in this election, notwithstanding the evident favour with which he was regarded by the King, who appeared very openly indeed as a supporter of his claims, and notwithstanding also the strong wish which St. Teresa had always evinced that he should be in office. Perhaps Gratian was not voted for as Definitor, because it was thought that he would be elected Provincial. But this does not seem likely, as he had, for the Provincialate, the slenderest possible majority, and as Antonio of Jesus, who was nearly elected, was also voted for as

Sagra Escritura y de Filosofos y razon que la division que se haze entre hermanos por major paz y union no merece nombre de division sino de conformidad." (*Reforma de los Discalços*, t. 1, lib. 5, c. 9.)

Definitor. The Commissary seems to have noted the fact, or to have been prepared for it. The historian of the Reform tells us that there was great difference of opinion as to the person to be chosen Provincial, and that the Commissary was well aware of this difference before the voting took place. He made a speech before the election for Provincial. He spoke of Gratian's great favour with the King, of his acceptableness to the grandees, whether secular or ecclesiastical, of his literary acquirements, his talents, and ability in the management of business. All the Court honoured his father, the Secretary. The friars and nuns loved him for the gentleness and sweetness of his government. He was esteemed beyond all by the good Mother Teresa, for his immense labours and services in the troubles the Order had passed through. Without absolute dictation as to the choice which they were to make, the good Priors, under the circumstances, had thus at least a very clear intimation as to the wishes of Philip.

Fra Juan de da Cuevas, the Commissary, did even more than this in favour of Father Gratian. If we understand the historian rightly, and if it is an actual speech of the Commissary that he is reporting, he went on to anticipate the objections to Gratian which were current in the Chapter. "From his noviceship he had governed, not obeyed. He had been made Apostolic Commissary within a few months, and had had no time to be well grounded in the virtues of penance, mortification, retirement, and obedience. He had shown more inclination to actions which made a show before the world, than to silence and prayer. Popular applause had much weight with him, and to gain it he could slight the Rule and the Constitutions. He spent more time on the souls of others than on his own, and he had endeavoured to plant the same spirit in the Reform, where it was already infectious." It is impossible either to doubt the fact, that there was much truth in some of these objections, which were quoted by the Commissary for the sake, of refuting them, or the other fact, that Gratian had rendered the greatest possible services to the Reform, had suffered immensely for it, and was even still almost indispensable to it.

The Commissary was partly successful, and these considerations prevailed so far, that Gratian was elected by a majority of one. An issue of this sort could hardly be called either a ratification and approval of everything that had been done by him while he was Superior of the Discalced, as Apostolical Commissary and Provincial, or as a promise of harmonious support to him in the office of Provincial for the future. It must be remembered that the friars of the Reform were few, and had among them fewer men still possessing the particular qualifications required for the moulding of the new Province after the trials which it had passed through. St. Teresa herself seems to have thought that Gratian and Nicolas Doria were the only two fitted for the post, though she put in Father Juan de Jesus to make a third. It may well be asked, why no one thought of St. John of the Cross? But we often see in the histories of the saints of God that the highest spiritual gifts are

frequently unaccompanied by the gifts of government and ability in affairs. It might seem almost
that the extreme purity of soul, love of suffering, and
closeness of union with our Lord, to which St. John
reached, might have suffered, if he had been cast into
the comparative hubbub and disquiet of the government of a Province of Carmelite friars. On all the
occasions in which we find St. John taking for the
moment a prominent part in the affairs of his Order,
his judgment would seem to have been as sound and
practically wise as that of Teresa herself. He was
to be the model of a Carmelite friar, but he was not
to be put to the grindstone of the work of a Religious
Superior in a time of great difficulty. It was not so
much that he was unequal to it, or that he had not
talents for it. But it was not his vocation. That was,
above all, to suffer, even at the hands of his brethren.
Wherever he went, he was always a burning and
shining light, such as no active and bustling Superior
could have been. He taught by example the most
perfect possible imitation of the character of the
Man of Sorrows. The Reform was immensely the
gainer. As its Superior, St. John might have guided
it through the next few years far better than Gratian,
or Doria, or any one else, and he might have saved
it many troubles and some deplorable losses. He
would not have been, as we may venture to say, the
St. John of the Cross whose history stands out
before the Church with that pure and characteristic
brilliancy which we so intensely venerate and love.

Putting aside St. John of the Cross, the Carmelites
of the Reform had hardly any choice between Gratian,

Antonio of Jesus, and Nicolas Doria. If the Superior who was to be chosen could have been a nun of St. Teresa's training, or St. Teresa herself, there would have been no difficulty. There were three or four women among the nuns who might have been admirable as rulers. But the alternatives among the friars were few indeed. So Teresa wished, as we shall see, that it might be Doria if it could not be Gratian, but what she wished most of all was that it might be Gratian, only strengthened by Doria, or Doria sweetened by Gratian. Father Antonio of Jesus was a bad governor. He had mismanaged the visitations that had been committed to him. His great merit was that he was a natural Superior, on account of his age and services. But, besides, it seems that he had a foolish ambition for the post, which was quite enough to make him unfit for it.

It is undoubted, on the other hand, that Doria was a man of strength, of devotion, of ability, of dexterity. But he was as much too severe as Gratian was too gentle, and besides, he was very new in Religion, although he was not very young in age. The favour of the King, after all that he had done for the Reform, probably decided the votes of a few waverers or timid Religious, and thus turned the election. Under all the circumstances it might have been even dangerous to offend the King at the very moment that he had been, under God, the visible providence to which they owed everything. So Teresa's sanguine soul rejoiced sincerely in the election of Gratian, as at all events the best thing that could be done at the moment. We have many

intimations, however, that she was not blind, either
to the defects of character in Gratian which threatened
mischief to the Order if they were not corrected, or to
the danger of a possible outbreak against his method
of government which might have disastrous effects.

Her letters to him, many of which, however, are
lost, while we have not a line on his side of the correspondence, are sufficient to show this. It is true
that she speaks always, as to him, with the greatest
reserve on such points. She had been especially
directed to trust to his guidance from the very
beginning of their acquaintance, and she was
faithful to the direction. She regarded him with a
motherly love, he was her *hijo querido*,[1] her *Sancta
Sanctorum*, and she looked upon him as having been
raised up to help her in her work in a singular way.
As subject, she always treated him with the greatest
deference, and this must be taken into account when
we consider the complaints at which she so often
hints. We owe him much for having preserved her
letters, especially as they contain so many hints of
her consciousness of his occasional defects—rather,
we should say, of the features in his character and
history which made him occasionally unfit to govern
the Carmelite friars and nuns committed to him with
perfect wisdom and invincible firmness. She was
herself eminently trustful and sanguine—all the persecutions and disappointments she had met with
were not enough to make her otherwise. She saw
all the good in Gratian, as she saw the good also in

---

[1] This name was used of him by himself, but it was adopted by
St. Teresa. See vol. ii. p. 298.

Nicolas Doria. She was inclined to hope that the two would supply each the deficiencies of the other, instead of allowing those defects to produce the divisions and mischief which she did not live to see.

It must, moreover, be remembered that the difference was probably not simply personal, nor does it appear to have anything of jealousy and self-seeking in either of these two good men. There was great difference of character between them, and each thought his own way was the best. Each of them came to the Reform more or less of a formed man. Neither of them had much experience of it before he was placed in a position of special pre-eminence and power. The great difference between them was probably that of their conception what the Order of Carmel was intended for, what was the perfect ideal of a Carmelite. Both would certainly have acquired influence and authority, even if they had not possessed a title to each in their personal qualities as well as in their connections. In this respect the new Province had few men who were to be compared to them in all that secures consideration among men. Moreover, it became naturally very dependent on its own resources, and could not expect much help in its formation from the existing authorities of the Order, the General and his Definitors. All these causes produced a state of things which was not hopeful, and even if St. Teresa had lived, she would have had a hard task indeed to prevent the smouldering evil from kindling itself into a fire.

The letters of St. Teresa at this time were, we cannot doubt, full of even more than ordinary wisdom,

and she seems to have written a great many, notwithstanding the very poor state of her health. But it is
just at this time that they fail us. At least, although
we have several, we know there must have been
many more. Even those to Father Gratian, through
whom she communicated to the Commissary and
the Fathers of the Chapter a great many requests
and suggestions, are comparatively few and fragmentary. There were reasons of prudence, no
doubt, which may have induced Father Gratian
sometimes to mutilate the letters he received at this
time, and sometimes to suppress them. St. Teresa
more than once desires him to tear them up. She
speaks of other documents which she had forwarded,
which were of a more formal character. Every one
at the time recognized her right to have a voice in
the deliberations, especially as regarded the nuns,
whose Constitutions were now for the first time
submitted to the Chapter. But none of these formal
documents exist, and the Commissary, to whom they
were submitted, did not probably think it necessary
to preserve them, especially as what she urged was
generally acted upon, on account of its intrinsic
reasonableness as well as on account of the great
authority which naturally belonged to whatever came
from her. There were, however, no doubt, some
points on which the importance of her suggestions
was not so obvious to others, of less experience, as
to herself. On one matter, that of the selection of
confessors for the nuns, she does not seem to have
been listened to, at least to the full extent of her
demands.

At the beginning of her Reform, St. Teresa had drawn up Constitutions for the government of her Religious—as yet there were no friars, but only nuns—which had been shown by her to the General, Rossi, at the time of his visit in 1566, and approved by him, and afterwards by the Pope, Pius V., who also gave leave to Teresa to make any alteration from time to time which she might think necessary. She used this liberty very sparingly indeed. These were the Constitutions by which all her convents were governed, and which preserved them in that admirable unity of spirit which was sometimes absent from the monasteries of the friars. These Constitutions were now to be "revised" by the Chapter, not, apparently, because of any complaints that had been made, but in order that they might be finally settled and again authorized by the highest powers in the Church. Teresa was naturally consulted, and there seems to have been no desire whatever to depart from her recommendation. It would, however, be a most valuable help to us in our study of her character if we possessed what she wrote on the subject—all the more so, as among the evil effects of the troubles which befell her Order, not long after her decease, must be reckoned the disputes that arose about these very Constitutions, which have resulted in their original text being almost entirely lost until the present time.

The few letters which remain to us of this interesting series have been given in due order, fragmentary as they are, and it will be enough here to refer to those most striking points which illustrate especially the character of St. Teresa, her views as to the dangers that might arise, and the matters on which it was well to insist as most important to the stability of her work. One of the points on which she speaks most strongly is that the confessors of the nuns are not to be their Superiors. She may have had in her mind the miseries which she had known of in the Convent of the Incarnation at the time of the persecution on account of the Reform. At all events, she tells Gratian that though she agrees with him that it was well the nuns should confess to the friars, she would rather give up that advantage than incur the evil of having a confessor their Superior. She begs him to trust her as to this. When St. Joseph's at Avila was founded, the question was fully discussed by grave and experienced men, and it was settled that the convent should be under the Ordinary, with this object in view among others, that thus the Superior could not be the confessor. The inconvenience she mentions is enough, but she evidently had a great many more in her mind. A Superior can always speak to a Religious whenever he pleases, and the Prioress cannot prevent it on account of his authority. If, therefore, he is confessor too, there could be no check on such evils as those which led to the troubles at Seville. It is the same if the Priors of the monasteries in any place are also Superiors of the convents. These must be under the Provincial alone. The greatest good the Fathers of the Chapter can do, is to make it plain and certain that the confessors have nothing to do with the Religious, except to hear their sins in the confessional.

She says it is so with the Dominicans, of whom the Commissary was one : the Fathers hear the nuns in confession, but are not their Superiors.

Other points on which St. Teresa insists are the carefulness with which the rules as to enclosure, the persons by whom the nuns are to be seen with their veils lifted, the treatment of the sick, the prayers and Masses that are to be said for the deceased of the Order, and the like. In all points she is against ambiguity, and all unnecessary severity, while she wishes poverty and seclusion from the world to be strictly observed. There is a very strong passage about the injunction which she wishes to be laid on the Priors to give the friars a sufficiency of food. Here she travels beyond her peculiar province, and, that she does this, shows how much importance she attaches to the matter. We have seen the excesses to which the love of mortification led in the case of the famous Monastery of Calvary. There is another passage about cleanliness, which also she desires to be put into the Constitutions of the friars.

In many of these matters St. Teresa's wishes were listened to. Another thing she desired was the printing of the Constitutions, which, as long as they were in manuscript, might be, and, as a matter of fact, often were, altered at the caprice of individual Superiors. We gather from occasional hints in her letters that she did not feel secure as to the future. But in any case the great work on which she had so long laboured was now sanctioned and confirmed by the Church, and she could sing her *Nunc dimittis* with great thankfulness.

We shall now resume the story of her foundations, where it has been interrupted.

———

CHAPTER VIII.

Soria.

ST. TERESA seems to have left Palencia at the end of May, 1581, and proceeded at once to her next foundation, which was made at Soria. The Reform was now beginning to expand itself, and we hear of a new monastery of the friars at Salamanca, as well as a college, which became afterwards a famous seat of learning. The distance was not great, and Teresa had personal reasons for wishing to confer with the good Bishop of Osma, who was no other than the Canon Velasquez of Toledo, to whom she was in the habit of confessing during her stay in that city. But we must, in a great measure, let her tell the story in her own words.

When I was in Palencia, on the business of the foundations now described, I received a letter from Dr. Velasquez, Bishop of Osma. I had had relations with him when he was Canon and Professor in the Cathedral of Toledo, and when I was harassed by certain misgivings, for I knew he was a most learned man, and a great servant of God, and so, after many importunities, I persuaded him to take upon himself the care of my soul, and to hear my confession. Notwithstanding his many occupations, yet, because he saw what straits I was in, he consented so readily that I was surprised, and he confessed and directed me all the time

O 3

I remained in Toledo, which was long enough. I laid before him the state of my soul with exceeding plainness, as I am in the habit of doing. The service he rendered me was so very great that from that moment my misgivings began to lessen. The truth is, there was another reason, not to be told here. Nevertheless, he really did me a great service, for he made me feel safe by means of passages from the Holy Scriptures, which is a way that has most effect upon me when I am certain that he who speaks understands it, and is also of good life: I was certain of both in his case.

That letter was written by him in Soria, where he then was. He told me that a lady, who was his penitent there, had spoken to him about founding a convent for our nuns, of which he approved; that he had promised her he would persuade me to go and make a foundation there; that I must not fail him; and that if I thought it right to do so I was to let him know, and that he would send for me. I was very glad, for, setting aside that it would be a good work to make a foundation there, I wished to make known to him certain matters relating to the state of my soul, and also to see him, because I have a great affection for him, the fruit of the great service he has done me.

The lady, the foundress, was Doña Beatriz de Veamonte y Navarre (for she was descended from the Kings of Navarre), the child of Don Francis de Veamonte, of noble and illustrious lineage. She had been married for some years, had no children, was exceedingly wealthy, and for some time past had resolved to found a convent of nuns. She spoke of it to the Bishop, and he told her of the Order of our Lady, the Barefooted Carmelites. She was so pleased that she made great haste to carry out her purpose. She is very gentle, generous, and mortified; in a word, a very great servant of God. She had in Soria an excellent house, well built, and in a very good situation, and said she would give it to us, with everything else that might be wanted for the foundation. She gave it, together with a sum of money which would bring in five hundred ducats a year. The Bishop undertook to give a very fine church with a stone roof; it belonged to a parish in that part, and by adding a passage it has been made such as we could use. He could do this well, for the parish was poor, and there are there many churches, so he transferred the parish to another. All this he told me in his letter. I spoke of the matter to the Father Provincial, who was then here, and it seemed to him and to all my friends that I should write to them to come for me, as the foundation of Palencia was now made. I was very glad of it, for the reason I gave before.

I began to send for the nuns I was to take with me: they were seven (the lady would rather have had more than fewer), with one lay-sister, who is my companion, and myself. A person came for us in time, and with much diligence, as I had said, I had to bring with me two Barefooted friars. I took the Father, Fra Nicolas of Jesu Maria, a man of great perfection and discernment, a Genoese by birth.

It is worth while to give at length St. Teresa's account at this time of Father Nicolas, of whom we have heard so much, and whose career was to be one which left a lasting impression on the Reformed Carmel.

He was more than forty years old, I believe, when he received the habit—at least, he is now upwards of forty, and it was not long ago—but he has made such great progress in a short time, that it is clear our Lord chose him to help the Order, which he did in these days of persecutions, that were so full of trouble, and then the others who could have helped us were some of them out of Castile, others in prison. Since he held no office—for, as I have said, he had not been long in the Order—he was not thought of so much account: this being the work of God, that he might remain to help me. He is very prudent, for when he was staying in the monastery of the Mitigation in Madrid, he was so reserved, as if he had other affairs to transact, that they never discovered he was engaged in ours, and so allowed to remain. We wrote to each other continually, for I was then in the Convent of St. Joseph's in Avila, and discussed what was necessary to be done, which was a comfort to him. This shows the difficulties of the Order at that time, seeing that they made so much of me, according to the saying, "For want of good men," &c. During the whole of this time I had experience of his perfection and prudence, and hence he is one of those in the Order for whom I have a great affection in our Lord, and highly esteem.

He, then, with a companion, a lay-brother, went with us. I had no trouble on the road, for he whom the Bishop had sent for us took great care of us, and helped us to the utmost of his power to find good lodgings, for when we entered the diocese of Osma the people provided us with good lodgings on being told that our coming was the Bishop's doing, so great is their affection for him. The weather was fine, and we made short stages each day, so that there was no fatigue in travelling, only joy, for it was to me an exceeding great joy to listen to what people said of the holy life of the Bishop.

We arrived at Burgo [1] the day before the octave of Corpus Christi, and went to Communion on Thursday, which was the day of the octave, the morning after our arrival, and dined there, because we could not reach Soria that day. That night we spent in a church, for there was

---

[1] The Burgo de Osma, where the Cathedral and Bishop's Palace stand, forms one side of the River Duero, Osma being on the other.

no other place to lodge in, and no harm came of it. The next morning we heard Mass there, and reached Soria about five in the afternoon. The saintly Bishop was at a window of his house when we passed, and thence gave us his blessing; it was a great comfort to me, for the blessing of a bishop and a saint is a great blessing.

The lady our foundress was waiting for us at the door of her own house, as it was there the convent was to be founded; we did not see how to make our way in, because of the great crowd present. That was nothing new, for wherever we go, so fond is the world of novelties, the size of the crowd would be a grave annoyance were it not that we cover our faces with our veils, which enables us to bear it. The lady had a very large and very fine room made ready, wherein Mass was said for the present, because a passage had to be made into the church which the Bishop was to give us, and forthwith the next day Mass was said in honour of our Father St. Eliseus. The lady most abundantly furnished everything that we had need of, and left us in that room, wherein we kept ourselves enclosed until the passage was made, and this lasted till the Transfiguration.

On that day the first Mass was said with great solemnity, a large congregation being present in the church. A Father of the Society preached, the Bishop having gone to Burgo, for he never loses a day or an hour, but is always at work, though he is not strong, and the sight of one of his eyes is gone. I had this sorrow there, for it was a very great grief to me that his sight, which was so profitable in the service of our Lord, was lost. God's judgments are His own. This must have happened to enable His servant to gain more merit, and to try his conformity to His will, for he did not refrain from labouring as he did before. He told me that he did not grieve over his loss any more than if it had happened to another. He felt sometimes that he should not think it a matter of regret if he lost the sight of the

other eye, for he would then live in a hermitage, serving
God without further obligation. That was always his vocation before he was made Bishop, and he spoke of it to me
occasionally, and had almost made up his mind to resign
everything and go. I could not bear that, because I thought
that as a Bishop he would be of great service in the Church
of God, and accordingly wished him to be what he is,
though on the day he was offered the bishopric—he sent
word of it to me at once—I fell into very great distress
about it, seeing him laid under so heavy a burthen, and I
could not rest nor comfort him. I went into the choir, and
prayed for him to our Lord, and His Majesty made me
calm in a moment, saying to me that he would serve Him
greatly; and so it seems.

Notwithstanding the loss of an eye, certain other very
painful infirmities, and unceasing work, he fasts four days
in the week, and inflicts other penances on himself; his
food is very plain. When he visits the diocese he goes on
foot; his servants cannot bear it, and have complained of
it to me. His servants must be pious persons, or they may
not remain in his house. He does not trust important
affairs to his Vicars-General; they must pass through his
own hands, and indeed I think everything does. For the
first two years of his episcopate here he underwent a
most unrelenting persecution from slanders, at which I was
amazed, for in the administration of justice he is upright
and true. That has now come to an end, for, though
people went to the Court to complain of him, and to every
other place where they thought they could work evil against
him, they did not prevail, for the good he was doing
throughout his diocese became known. He bore it all so
perfectly that he made them ashamed, doing good to those
whom he knew to be doing evil to him. Though he had
much to do, he never failed to find time for prayer.

It seems to me that I am carried away when I praise

this holy man—and I have not said much—but I have done so that people may know who it was that really began the foundation of the Most Holy Trinity in Soria, and for the consolation of those who have to dwell there. My labour is not thrown away, and they who are there now know it well. Though he did not endow us, he gave us the church, and it was he, as I am saying, who put it into the heart of that lady to make the foundation, and he was, as I before remarked, a man of great piety, goodness, and penance.

Then, when the passage leading into the church was made, and everything necessary for our enclosure arranged, it became necessary I should return to the Convent of St. Joseph in Avila; and so I went away at once in the great heat, the road being very bad for the carriage. Ribera, a minor canon of Palencia, went with me; he had been a very great help in the making of the passage into the church, and in everything, for the Father Nicolas of Jesu Maria had gone away as soon as the deeds relating to the foundation were drawn out, being very much wanted elsewhere. Ribera had business in Soria when we were going thither, and went with us. From that time forth God gave him such an earnest desire to do us good, that we may pray to His Majesty for him among the benefactors of the Order. I would not have anybody else travel with me and my companions, for he was enough, because he is so careful, and the more quietly we travel the better am I on the road.

I paid now for the ease with which I had travelled on this road before, for, though the young man who went with us knew the way as far as Segovia, he did not know the high-road, and so he led us into places where we had frequently to dismount, and took the carriage over deep precipices where it almost swung in the air. If we took persons to show us the way, they led us as far as the roads were safe, and left us just before we came to a difficulty, saying that they had something to do elsewhere. Before reaching the inns, as we had no certain knowledge of the country, we had to bear long the great heat of the sun, and our carriage was often in danger of being overturned. I was sorry for our fellow-traveller, because it was often necessary to retrace our steps, though we had been told that we were on the right road; but in him goodness was so deeply rooted that I do not think I ever saw him annoyed, at which I marvelled much, and for which I gave thanks to God, for where goodness has taken root the occasions of sin have little influence. I gave thanks to our Lord because He was pleased to save us from the danger of this road.

On the eve of St. Bartholomew we reached St. Joseph's in Segovia, where our nuns were in distress because I was so late in coming; and I was late because the roads were bad. There they made much of us, for God never sends me trouble but He pays me for it forthwith. I rested for eight days and longer; the foundation, however, was made with so very little trouble that I think nothing of it, because it is nothing. I came away rejoicing, as the place seemed to me to be one where, I trust in the compassion of God, He will be served by those who dwell there, as He is at present. May He be praised and blessed for ever and everywhere! Amen. *Deo gratias.*

The letters of St. Teresa at this time begin by an affectionate fragment addressed to Mary of St. Joseph, at Seville, begging her to take care of her health. "Do be obedient, and do not kill me. I tell you that there is no Prioress whose loss I should feel as yours."[1] Teresa writes to Father Gratian[2] from Soria, June 27 (1581), in answer to his proposal that she should go at once to Avila, where she was urgently wanted. She says if she leaves the business

[1] Letter cccxli. [2] Letter cccxlii.

she is about now, she leaves it for ever : she will never be able to return. But if Father Gregory Nazianzene is there (as confessor), and she is made Prioress, it could well be arranged that she might be absent for some time. She probably considers the foundation of Burgos as the business she has in hand. She wishes she was nearer to him when he has to decide, and suggests more than one way by which a letter will reach her. She hopes he is well in all the heat of the season. All goes well at the new foundation. The Prioress, Catharine of Christ (she did not know how to read), did very well, and kept up her authority.

We have next a long letter to Father Gratian, dated the 14th of July.[1] She says she has not received a long letter which he had written to her. She is glad he is well. His Reverence may not have received a letter she had sent him about the affairs of Doña Elena Quiroga, begging him not to give leave for her entrance : she had sent the letters to Valladolid, where she thought he was. He will see how much displeased the Archbishop of Toledo was, and it was by no means prudent in them to have him as an enemy. But besides this, there were strong objections, as her daughter was already a nun in the convent. She repeats what she has before said about Father Balthasar Alvarez. She begs him to tear up this letter, since she does not want the family to know her reason against the entrance of Doña Elena. *Ya tenemos harta experiencia de estas viudas.* This letter was of course written before the

---

[1] Letter cccxliii.

change in the Cardinal's views as to his niece, of which we have heard in a former chapter.

Then Teresa proceeds to urge on him once more the printing of the Constitutions. (In fact they were printed before the end of the year.) She next speaks of the projected foundation at Burgos. She is surprised that some people seem to think she is already there. She has written to the Bishop of Palencia that her infirmities prevent her being there in the winter, as Gratian had told her. She has expressed no doubt as to the good-will of the Archbishop, for he and the Bishop of Palencia are good friends. She is afraid that there will be trouble, if the city (as she has been told is likely) should oppose the foundation, and as they would not care much for her, she waits till it is settled favourably in that quarter. What they must now think of is the foundation of Madrid. She thinks that when the Cardinal of Toledo sees that they are doing what he wishes (in the affair of his niece), he will soon grant the leave for Madrid. The Bishop of Osma is going to him in September, and he has promised her to obtain it. She will have finished her present business at Soria by the middle of August.

Thus, after our Lady's feast, if his Reverence pleases, she can go to Avila. The nuns do not seem to have been open enough with Father Nicolas, who had lately been there. It would be a great comfort to her not to be made Prioress at Avila, she is not fit for the place, and it is beyond her strength (she could not follow all the community exercises, which the Prioress should do), and so would have scruples. If Fra Gregorio is left as confessor, the present Prioress—for there is no other there—would do. She corrects herself, however, at once. She will not do, especially for the interior guidance. So his Reverence must settle as he thinks best. No trouble is too great for her to take for that house, which she cares for so much, and she might do some good till God arranges for Madrid. But her nature shrinks from being there, seeing that her friends and her brothers are gone—she means Salcedo and others, and Don Lorenzo—and the worst is that those left are such as they are—meaning chiefly her poor brother Pedro with all his melancholy.

She then gives her advice about the sending some one to Rome. It is necessary, she thinks, and there is nothing to fear, in sending some one to profess their obedience to the General—some of those who would not be much missed. Father Nicolas would be a loss to his Reverence, but, on the other hand, he was a person to set all things smooth. She thinks that the General will not require much of them, if they profess that they are his subjects, and show him some civility and politeness from time to time, as such. It will not be as of old. The expense of the journey, whatever it is, may be a burthen to the houses.

In the latter part of the letter she speaks of some trouble which was caused by Anne of the Angels, the daughter of the "Flemish" lady, who seems to have been a prey to melancholy. *Crea, que a una monja descontenta yo la temo mas que a muchos demonios.* We are glad to know that the person in question lived to be a very happy and exemplary Religious. There is also a good deal about her niece Beatriz, whom she is anxious at any cost to get away from her home at Alba de Tormes. We have already said something about her. She migrated to Avila, chiefly to please her aunt, and at the cost of some loss of reputation, for her leaving home seemed like an acknowledgment of the truth of the reports against her. She, too, as has been said, at last became a Carmelite nun, and very holy.

We have a fragment written in this summer from Soria to Father Gratian about the new College he was founding at Salamanca.[1] Then come three to Denys Peña, the chaplain of the Archbishop of Toledo, about Doña Elena de Quiroga, of which we have already spoken.[2] Then follows a rather long letter to the Canon Geronimo Reinoso of Palencia. Teresa writes to explain to him the private reasons which induce her not to go at that time to Burgos— it is dated the 13th of July.[3] She has already written to Catharine of Tolosa, the good lady who was to found the convent with so much liberality, and she has asked Inez of Jesus, the Prioress of Palencia, to show him the letter. That letter contains what she calls her public reasons. She will tell him and the Prioress some others which influence her. She says that if the formation of the Province was at stake, no doubt she would overcome all obstacles. There are many obstacles to her journey to Burgos, which for

[1] Letter cccxliv.
[2] Letters cccxlv. cccxlvi. cccxlvii.   [3] Letter cccxlviii.

want of time she will only touch on. It is not a
question of going a day or so out of the way. But
she cannot understand that she should make so long
a journey as to Burgos, without having something
certain before her. The Province has not fallen so
low as that. This foundation is necessary for it.
Since she has been at Soria two others have been
proposed, at Ciudad Rodrigo and at Orduna, which
also she thinks of refusing.

Then she comes to the point. The truth is, she
cannot depend on the Archbishop of Burgos. He
was a native of Avila, and had witnessed the first
foundation of the Reform at St. Joseph's. He had
seen the great good which had resulted from it, and
yet he had written to a Canon, her friend, that he
remembers the disturbance very well, and that on
account of his position he should feel obliged not to
take the responsibility of giving occasion to similar
troubles. St. Teresa asks, what can be expected of
such a person? He is afraid of what perhaps may
never be, and if any great storm were to come about
by the instigation of the devil, he would refuse his
leave for the foundation, and she should be blamed
for imprudence in taking part in such an enterprise.
He had also told a Father of the Society that the
municipality would not consent, and that without
their consent and without an assured revenue he
would not give his. Two different persons have told
her he is very timid and shrinking in character.
He will only be more frightened if she were to go
to Burgos. He would not act as Don Alvaro
de Mendoza had done, as to the foundation of

St. Joseph, and brave everything where there was no offence to God. These are in substance her reasons, and they certainly show how accurately she measured the character of the Archbishop beforehand.

What she recommends is that they should now try to negotiate with the municipality, and this is better done at a distance and with leisure. It is not a matter which can be done in a week or a month, and there would be the poor foundress in the house of a secular, which she could not leave without its being much noted! She thinks it therefore better to make a long journey and return hither by-and-bye, than incur all the inconveniences which might follow. If God chooses to bring it about, all will thus be arranged quietly, and the end will be gained, although the devil will not like it, and no force be used. She thinks all has been done that can be done, and she tells his honour that at first she felt no kind of pain in putting it off—rather, comfort—"only for that blessed Catharine of Tolosa, who has done so much. When I have read her letters, I think I should like to give her pleasure. We do not understand the ordinances of our Lord. Perhaps it is well I should now go elsewhere. So great a resistance from the Archbishop, who I certainly believe wishes for the foundation, must have some mysterious reason. I say nothing to the Bishop here,[1] for he is so much occupied that he has not been able to see me for some days." She says that she has not mentioned these reasons of hers against the journey—only alleging the

[1] The Bishop of Osma.

cold climate of Burgos, the bad effect it would have on her health at the beginning of winter. She tells the Archbishop that she won't expose him to all the outcry that might follow, until the negotiation with the city has been settled, and she thanks him for all his kindness. The rest of the letter relates to other matters.

We have already learnt that St. Teresa had left Soria about the middle of August, on her road to Avila. Before her departure, as the internal arrangements of the convent were not quite finished, Teresa left in writing some instructions for the direction of the nuns.[1] They chiefly turn on matters like the gratings, curtains, and the like, which were necessary for the perfect observance of the Rule in the parlours and other places, which included in this case the rooms to be used as parlours by the foundress, Doña Beatriz and her daughters. Teresa also instructs them to treat her in all things with the greatest submissiveness and attention, to consult her as to the reception of novices, and do nothing of importance without her consent. A great lady, who had been married to Doña Beatriz's nephew, Don Francesco, but whose marriage had been annulled on account of a diriment impediment, had become a novice before St. Teresa's departure. The chronicler of the Reform tells us that Teresa had been talking to her about Father Nicolas Doria, and had spoken of his vocation. She said that he had taken up warmly the affairs of the Reform while in Seville,

[1] This instruction will be found in Don Vicente de la Fuente's *Obras de Sante Teresa*, t. iii. p. 167. (Edit. 1881.)

and she in turn had taken to praying for him. In a year's time he had become a friar. Leonor de Ayans, the lady in question, had been so struck by what she heard, that she begged the Prioress, Catharine of Christ, to give her the habit. This was done soon after. We have two letters of St. Teresa to this novice, of which we shall speak in due time.

While in Soria, Teresa had seen for the last time her two earliest biographers. The first of these, who wrote the Life of the Saint only seven years after her death, was Father Francis Ribera, of the Society. He tells us that he spent four days in Soria this year on his way back from Rome, and that it was only after three of them had passed that the Bishop told him that Mother Teresa was in the place. He deeply regretted having missed so much of his opportunity, and did so afterwards, all the more, as he never saw her again. The second biographer of St. Teresa was Yepez, afterwards Bishop of Taragona, of the Order of the Hieronymites. He tells us that she arrived at Soria in the evening, and that he met her at the carriage door, but as she was closely veiled, she did not see who it was, and asked him, when he welcomed her. On his giving his name, she was silent. He afterwards inquired why she had not spoken, and she said that two things occurred to her mind and afflicted her; one, lest some penance had been laid upon him by his Superiors, and the other that she feared the meeting him was a recompense by which God meant to reward the trouble she was taking in the new foundation. He told her that the first matter was the case, but not the last. Yepez also tells us that, in giving Teresa Communion twice at Osma, he remarked two things which seemed extraordinary. One was that when she approached the priest to receive our Lord, her whole countenance, which was usually what might be expected from her age, long labours, and severe penances, became so beautiful and, as it were, beaming with light, that he was filled with devotion. He also remarked that her breath and clothes seemed fraught with an exquisite perfume. It made him doubt whether she did not use scents, and he asked Anne of St. Bartholomew, who said she never used such things, for they made her head ache.

Teresa herself has told us of the mistakes that were made by her guides on the road, and the dangers she incurred in consequence. She stayed about a week to rest in the convent at Segovia. We have a short letter written from this place to her sister, Juana de Ahumada,[1] begging that when she arrives at Avila she and her daughter Beatriz may come and see her. She was bent, as we know, on getting Beatriz away from her home, and it seems to have been arranged that she should stay with her relative, Peralvarez Cimbron, at Avila. The matter was very much on Teresa's mind, as we learn from her other letters. She speaks of her stay as short, and of her speedy departure for Soria, perhaps on the way to Madrid or Burgos. She says she shall expect them not later than the Vespers of our Lady—that is, the eve of her Nativity, September 7th. We have also a note written on her journey to Avila, from Villacastin, to

[1] Letter cccxlix.

Mary of St. Joseph, Prioress of Seville.[1] It looks like a mere note sent to greet the nuns at Seville, as she has a good opportunity, and she has heard some good news of them, that the plague has ceased. But it seems that she was still anxious about the money which the convent at Seville owed to the estate of her brother, Don Lorenzo. She has just heard that it has been paid to Father Nicolas Doria's brother, Señor Horacio. She says it is well, though she had begged the Prioress not to send it to Medina. Now she must give an order that it be paid to Teresa, otherwise it will not be put to the credit of the convent. This seems the real business of the letter. She speaks of beginning her brother's chapel at once, as it is on her conscience. But we are told that she never got the money, Señor Horacio retaining it for himself, as he also was a creditor of the convent at Seville, or rather of the whole Province, for the money he had lent had been for the expenses of the mission to Rome. Thus he had really not the slightest right to the particular sum which he diverted from its destination, and he thus prevented the discharge of a debt of justice.

The reason for the haste with which St. Teresa returned to Avila has been already mentioned. The convent was suffering both temporally and spiritually. The alms by which it was ordinarily supported had ceased, because it was known the nuns had had a legacy left them, which, however, they had not received. The confessor, Julian of Avila, had become too indulgent, all the nuns, for some pretext or other,

[1] Letter cccl.

were allowed meat, and the Prioress either aided the relaxation or was unable to remedy it. We notice in the letters of St. Teresa how easy it was for a fervent community to lose its fervour, and the smallness of the numbers in each house made it very easy for the contagion of laxity to spread till it affected half or more than half of the whole. There was also a continual danger of harm through any weakness of the Prioress or any want of spiritual wisdom in the confessor.

But the presence of St. Teresa seemed at once to set things in a way to be right. However, she was not able to escape the charge which she dreaded—that of Prioress. Father Gratian was either there when she arrived or came soon after. The term of the existing Superior was not yet at an end, but she was the first to suggest that it should be brought to an end by resignation. On the 10th of September the election was made. Teresa was chosen unanimously, except by her own suffrage. She pleaded her age and infirmities in vain. Gratian bade her kiss the ground in penance, intoned the *Te Deum*, and then the Religious led her into the choir and acknowledged her as their Prioress. She was able before long to get the debts paid, as well as to restore the spirit of fervent observance. She writes on the 9th of September, the day before her election, to the Canon Reinoso, who had helped her so much in various ways at Palencia. She tells him she is in Avila, and would willingly be again his child (in confession) if it were possible. She is very much alone where she is, and has no one to console her. The longer she lives, the

less she finds to keep her in life. " I tell your honour
that these journeys are very tiring," then she corrects
herself, "although one can't say that of the journey
hither from Soria, which was rather more a recreation
to me, because it was level, and often in sight of
streams of water, *que me hacia harta compania.*" She
has a pleasant word to say, too, of the ecclesiastic,
Don Pedro Rivera, who had accompanied her. Teresa
was fond of streams, and more than once speaks of
them as adding to the beauty of a view. " It is a
wonder how no one who tries to do me kindness is
able to escape much trouble ; may God give them all
charity to find pleasure in it, as your honour has.
Take care not to omit writing me a letter when you
have an opportunity, although it may bore you. I
tell you, I have very little which gives me comfort,
and many labours." She is glad that " Dionysia "—
probably a friend or relation of his—is to enter one
of her convents, it appears. Then she speaks of the
number of visitors she has had to see, and the letter
ends with kind messages.[1]

*   *   *

Before closing this chapter, which has been mainly occupied
with the foundation of Soria by St. Teresa, we may mention a
traditional custom which has come down from her times in
that convent. She left Soria for Avila about the feast of the
Assumption, which is not long before that of the Exaltation of
the Cross, the 14th of September, and she left behind her some
simple verses for the entertainment of the new community,
which have been preserved ever since. On the day of the
feast a large crucifix is carried into the recreation-room, with

[1] Letter cccli.

some branches of olive and some veils. After the recreation is
over, the Superior presents the crucifix to be adored by all
the Religious, and they then sing St. Teresa's verses, devoutly
walking in procession, with the olive-branches in their hands,
through the cloisters to the cemetery, where they sing a
Response for the Dead and fix the branches on the graves.

The verses are in very simple Spanish, and not very difficult
even to those who know some of the kindred languages only.
It seems better not to attempt to translate them, and they are
here given in the original.

En la Cruz esta la vida
  Y el consuelo
Y ella sola es el camino
  Para el cielo.

En la Cruz esta el Señor
  de Cielo y tierra,
Y el gozar de mucha paz
  aunque haya guerra,
Todos los males destierra
  En esto suelo,
Y ella sola es el camino
  Para el cielo.

De la Cruz dice la Esposa
  A su querido,
Que es una palma preciosa
  Adonde ha subido,
E su fruto le ha sabido
  A Dios del cielo,
Y ella sola es el camino
  Para el cielo.

Es la Cruz el arbol verde
  E deseado,
De la Esposa que a su sombra
  se ha sentado,
Para gozar de su amado,
  El Rey del cielo,
Y ella sola es el camino
  Para el cielo.

Es una oliva preciosa
　　La santa Cruz,
Que con su aceite nos unta
　　Y nos da luz;
Alma mia, toma la Cruz
　　con gran consuelo,
Que ella sola es el camino
　　Para el cielo.

El alma que a Dios esta
　　toda rendida,
Y muy de veras del mundo
　　desasida;
La Cruz le es arbol de vida
　　Y de consuelo
Y un camino deleitoso
　　Para el cielo.

Despues que se puso en Cruz
　　El Salvador,
En la Cruz esta la gloria
　　Y el honor;
Y en el padecer dolor
　　vida y consuelo,
Y el camino mas seguro
　　Para el cielo.

Caminemos para el cielo,
　　Monjas del Carmelo!
Abracemos bien la Cruz
　　Y sigamos a Jesus,
Que es nuestro camino y luz,
　　Lleno de todo consuelo,
　　　Monjas del Carmelo!

Si guardais mas que los ojos
　　La profesion de tres votos,
Libraros han de mil enojos
　　De tristeza y desconsuelo,
　　　Monjas del Carmelo!

El voto le la obediencia
　　aunque es de muy alta ciencia,
Jamas se le hace ofensa,
　　Sin quando ha y resistencia;
de esta os libre Dios del cielo,
　　　Monjas del Carmelo!

El voto de castidad
  Con gran cuidado guardad,
A soio Dios desead,
  Y en el mismo os encerrad,
Sin mirar cosas del suelo,
      Monjas del Carmelo !

El que llaman de pobreza
  Si se guarda con pureza,
esta llena de riqueza
  Y abre las puertas del cielo,
      Monjas del Carmelo !

Y si asi lo hacemos,
  Los contrarios vinceremos,
Y la fin descansaremos,
  Con El que hizo tierra y cielo,
      Monjas del Carmelo !

NOTE TO CHAPTER VIII.

The letters which belong to this chapter are the following :

1. (cccxli.) *To Mary of St. Joseph, Prioress at Seville.* From Soria, June 16, 1581.

Mentioned at p. 216.

2. (cccxlii.) *To Father Jerome Gratian.* From Soria, June 27, 1581.

An account is given at p. 216.

3. (cccxliii.) *To the same.* From Soria, July 14, 1581.

An account is given, p. 217.

4. (cccxliv.) *To the same* (about the same date).

Mentioned at p. 221.

5. (cccxlv.) *To Dionysio Ruiz de la Peña, Confessor to the Cardinal Archbishop of Toledo.* From Soria, June 30, 1581.

6. (cccxlvi.) *To the same.* From Soria, July 8, 1581.

7. (cccxlvii.) *To the same.* From Avila, September 13, 1581.

These three letters are mentioned at p. 220, and also in ch. vi. pp. 180—184.

8. (cccxlviii.) *To Don Geronimo Reinoso, Canon of Palencia.* From Soria, July 13, 1581.

An account is given, p. 220.

9. (cccxlix.) *To Juana de Ahumada, her sister.* From Segovia, August 26, 1581.

An account is given, p. 225.

10. (cccl.) *To Mary of St. Joseph, Prioress of Seville.* From Villacastin, September 5, 1581.

An account is given, p. 226.

11. (cccli.) *To Don Geronimo Reinoso, Canon of Palencia.* From Avila, September 9, 1581.

An account is given, p. 227.

CHAPTER IX.

Last stay in Avila.

SOON after her return to Avila, Teresa received a
blow in a very tender part of her heart. We shall
easily call to mind the bright child of high birth
and wealth, Casilda de Padilla, the daughter of the
Adelantado of Castile, who came to the Order of
Mount Carmel against the will of her relatives, when
she was still too young to be made a nun, and
whose vocation and perseverance, as it seemed, are so
beautifully commemorated by Teresa in the *Book of
the Foundations.*[1] More than four years had now
passed since Casilda's profession, and whenever she
has been mentioned in the letters of St. Teresa, it has
always been as a cause of consolation and joy. And
now the news came suddenly that a Brief had been
obtained at Rome, by which she was transferred to
a convent of another Order, where she was to be
Abbess. This kind of transference might be represented as a gain to the convent in which she was to
be Superior, and thus the Brief may have been
obtained without her previous consent. This, however, is conjecture. Casilda's new convent was

[1] *Foundations,* chs. x. xi.

that of some Franciscan nuns at Burgos. Her
family had always been unwilling to see her as a
common Religious in a community which was small
and poor. They wished to see her, if she must be a
Religious, at least in some famous and distinguished
convent, of which she could be Superior. We do
not know whether the young lady was herself in
any way a consenting party to the change, though it
is hard to suppose she could have been determined
not to make it. Perhaps she was beguiled by the
importunities of her relatives. In the letter which
St. Teresa writes to Father Gratian on the subject,
she tells him that the mother, Doña Maria de Acuña,
had made many apologies to the convent, that they
were to be paid for the maintenance of Casilda all
the time she had been there, and that it had been
alleged that she had been professed before the proper
time. Teresa says she does not see how that can be
said. They had had a Brief from the Pope. In any
case, Teresa's heart was deeply wounded, but she
speaks of the matter with her accustomed cheerfulness and resignation.

She writes to Gratian the same day that the news
reached her from Valladolid. She has been quite
upset. The judgments of God are just, and He loves
the Order, and intends to draw some good out of
this, or to prevent some evil. Let not his Reverence
be pained. She pities the poor girl. It is absurd to
say she was unhappy—so joyous as she always was.
His Majesty evidently does not wish them to be
exalted with the lords of the earth, but with poor
people, like the Apostles, so they must not think

much of it. The other sister[1] also has been taken from her convent at the same time, that their mother may have them with her, and so no slur will be cast on the Carmelites. God be with her! But may He save us from these great people, who can do everything they like, and change so wonderfully! Perhaps the poor child does not understand what has been done—for she seems to think she can come back again, which Teresa thinks will not do. She does not believe she can have been unhappy, she could not have dissembled it. "If she had only shown such signs of discontent as the novice they have here at Avila!" We shall hear more of this. She repeats in her postscript that Casilda's love for the Order was certainly very great.[2]

The next letter is dated nearly a fortnight later, the 9th of October.[3] It is addressed to Don Sancho Davila, who was afterwards Bishop of Jaen. The letter is an answer to one she has received from him. It contains various bits of spiritual advice. It begins by condoling with him on the loss of his mother. He tells her that he has ceased to feel so much excessive pain at what has happened. Teresa replies that is a gain, not a thing for which he might reproach himself. Such grief can do no good to the soul. She mentions that she thinks it impossible to avoid distractions in reciting the Divine Office, which she sets down to weakness of head, and therefore there is no sin, and she says that she has been to confession to Fra Domingo Bañez, who told her not to mind it,

---

[1] Casilda's elder sister, who became a nun before her.
[2] Letter ccclii.　　[3] Letter cccliii.

and so she begs his honour not to do so. It is an incurable evil. She then goes into the question how to get rid of a toothache. He seems to have been writing the life of his mother, of which she is very glad. The letter ends with kind messages. It seems that Don Sancho was her cousin. She mentions the nasty stories about her niece Beatriz, whom she has been trying to get away from Alba. Some learned men have said that she is obliged to leave it, and Teresa thinks that even if she were not, it would be prudent to fly, as from a wild beast, from the tongue of a passionate woman. This looks as if the calumniator of Beatriz was still alive, although the wife of the gentleman whose name was mixed up with that of Beatriz was now dead.

We pass over a short note of condolence to Doña Guiomar Pardo y Tavera, daughter of her friend Doña Luisa de la Cerda. "Our Lord did not choose me to enjoy seeing your honour's letter, since the cause of its coming took away my delight. May He be blessed for all. It seems that He is well loved in that house of yours, since in so many ways He gives you sorrows, in order that He may give you yet greater boons for the patience with which they are borne." This is quite in St. Teresa's manner.[1]

Then comes a letter to Father Gratian, about various matters. The first is the case which has been already more than once alluded to, the "discontented" nun. She was Anne of the Angels, daughter of Anne of St. Peter ("the Fleming"). She was scrupulous and melancholy, and St. Teresa had told her that she

[1] Letter cccliv.

would not have her professed there. She was to
go to the Convent of the Incarnation, and there be
professed of the Mitigated Rule, and then come
to St. Joseph's, as many others had done from that
convent. She would have to pay a dower in both, that
was all. Her mother was the one who was most strong
in saying she was not fit for St. Joseph's. Then the
novice began to beg that she might be tried as long
as the nuns of St. Joseph's liked. She would abide
by what her confessors said. If they thought it well
for her to go, she would do it. In short, she took
quite a new turn, and all her troubles vanished.
This has lasted now nearly a fortnight. If she goes
on thus, Teresa thinks she cannot in conscience refuse
to profess her. She is told by the confessors of the
novice that she is not naturally melancholy. This
fit has been on her not more than a year and a half.
She had been told before it was habitual. She begs
Gratian to pray about it. She fears some delusion, and
that the good state may pass, but her mother, who
had been tormented also, is quite well now. The
matter ended in the novice making her profession in
St. Joseph's, some weeks later.

There is an amusing passage about a certain
Canon Castro. He had been a student at Alcala
with Gratian, and had charmed Teresa with his intelligence, cleverness, and good language.[1] She wants
to know his character. He reminds her of Gratian.
He has preached to them once. "He will not hear
any confessions, but it seems to me he would like to
hear mine, and I suspect, as he is such an enemy of

[1] "Romance."

the thing, that it is out of curiosity. He says he is most hostile to revelations, and does not even believe St. Bridget's. He does not say this to me, but to Mary of Christ. At another time, I should have taken pains to speak to him of my soul, because I was always well disposed to do so with persons of that opinion, thinking they would undeceive me, if I were deluded, better than others. But now that I have not those fears, I don't care so much for it, except a little, and if I had no confessor, and your Reverence thought it well, I would do it, although I do not converse on those things much with any one, now that I am settled, except with my former confessors." This confirms what is said in her letter to the Bishop of Osma, given above. We shall see that the Canon Castro came round entirely, and that Teresa was delighted with him as her confessor.

She sends him a letter from Villanueva, where the Prioress has much to suffer from the Subprioress. This is a great trouble, and she is afraid, in consequence, of giving some of the nuns their profession. She would like his Reverence to go thither, and suggests that if the foundation at Granada is made, the Subprioress should be sent to it. She would do better with Anne of Jesus, and also one or two of the Sisters from Villanueva. At Granada the place would be larger, and they would have the friars to confess them. Nevertheless, she thinks Villanueva will go on well, they are good souls. Father Nicolas wants Gratian to go to Seville, as his brother has written some bad news about the convent there, but Teresa believes it is all nothing. She has told Father

Nicolas so, as she has heard lately from the convent. Gratian cannot leave Salamanca at present.

She says she has made a rule in her convent that when any one is ill, the nuns are not to go together to visit her, but one at a time. There is much inconvenience in the other way, loss of silence, breaking up the community, and sometimes perhaps "murmuration." If he thinks it well, she asks him to make the rule in other places. Then she breaks out about the state of things with some of the Religious and their confessor. "Oh, my Father, in what a peevish state Julian is! Mariana (one of the nuns) is every day wanting him, and I can't deny him. It is all holy, but God deliver me from confessors who have been so for many years! It will be good luck if we manage to root out the evil. What would it be if they were not such good souls!" And she adds that since she has begun her letter, something has occurred which has put her out very much. She thinks the only remedy is to remove certain nuns, if the foundation at Madrid is made. The letter ends with asking the habit for the bearer of her letter, who wished to be a friar, and that suffrages should be ordered for Mary Magdalene, one of the nuns of Toledo who has just died.[1]

We have next the letter to the Cardinal Quiroga, about the clothing of Doña Elena, his niece, which has already been mentioned.[2] It took place at the Convent of Medina del Campo, in the foundation of which she had so large a part. After another letter of courtesy and compliment to the Duchess of Alva,[3]

[1] Letter cccliv.   [2] Letter ccclvi.   [3] Letter ccclvii.

we come to another to Mary of St. Joseph, Prioress
of Seville, on which a few words may be said.   It
begins with one of St. Teresa's outbursts of affection.
Mary's letter delighted her.   It is no new thing for
her to find in her letters the pleasure which she wants
after those of others have wearied her.   If Mary
loves her well, she pays her well back, and she likes
her to tell her of her love.   " It is certainly a part
of our nature to love being loved in return.   It can't
be bad, for our Lord does it as well as we, although
there is no comparison between the love we owe His
Majesty and what He deserves.   But let us be like
Him, in whatever it may be."

  ,   She is not surprised that the nuns at Seville are
well and quiet, as when they were in great straits so
many prayers were made for them in Castile.   Now
that Seville is without trouble, let the nuns there pay
the others back—" especially this house of St. Joseph
in Avila, where the nuns have just elected me
Prioress out of sheer hunger !   You may understand
how I can manage, with my years and occupations."
She then gives her own account of the circumstances
which caused the convent to need her so much.
A gentleman of Avila—her old friend Don Francisco
de Salcedo—had left them a certain property, which
was not a fourth part enough to sustain them, and
which they were not to come into for a year.
Immediately nearly all the alms which they used to
receive from persons in the city ceased, and a great
many debts were the consequence.   This is the state
of the case, which she has to remedy.   Of course she
finds it hard on her to be Prioress, with all her

troubles, but if God is served by it, all is as nothing. Mary of St. Joseph has been telling her of her own maladies. She is sorry that she resembles her in anything—she is all bad. The pain in the heart she does not care for so much, as it is a disease which stops others and is not very dangerous. She was threatened with dropsy, and she is glad to have this instead. She reminds her that she must not take too many remedies at once, and sends her a receipt for some pills which have done herself much good, begging her to try them. " Mi Gabriel " has been very ill, and she is so glad to hear of her being better. Teresita loves them all very much, and there is a passage about her growth in perfection, which shows her aunt's great hopes for her. She desires news of Fra Garcia de Toledo, her old director and friend, who has arrived at Seville. She gets nothing in the way of money from America, for Lorenzo has now heard of his father's death, and waits to hear from Francis. He is well married, and has a good income of six thousand ducats. His brother in Madrid gets on badly, and his relations give him trouble.

There follows next a long passage about the money which ought to have come from Seville to the convent at Avila, about which we already know something. We have already stated the facts. The important thing is, Father Nicolas Doria seems to have been interfering rather unwarrantably, and the passage was left out of the letters of St. Teresa when they were first printed, the editors having been some of his partisans. His brother Horacio had lent some

Q 3

money for the expenses of the affairs at Rome,
which were to be borne ultimately by all the
convents of the Province. The money which the
convent at Seville was sending to Avila for the
payment of the debt to Don Lorenzo, the father,
had fallen into his hands by mistake. It was quite
wrong to appropriate it to another purpose. Teresa
says this plainly, and has evidently been much
displeased at his having been obstinate and self-
willed in the matter, and acted without her. Now
she does not know what to do for the money, as
many of the convents cannot pay for their share in
the common expenses of the Province, to which by
this act of Doria's they have been applied. Her
brother has left her the money owing to him from
Seville for the chapel at St. Joseph's, and if she
dies she fears it may never be built. We do not
know whether the money was ever paid.

She then passes to other subjects, asks about
the spiritual state of the convent, and gives directions
about the recreations and other matters, insisting
strongly on the rule of the nuns not going into the
church out of the sacristy, and especially about the
porteria, the going into which had been forbidden
by the Pope under pain of excommunication. She
also tells Mary of St. Joseph to see Father Rodrigo
Alvarez, under seal of confession, to read to him the
last "Mansion" in her book of the *Interior Castle*,
and tell him that that describes the state of "the
person he knows" (herself), and that she is quite at
peace, that very learned men say that it is right.
The book is to be kept secret, and Father Rodrigo

is just to send her a line what he thinks. The rest of this letter speaks of less important matters. It is dated November 8, 1581.[1]

On the 13th of November, Teresa wrote to the Canon Martin Alonzo de Salinas of Palencia, of whom we have heard in connection with the foundation at Palencia. Teresa gracefully thanks him for his kindness in writing to her, which she begs him to do again sometimes, although his letter revives the sorrow she feels at being at a distance from him. She is very lonely where she is. She takes advantage of his being at Burgos to ask him to exert himself in promoting the foundation there, about which there is some mystery. She asks him to write some letters to persons of influence, though perhaps their fears may be groundless, for Doña Catalina de Tolosa writes that since the beginning of this negotiation for their convent, the Corporation have given leave for others. She does not see why there should be so great a difficulty about thirteen women, except that the devil dislikes their coming very much. If it is his work and our Lord wishes them to come, he won't make much mischief. She mentions that there is much snow at Avila now, but she does not feel the cold as much as usual.[2]

The next letter brings up again the great anxiety in which Teresa was concerning her niece Beatriz. The girl herself seems to have been at Avila, staying with an uncle. But Teresa wanted a stronger step, that is, the removal of the whole family from Alba de Tormes to Avila. She writes to her brother-in-

---

[1.] Letter ccclviii.   [2.] Letter ccclix.

law, Juan de Ovalle,[1] in this sense, asking whether he is in Alba, what he is about, and entreating him not to neglect what she considers a duty. Beatriz cannot stay for ever with her relations, but Teresa mentions one or two who have invited her. The latter part of the letter is about news from America. Her brother Augustin has written to say that he is coming home next year, that he has not made a fortune, but expects something from the King. She mentions Lorenzo's marriage with a daughter of an auditor, a high official, and that he is getting on very well. He did not send anything to his family, as he has had great expenses. There is a message to Beatriz at the end, and her brother Don Gonzalo, who is to remember what he has promised to his aunt. As for Beatriz, Teresa says she has been praying for her so much that she does not know when she will be paid. But Beatriz was to pay her very well in the end, though not till after her aunt's death. This letter is dated the 14th of November.

We have next as many as three different letters from Teresa to the Canon Pedro de Castro, of whom we have heard her speak in her letter to Father Gratian. He was the man who declared himself a resolute enemy of all revelations, and said he would not believe even those of St. Bridget. He had, however, been reading St. Teresa's Life, and, as it appears, had written her a letter declaring himself entirely converted. He was Bishop of Segovia at the time of the informations that were taken for her canonization, and he then deposed that he had begun

[1] Letter ccclx.

to read her writings with the greatest indifference, intending not to pass over any point that he could fasten on, but they gained him over so that he said no book of devotion ever moved him more, and very few as much. The letter before us[1] is an outpouring of Teresa's delighted gratitude in finding that her book had seemed to him quite right and sound. She says that the kindness which his honour had done her by his letter so overpowered her that she began by thanking God with à *Te Deum*, before thanking him, for it seemed to her that the kindness came from above. Then she "kissed his honour's hands," and should have liked to thank him by word of mouth. "My misdeeds have done your honour good. You see me saved from Hell, which I have deserved much, and the title of the book is, *Of the mercies of God.*"

We have said she had asked him to be her confessor, and she had spoken of this in her letter to Father Gratian. She tells him that she never expected a favour less than she expected this, and yet she had felt troubled at every word of disapproval that he had addressed to her. She will not say more on paper, but she begs that he will see her next day, which is the eve of the Presentation of our Lady. She will bring before him a soul that has often undone itself, that his honour may do to it all that he shall understand to be convenient, in order to please our Lord, and she hopes that His Majesty will give her grace to obey him all her life—for she does not think that absence from her confessor gives

[1] Letter ccclxi.

her liberty, nor does she desire it, for she has known dangers to come from such desires, and great good must come from the other way, if his honour does not desert her—and he will not, and she keeps his letter as a pledge, although she has a better security than that. What she entreats of him is that he will always keep before him what she is, that he may not think better of her for the great mercies God has shown her, but rather worse, because she serves God so poorly that it is clear her case is one of continual receiving, and yet remaining all the more in debt. He must avenge God upon her, for His Majesty only punishes her by favours, which is no slight punishment for a soul that understands itself.

She says that when his honour shall have finished reading the papers he has of hers, she will send him more, and when he sees them he cannot fail to abhor one who ought to be so different from what she is. She thinks his honour will be pleased with them. "May our Lord grant it. Amen." There is a little compliment about his style of writing, for which he seems to have made some apology, and she says she had such joy to-night as never before.

Teresa's next letter to the Canon de Castro[2] is a note thanking him for a sermon he had preached in the convent. It is full of little graceful touches, as when she says she would rather not have heard him if his honour does not help her to carry out his doctrine, and that she desires for him, not only that he may go to Heaven, but that he may be something great in the Church of God. He is to let her know whether

[1] Letter ccclxii.

he is tired, but not to write, because she thinks it may be a fresh fatigue. This letter is written in the same month, of November, as the former, and it is followed by another,[1] after the Canon had said he could not preach on the profession of the novice about whom we have already heard.

We have next a letter to Mary of St. Joseph, the Prioress of Seville, asking her to give two nuns, and of her best, for the projected foundation of Granada, which is now being prepared.[2] We shall speak of it more at length presently. She also writes about the same time to Juan de Ovalle again,[3] on the subject of Beatriz. She says she has thought that if Beatriz had any intention of being a nun—as, in fact, she became, but not till after St. Teresa's death—she might take her with her to Burgos, giving her the habit first at Avila, and then take her to Madrid, and she evidently was looking forward now to the foundation in that city. Then if Beatriz did not like the place, she might come back to Avila. She speaks of what is very evident, her great anxiety for her niece's welfare. The plan, however, never came about. She changes her plan, indeed, before the letter is sent, and proposes that on her way to Burgos she should go to Alba to see her sister, which is reason enough for the journey, and then say she wished to take her niece with her, and nothing need be said at Avila. She mentions this plan a little later in a letter to Father Gratian,[4] and says it will have one inconvenience, because she wishes to keep Teresita, who is

---

[1] Letter ccclxiii.

[2] Letter ccclxiv.   [3] Letter ccclxv.   [4] Letter ccclxvi.

to go with her, apart from Beatriz. The letter speaks
first about the foundation of Granada, which we have
already postponed to another chapter. She mentions
Teresita as a little downcast by the thought of her
aunt's going to Burgos without her, and so she has
given her hopes. "The Fleming's" daughter has
been professed, and mother and daughter are both
mad with joy. She writes to him again[1] on the 1st
of December, sending him some money from Antonio
Ruiz by Father Ambrose. She has taken, out a
small sum for good reasons. It seeems she is learning
how to beg. She inquires carefully about the good
Provincial's chilblains.

We have a fragment of a note written to Father
Gratian on the 4th of December. The only important
portion of its contents seems to be an intimation that
the family of Doña Orofrisia, the wife of Don Francis,
St. Teresa's nephew, were thinking of trying to in-
validate the will of his father. She says she has
been told by learned men that they set it aside
without mortal sin. She says also that she thinks
she must keep Teresita with her. This refers to the
question of her having her as a companion on her
journey to Burgos.[2] Then comes the letter in which
St. Teresa, writing to Father Gratian, says she does not
understand certain "sanctities," and seems to reflect
sorrowfully upon the way in which some of the friars
were already beginning to treat him. We may speak
of this letter presently. There is also a passage
showing her continued anxiety about Beatriz, whom
it was proposed, apparently, to lodge in the Convent

[1] Letter ccclxvii.   [2] Letter ccclxviii.

of the Incarnation. Her aunt, however, altogether disapproves of this. Teresita is well, and writes a pretty little postscript to the letter, thanking him for a diurnal which he has sent her. Dr. Francisco has been asking to send him one of the scapulars which Gratian has sent. She says she gets on very well with Canon Castro. The best way of enabling a confessor to understand her is to send him one of her books to read.[1] The next fragment is one of only three or four lines, and has reference to her journey to Burgos.[2]

There remain but two other letters written during this last stay of St. Teresa at Avila. The first is to her nephew, Don Lorenzo, in America. It is written after the news of his marriage, on which Teresa congratulates him warmly. Things in Spain are very different from the state in which she would wish to see them with her family. Although Don Francisco has made a most excellent match, and could not have a more charming wife in all respects, yet his affairs are in a poor state already. What with the legacies left by his father, besides what must go to Teresa, his sister, his debts, and the like, she does not see how he is to live.[3] She sends a kind message to the bride. "She has a good bedeswoman here, and many of them." She should like much to see her, but if her coming to Spain involved her sharing in the troubles of the family, she had better stay where she is in

---

[1] Letter ccclxix.

[2] Letter ccclxx.

[3] According to the Spanish law, if the legacies exceeded a fifth of the property, they might be reduced, though not annulled.

peace. Then she breaks out into the praises of
Teresa, his sister. She has grown into a woman,
and is always increasing in virtue. Lorenzo may
well take the advice she gives him—truly she made
her laugh when she read the letter she has written to
Lorenzo—God speaks in her, and she does what she
talks about, our Lord holds her by the hand, and she
gives edification to all. He must not forget to write
to her, for she is very lonely, and when Teresa
remembers the affection and the presents of her
father to her, she compassionates her much, for she
has no one now. Francis loves her tenderly, and
would like to make her presents, but can do little
more. She tells him his letters are too short, considering they come such a great way. It is a great
mercy of God that he has fallen in with such a wife,
and so soon.

Then Teresa goes on to speak of the necessities
of the convent, after the legacy of Don Francisco de
Salcedo. The dowry of Teresita will do much good
there, if she is professed, as she much desires. She
tells him of the foundations she has made since he
left. She is expecting her sister, Juana de Ahumada.
She and her husband are in great poverty. She
mentions Beatriz as not having anything to become
a nun with, even if she wished it, and she begs him
to send them something, even if it is but a little.
She mentions the intention of her brother Augustin
to come here, and begs that he may see the letter,
as she has not head to write much. It is a risky
thing to take so long a voyage as Augustin thinks of,
merely on the chance of bettering himself. She ends

by saying that she leaves other things to Teresita's letter, and that he will do well to follow her advice. The letter is dated the 15th of December.[1]

Our last letter from Avila is one of thanks to the new community of Soria, who had sent an alms to the Convent of St. Joseph. It is written with all her usual affectionateness and gaiety. She is in a great hurry, and is to start for Burgos the same evening. So she writes to them a letter common to all. She thanks them for their alms, and is very grateful, though they still owe her something. She says that their friend, Don Diego Villejo, is being treated by our Lord with great marks of His favour, for the more he serves God the more crosses does he get. It seems that Doña Leonor de Ayans, who has been already mentioned as the niece by marriage of Doña Beatriz de Veamonte, was about to enter the Novitiate at Soria, and Teresa now begs them to treat her with the greatest kindness and consideration. She mentions afterwards that Doña Leonor had already been a benefactor to the convent in the way of building. She says that the Subprioress is, according to the Rule, to eat meat whenever her health requires it, even in Lent, although she is glad to hear that she is better.[2] The letter is dated December 28, 1581.

We have already mentioned Leonor de Ayans, who entered about this time as a novice in the Carmel of Soria. Her connection with Doña Beatriz de Veamonte, who was the foundress of the convent in that city, consisted in her having lived as wife to the

---

[1] Letter ccclxxi.   [2] Letter ccclxxii.

nephew of Doña Beatriz for eight years, when a diriment impediment was discovered, and the marriage annulled. She is the lady who was moved to wish for admission by hearing St. Teresa talk about Nicolas Doria. We have a letter of St. Teresa to her, written soon after her entrance, though the precise date is not given.[1] It seems to have been written after Teresa's arrival at Burgos, of which we shall soon speak.

She begins affectionately, calling the novice her daughter, and saying how much she likes to hear from her and to answer her. She is never to let the devil tempt her into believing that she does not care for her letters. Leonor was suffering greatly from dryness and desolation. Teresa tells her that our Lord treats her as one who already belongs to His household, whom He knows He shall not lose, and to whom He gives great occasions of merit by suffering. "He may hitherto have given you tender feelings, and the like, wishing to disentangle you from other delights."

Then she tells a story of a celebrated lady at Avila, whom she knew in the earlier years of her religious life, when she was under the direction of Father Balthasar Alvarez. This was Mari, or Maria, Diaz, of whom Father Luis de la Puente speaks in his Life of that venerable Father. She was much older than Teresa, having died in 1572. She was more than eighty years of age when she died, and had lived in Avila for more than forty, practising great poverty, for she lived on alms, having given away all she had to the poor. The Bishop let her live in the tribune of a church, close to the Blessed Sacrament, and she

[1] Letter ccclxxiv.

never left the place except to confess and to communicate. Father Balthasar Alvarez mortified and humbled her continually, in order to try her virtue and make it more perfect. St. Teresa's story is that she had given away everything but a coverlet, which she used for herself, and then gave that away also. Then our Lord sent her great dryness, desolation, and interior trials, and she said to Him, by way of complaint, that this was an odd way of treating her, that when He had left her nothing else He took Himself away! And so Teresa tells Leonor that this is our Lord's way to repay great services by great troubles, which are the best of all pay, because they are the way to gain the love of God. She tells her to serve the King of Heaven at her own expense, as the grandees serve the King. Let Him do as He will with her soul, His own spouse, and He will give a good account of all. It may be that the novelty of the life, and the daily routine she has to observe, have disturbed her a little. But peace will come back at once and abundantly. There are two more notes by St. Teresa to this Sister Leonor de la Misericordia, for whom she seems to have had a special predilection.

There exists another letter of St. Teresa's about this date, which may at all events be placed here, as we have already heard of the affair to which it relates, and it has less to do with the subject of the next chapter. It is addressed to Doña Beatriz de Mendoza y Castillo, the mother-in-law of Don Francisco, and explains St. Teresa's position with regard to the will of Don Lorenzo. Doña Beatriz seems to have complained that Teresa had expressed a wish to have no letters from her. Teresa says she thinks what she has said was to the effect that she did not wish to hear from her on the particular matter now at issue, for she is always glad and grateful to hear from her honour. But she is much pained when the correspondence turns on matters which it is against her conscience for her to agree to, and which, as she is told, it would also be wrong for Don Francisco to do. Her honour, Doña Beatriz, has been told otherwise, and may therefore have some doubt as to her goodwill. This is very painful to her. She desires to see these matters ended. May God so manage it according as it may be most for His service! which is what her honour also desires, and Teresa declares she has never had the slightest wish for anything else. She always wishes what may give comfort to her honour, and she knows well the worth of Doña Orofrisia.

She does not pay much attention to the claims of Don Pedro de Ahumada. She is so weary of the business that she would have refused to have anything to do with it, but that Peralvarez, her cousin, had told her that Doña Beatriz thought it ought not to be so, as the interests of St. Joseph's were engaged. For her sins she has been made Prioress, and so she sees it is right for her to act. But she thinks that the convent should have its rights insisted on, and that the work (her brother's chapel) should be finished quickly. Although her brother's children may agree to annul his will, the convent does not lose these rights, and no one can tear up the will without many suits, which are terrible things, and therefore it is right to wish all to be made safe. "May our Lord settle it, as He can, and preserve your honour for the benefit of your children. Amen!"

It may not be easy for us to understand the matter perfectly. But it is clear that it was proposed to quash the will of Don Lorenzo, and that his children might have been led to consent. But the legacy to the convent could not be quashed without the agreement of the convent, and St. Teresa, standing up for this as Prioress, and being also executrix, could prevent it. This probably brought her into collision with the advisers and connections of Don Francisco. Lorenzo was in America, Teresita with her, and she was careful to keep her with her for fear of other influences. It would seem that some of the relatives, Mary Baptist at Valladolid among the number, took part against her, and in consequence poisoned, as far as that was possible, the happiness of the end of her life, in a manner which they must have most bitterly regretted.[1]

We have another short letter of St. Teresa of this date, apparently, which has a sentence or two of some importance. It is addressed to Father Nicolas Doria,[2] and shows us that St. Teresa was already aware, so soon after the formation of the Province, of the discord which was likely to arise, though it did not break out till after her death. Father Nicolas was about this time sent to Italy, in order to arrange matters with the General. He sailed to his own home, Genoa, when he was met by the news that the General would soon be there also. This note of St. Teresa was written before his departure for Italy.

[1] Letter ccclxxv. [2] Letter ccclxxvi.

She speaks, apparently, of an attempt to thrust some dignity on him. We hear that the Pope once wanted to make him a Cardinal. St. Teresa speaks of his humility as shown in a letter to herself. But she adds, " Do consider, my Father, that all beginnings are laborious, and so it will be with your Reverence." Then she speaks of the question of hard studies for young Religious, in which she seems to see much danger to the spirit of recollection. It was an important matter at this time, as the College at Salamanca was making its start. Then comes a sentence which seems to allude to his relations with Father Gratian. "You must not consider that in government the chief matter is to be always noticing faults ; it is necessary often to choose to forget them. The Superior is in the place of God, to do his office, and He will give what may be wanting, and no one can be expected to be perfect. So do not dissemble,[1] or leave off writing to our Father whatever you think well."

This passage throws some light upon a letter of St. Teresa to Gratian, which has already been mentioned,[2] in which she says that she does not understand certain " phases of sanctity"—*algunas santitades.* She says that she writes thus with reference to that

---

[1] " No se haga mojigato." There seems some ambiguity about the exact meaning of the word. Doria was one of the Definitors, and may have held back, somewhat sulkily, from exercising his office, disapproving of the way in which Gratian governed, and finding himself not always listened to. St. Teresa also often enough found herself not attended to, but was too perfect in charity to desist from admonitions merely on that account.

[2] Letter ccclxviii.

person "who does not write to your Reverence, and that other, who will say that everything must be done according to his own opinion, which has caused me a temptation"—that is, to judge him hardly. It seems to have been Doria who would not write to his Superior,—the other may perhaps have been Antonio of Jesus. It is clear that St. Teresa was to be soon forced to lay aside her dream of a perfect union between Gratian and Doria, and that already the seeds of a fatal difference between them were beginning to be perceptible. It is not our business here to enter into the details of the dissension, or to say whether or not there were, now or at any future time, good grounds for the dissatisfaction with the government of Gratian which revealed itself at the next General Chapter. But it is not easy to see what can be said in defence of one in Doria's position, who was undoubtedly Gratian's subject, as well as Definitor, if he did not help him in every possible way towards the right government of the Province, as long as he had a reasonable hope that his representation would be listened to.

The letters which have now been mentioned as belonging to this short period of the last stay of St. Teresa in her native city, taken together with those of four or five months before her return, give us more or less of a picture of her state during the last years of her life on which she had now entered. The letters are but fragments of her correspondence, and yet they contain numberless traits of character, which we should have missed if we did not possess them. The habitual state of her soul, her constant

R 3

sense of the Divine Presence, her longings for the eternal possession of God so perfectly controlled by union with His will, which softened down even the pain which she was wont to feel at seeing Him offended and at the loss of souls, we find described for us in the beautiful letter to Bishop Velasquez,[1] written in the early summer of 1581. The time of rapts and ecstasies has passed with her, as well as that of anxiety and scruple about the preternatural communications with which she has been favoured. She does not care so much now to set the state of her conscience before learned men—and yet she shows a childlike delight in finding fresh approval of the path along which her soul has been led, from the last guide with whom she made acquaintance, the Canon Castro. She is at peace, too, as to the Reform which she has been the instrument of carrying out. Her name is now connected for ever with one of the greatest spiritual benefits received by the Church in the great century in which she lived, the century of the Council of Trent and the Catholic revival, the century of St. Pius V. and St. Charles, of St. Ignatius and St. Philip and St. Francis Xavier, and of a score more of the great restorers and enlargers of the Kingdom of God.

History has shown the greatness and the solidity of the work for which she had been raised up. And now her Reform had survived the tempests which raged round its birth, and was too strong to be shaken by the internal storms which were brewing even ere she died. Her friends and disciples

[1] Letter cccxxxvi.

were at work all around her, St. John of the Cross, Venerable Anne of Jesus, as well as a crowd of less famous souls as great before God as many of those of whom the Church knows more. At the same time, God does not spare her the most precious of His rewards, continual and great suffering. Her affections are wounded in their tenderest feelings. Indeed her life has become a succession of crosses. Casilda has gone out from her convent; Lorenzo, her dear brother, is dead ; Avila, her beloved house, is a solitude. Avila almost leaves her alone before she quits it. Her crowd of brothers are all gone, except the melancholy and restless Pedro, and there is a doubtful expectation that Augustin may come home. Juana de Ahumada can scarcely be persuaded to return to her to save, as St. Teresa thinks, the reputation of her dear niece, whose features reminded her of her own mother's. Francisco de Salcedo is dead, Julian of Avila has come to be a cause of pain, the good Bishop Don Alvaro and his sister Doña Maria are gone away. Balthasar Alvarez, to whom she owed so much and whom she always regarded as her father, had long been out of her path, and her feelings towards him had lately been revived by his death, over which she wept tenderly.[1]

The state of divine consolation in which she

---

[1] It was at Medina del Campo, on her way from Segovia to Avila, in 1580, after the death of Don Lorenzo de Cepeda, that St. Teresa heard of the death of Father Balthasar Alvarez. She wept for an hour, saying it was for the great loss to the Church. She remained in prayer two hours longer. It was at this visit that she cured by her touch the frightful erysipelas of a nun in the convent, who had kept away from meeting her on account of her disfigurement.

ordinarily lived, did not make her less, it made her more, tender in every holy feeling of affection. The nuns who leave St. Joseph's for Granada leave her in great loneliness, though one of them, at least, was not sorry to go. She is torn with anxieties about her niece Beatriz. Francis, her nephew, causes her much trouble. Only Teresita remains to her, and she is obliged to take her with her to Burgos, for fear of the influence of others. And the one consolation which she looked forward to at Avila, the profession of this much loved child, she was to be denied from seeing while alive. Between it and her lay all the crucifixion which she was to meet with at Burgos, and even Anne of Jesus, "her daughter and her crown," was to have some share in making her suffer, although we have reason for thinking that there was much misconception as to the degree in which she occasioned it.

NOTE TO CHAPTER IX.

The letters belonging to this chapter are the following :

1. (ccclii.) *To Father Gratian.* From Avila, September 28, 1581.

A full account is given, p. 234.

2. (cccliii.) *To Don Sancho Davila (afterwards Bishop of Jaen).* From Avila, October 9, 1581.

An account is given, p. 235.

3. (cccliv.) *To Senora Doña Guiomar Pardo y Tavera.* From Avila, apparently October 22, 1581.

An account is given, p. 236.

4. (ccclv.) *To Father Gratian.* From Avila, October 26, 1581.

A full account is given, p. 236.

5. (ccclvi.) *To the Most Eminent Cardinal Quiroga, Archbishop of Toledo.* From Avila, October 30, 1581.

This letter has been already spoken of at p. 179, ch. vi.

6. (ccclvii.) *To Senora Doña Maria Enriquez, Duchess of Alva.* From Avila, beginning of November, 1581.

Mentioned at p. 239.

7. (ccclviii.) *To Mary of St. Joseph, Prioress of Seville.* From Avila, November 8, 1581.

A full account is given, p. 240.

8. (ccclix.) *To Martin Alonzo de Salinas, Canon of Palencia.* From Avila, November 13, 1581.

A full account is given, p. 243.

9. (ccclx.) *To Juan de Ovalle, her brother-in-law, at Alba de Tormes.* From Avila, November 14, 1581.

A full account is given, p. 244.

10. (ccclxi.) *To Señor Pedro Castro, Canon of Avila.* From Avila, November 19, 1581.

A full account is given, p. 245.

11. (ccclxii.) *To the same.* From Avila, November, 1581.

12. (ccclxiii.) *To the same.* From Avila, November, 1581.

Both these are mentioned, p. 247.

13. (ccclxiv.) *To Mary of St. Joseph, Prioress of Seville.* From Avila, November 23, 1581.

Mentioned at p. 247.

14. (ccclxv.) *To Juan de Ovalle.* From Avila, November 29, 1581.

An account is given, p. 247.

15. (ccclxvi.) *To Father Gratian.* From Avila, November 29, 1581.

Mentioned at p. 248.

16. (ccclxvii.) *To the same.* From Avila, December 1, 1581.

Mentioned at p. 248.

17. (ccclxviii.) *To the same.* From Avila, December 4, 1581.

Mentioned at p. 248.

18. (ccclxix.) *To the same.* From Avila, December 4, 1581.

Mentioned at p. 249.

19. (ccclxx.) *Fragment, apparently to Father Gratian* (end of 1581).

Mentioned at p. 249.

20. (ccclxxi.) *To Don Lorenzo de Cepeda, her nephew in America.* From Avila, December 13, 1581.

An account is given, p. 249.

21. (ccclxxii.) *To the Prioress and Discalced Carmelites of the Convent at Soria.* From Avila, December 28, 1581.

An account is given, p. 251.

22. (ccclxxiii.) *To the Licentiate Peña, Confessor to the Cardinal Archbishop of Toledo.* From Medina del Campo, January 8, 1582.

This letter has already been mentioned in ch. vi. p. 168.

23. (ccclxxiv.) *To Sister Leonor de la Misericordia, at Soria.* From Burgos, early in 1582.

An account is given, p. 252.

24. (ccclxxv.) *To Señora Doña Beatriz de Mendoza y Castillo.* No date; apparently at the end of 1581 or beginning of 1582.

An account is given, p. 253.

25. (ccclxxvi.) *To Father Fra Nicolas Doria.* Beginning of 1582. No date.

An account is given, p. 255.

CHAPTER X.

Granada and Burgos.

ALTHOUGH it hardly falls naturally to the biographer of St. Teresa to include in his narrative those foundations of her Reform which were not made by herself, even though they were made in her lifetime, yet there is reason for mentioning some of them as incidents in the development of her work. We have already mentioned that the foundation of a monastery of friars was made at Salamanca in the months which elapsed immediately after the Chapter of Alcala, and that in the same place the College in which the theologians who are known under the name of the Salmanticenses resided, was founded about the same time. This was apparently the chief work to which Father Gratian devoted himself at the time. A hardly less important step was taken by the Reformed Carmel soon after the date at which we have arrived, the beginning of the last year of St. Teresa's life, 1582. This step was the extension of the Reform to the capital of the newly "annexed" kingdom of Portugal, which for the time was united to Spain. The work was committed to the energetic and zealous Father Ambrose Mariano, and supported by the influence of the King. Mariano, as an Italian, was more acceptable to the Portuguese than a Spaniard might have been, and he was probably well fitted for an enterprise of this kind. The foundation is said by the Annalist of the Reform to have been made on February 19, 1582.[1] The monastery of Lisbon soon became popular in the city, but its beginnings were saddened by the loss of many valuable lives, if indeed the deaths of missionaries, which so often seem to presage future successes to the work of the Gospel, can be called altogether a loss. The Reformed Carmel, after occupying its monastery at Lisbon, embraced for the first time the work of missions to the heathen, in which it was afterwards to become so fruitful. Five Fathers were sent to the coast of Guinea, either this year or the next. They sailed on the 20th of March, the day after St. Joseph's feast, but before they had proceeded far on their voyage the small vessel in which they were embarked came by accident into collision with a larger ship, and the missionaries were all drowned.

But we are almost obliged to speak at some length of the story of another foundation, begun in this year, 1582, in which St. Teresa did not indeed take part personally, being occupied at Burgos, but to which she contributed largely in many ways. We have noticed that shortly before

[1] The historian of the Order, in the *Reforma de los Descalços*, t. i. l. v. c. 24, fixes the date in the spring of 1582. We are inclined to suspect a mistake, for perhaps it would be more accurate to say 1582-3, according to the old reckoning. First, there is utter silence in the letters of this spring of 1582, concerning this step. Then, both Ambrose Mariano and Jerome Gratian are mentioned as in other places during this time.

leaving Avila on her last journey, she speaks of the gaps occasioned in the small community of St. Joseph's, as one of the causes of her feelings of loneliness. These gaps were partly caused by the foundation of which we are to speak, for which two of the community of St. Joseph's left, one of whom was the Subprioress, and another Antoineta of the Holy Ghost, one of the four original novices of the foundation, who seems never to have left it before. This was the famous foundation of Granada, made by Anne of Jesus, under the authority of St. Teresa, almost simultaneously with Teresa's own last foundation of Burgos. It will perhaps be most convenient if we place our account of it here, before proceeding with the last journey of Teresa herself.

It appears that when the Chapter of Alcala was concluded, the new Provincial, Father Jerome Gratian, appointed two Vice-Provincials under himself, one for Andalusia, the other for Castile. The Vice-Provincial of Andalusia was Fra Diego of the Trinity, that of Castile was Fra Antonio of Jesus. It does not seem certain how far these Vice-Provincials shared the authority of Father Gratian, who perhaps may have been over-hasty in ridding himself of a burthen which he certainly disliked, though it was no doubt a very heavy one, especially as the monasteries and convents were very much scattered, and the means of communication were very uncertain. Our business now is with Anne of Jesus.

Anne had been left at Veas as Prioress on the foundation of that convent in 1575. She had been re-elected for another term of three years in 1578, and would no doubt have been continued longer in the post if the choice had been left to the nuns of the convent, who had been formed by her to a very high perfection. We are told that, shortly before the time of election, in 1581, St. Teresa wrote to the nuns at Veas, saying that they must not re-elect Anne another time, because she would be wanted for the foundation of Granada. Teresa would not have spoken in this manner merely upon her own judgment, still less upon the authority of some private relation which she might have had on the subject. We must suppose, therefore, that the project had already been discussed, and the foundation much desired by the nuns. It cannot be considered that it was anything but an extremely important step in the onward progress of the Reform.

The only question would be about the possibility of gaining permission to make the foundation, and about the person who was to be the leader of the little band of Religious who might be sent. Caravaca had been founded by Anne of St. Albert in 1576, when it was for the time impossible for Teresa to leave Seville. All the other convents of the Reform had been founded by herself in person. Anne of Jesus, who had shown herself so wonderfully like St. Teresa in the training of her novices, was considered by some of the few persons capable of forming a judgment on such matters, to be almost her equal in spiritual and mental gifts. It is said that Teresa had told her that she was destined to be the foundress, not only of the Carmel of Granada, but also of that of Madrid. On the occasion of which we are speaking, the nuns at

Veas obeyed the injunction of St. Teresa, and Anne was left in her convent, when the three years of her office expired, as a simple Religious. This did not prevent the nuns from treating her as if she was their Superior, especially in all that concerned the affairs of their souls, which they were in the habit of manifesting to her as freely as before. The new Prioress must have been one of her own spiritual children, and thus there would have been no jealousy between them. We shall see, however, that St. Teresa saw a little danger in the great personal devotion with which Anne was regarded, and perhaps Anne herself had unconsciously caught some of the ways of a "perpetual" Superior.

In the October of the year 1581, Fra Diego of the Trinity, the Vice-Provincial, came to Veas to confer with Anne of Jesus about the founding of the convent at Granada. The Discalced Friars were already in the city, and had prepared the way by the great edification which they had given, and by the interest in the Reformed Carmel which had thus been created. Many ladies had talked of becoming Carmelite nuns. Fra Diego was one of the simplest of men, and he had the happy gift of supposing that every fair appearance and hopeful promise was certain to be fulfilled in fact. Anne of Jesus was more of the mind of St. Teresa on such matters. She took into consideration the certainty of the opposition of the powers of evil to any project involving the glory of God, and the way in which difficulties might gather, like clouds over a fair sky, from all quarters, and not least from the narrowness of good people. Anne told Fra Diego that the promises which had been made him were fair words, and nothing more. The Archbishop of Granada would almost certainly oppose the foundation of a new convent. Granada was a half-ruined city, there had been a number of bad seasons, the scarcity was great. Fra Diego had been promised help from the Licentiate Laguna, a man of great influence with the Archbishop, and Father Gaspar de Salazar had secretly promised to gain the prelate's consent. Anne made it a matter of fervent prayer, and at last she was brought to understand that her fears were true, and that they could not reckon upon any human help. Nevertheless, our Lord promised to take a special care of the nuns, and said that He would be greatly served in that convent.

Anne of Jesus sent at once for St. John of the Cross, who was the confessor of the nuns at Veas. She told him what had passed, and he advised her to communicate it to Father Gratian. It was agreed that Fra Diego should return to Granada to prepare matters, and that St. John himself should go to Avila for St. Teresa, who was still expected to come, and for the Religious whom she might choose as her companions, to make the foundation. St. John was the bearer of letters asking for the permission of Father Gratian, and also that St. Teresa might choose three nuns from Castile to be the nucleus of the new community. The rest were to be taken from Veas.

St. John of the Cross found St. Teresa at Avila. Father Gratian was still engaged on the beginnings of the College of Salamanca. He willingly left the

choice of the nuns to St. Teresa. The letter of
St. Teresa to Father Gratian, on the arrival of
St. John, has been already mentioned in the last
chapter.[1] She tells him that Mary of Christ, the
late Prioress, was glad to go away. Teresa had
some scruple in sending her, either because Gratian
had named some one else, or from some other cause.
Teresa says that Canon Castro satisfied her scruple.[2]
It was impossible for Teresa herself to go into
Andalusia. Burgos, which was to be a most
troublesome foundation, engaged all her care. He
said, moreover, that her presence was not required.
Anne of Jesus could secure success better than
herself. She wrote to Anne at the same time,
saying that she was certain all would go well, and
that our Lord would let them feel that He was
helping them powerfully.[3] The subjects whom she
chose from Castile were certainly excellent. Such
was the Subprioress of Avila, Mary of Christ.
Such, too, was Antoineta of the Holy Ghost, one of
the four first novices of St. Joseph at Avila. Beatriz
of Jesus, Teresa's cousin, was the third. Anne of
Jesus was herself to choose three from the community of Veas, which she knew so well, and which
she had formed to such perfection. She was to have
two more from the convent at Seville, and two from

[1] P. 247.
[2] This letter is No. ccclxvi.
[3] The letter to Anne is lost, as are all from St. Teresa to her,
because the latter ordered her to destroy them. The two or three
exceptions prove the rule, as is so often said,—because some special
reason may be given for their preservation.

Villanueva de la Jara.[1] Teresa wrote at once to Mary of St. Joseph at Seville, asking her to give of her best, as she knew how important it was that those chosen for such a work should be very good. Very good, also, were the two lay-sisters who were taken from the newly-formed community at Villanueva de la Jara. We know in what poverty that convent had been founded, and it was probably a relief to it to have a smaller number of mouths to feed.

St. John left Avila on the 28th of November, with the two nuns who were sent from St. Joseph's. He passed by Toledo, where he took Beatriz of Jesus to join the others, and reached Veas on the 6th of December. About this time he was elected Prior of the monastery at Granada, and was thus fixed on the spot where he could most help the new foundation. He found Anne of Jesus overwhelmed with sorrow, first at hearing that St. Teresa was not to come, and still more because she herself was to take her place.

In the meantime, Fra Diego had been working at Granada, and was still full of the most brilliant anticipations. St. Teresa's letters to the nuns mention the great expectations which his reports had raised. St. Vincent de Paul said that a good work talked about was already half defeated, and this good work was talked about almost before it had been begun. One strong fact was already against it. The

---

[1] In the letter just quoted in the text St. Teresa gives their numbers. "Three from hence (she means Castile, not Avila, as Beatriz of Jesus was at Toledo), four from Veas, one of whom was Anne of Jesus, two from Seville, and two from Villanueva de la Jara." The reason for noting the number carefully will be seen by-and-bye, as Anne of Jesus was blamed for taking more.

Archbishop of Granada steadily refused his leave. Anne wrote to Fra Diego that nothing could be done unless he could hire a house. The nuns from Castile were already at Veas. Diego could neither find a house, nor bend the Archbishop. He took his two influential friends, Don Luis de Mercado and the Licentiate Laguna, with him to the prelate. The Archbishop still formally refused. He would be glad, he said, "to suppress all the convents he had, and he was astonished at their thinking, in a time of such scarcity, of founding new houses, which could find no means of subsistence." He added more to the same purpose. At the same time the letters from Veas were pressing. The nuns were waiting—surely it would not require much to support them on their arrival? At last, by favour and interest, a magistrate of the town consented to let them a house. Fra Diego wrote sorrowfully, that he was grieved to have no more to offer them. But it had been agreed that they should start at the least word of encouragement from him.

Anne of Jesus tells us, that she was making her prayer as usual, on the 13th of January, the octave of the Epiphany—on which feast the Church commemorates also the Baptism of our Lord and the miracle at Cana—and thinking of the words of our Lord to St. John Baptist, "So it behoves us to fulfil all justice." Suddenly she heard a noise of a multitude of threatening voices and cries, which threw her into great alarm, and obliged her to lean her head on the nun next her, who was the Prioress. She begged the Prioress to send to see who was ringing at the door, and it turned out to be, as Anne had expected, the messenger to tell her to start at once with her companions for Granada. A most violent storm followed, rain and hailstones falling in abundance, while she herself was taken suddenly and inexplicably ill. Notwithstanding all her pains, she urged that all might be ready for the Sunday morning, it being already Saturday night. She was too ill next day to hear Mass, but nevertheless started with her little band at three on the Monday morning. The nuns were full of joy, thinking that our Lord would certainly be greatly honoured by the issue of their journey. The weather was fine, but the late storm made the roads very difficult.

They arrived the same night at Dayfuentes, a small town about five leagues from Granada. There a consultation was held as to the means to be employed for inducing the Archbishop to change his mind. It was agreed that St. John of the Cross and Peter of the Angels, the other Father who accompanied the nuns, should go the next morning to make a final effort. There was a thunder-storm that night, which struck the Archbishop's palace, destroyed a part of his library, and killed some mules in his stables. He himself fell ill in consequence. The next morning a further obstacle was raised. The person who had promised to let the nuns a house withdrew the promise, and was vainly offered a security to the amount of fifty thousand ducats. They did not know where to turn. But Don Luis de Mercado, already mentioned, had a widowed sister, Doña Anne de Penalosa, a widow who had lost her only child, and spent her days in mourning and retirement. Her brother asked her to shelter the newly-arrived Religious for a time, and she immediately prepared a lodging in her house, and arranged everything for a chapel.

The apartment which was thus placed at their disposal was convenient, though small, and the Religious stayed there a much longer time than had been thought of at first. They could thus enter Granada, and reached the lady's house at three in the morning of the 20th, the feast of SS. Fabian and Sebastian. Anne de Penalosa received her guests at the door of her house, weeping with devotion. They immediately set to work to arrange for Mass the little chapel, which was the porch of the house. Fra Diego was desirous of forcing matters with the Archbishop. Perhaps he knew how the foundation at Seville had been carried out, as it were, by a *coup de main*, and thought that Granada might have the same history. The Archbishop would give way when he had an accomplished fact to deal with, and if Mass was said, he would yield his permission. The attempt would apparently have been made, but for Anne of Jesus. She begged that the door might be shut, no bell rung, and no Mass said, till the Archbishop gave his leave. She wrote to him at once, informing him of their arrival, begging him to come and give them his blessing, and place the Blessed Sacrament in the chapel. She added, that though it was Sunday, they would not hear Mass till he gave leave that it should be said for them. The Archbishop had not risen when the letter was brought to

S 3

him, being ill : but he answered very kindly, saying
he was sorry he could not come and say Mass for
them, but that he would send his Vicar-General to do
whatever they asked. All was therefore gained. The
Vicar-General came at seven, when the Mass was
said, and Communion given to the nuns. He also
placed the Blessed Sacrament in the tabernacle ;
there was a fine function, attended by some magistrates and a large concourse of people. In truth, the
devotion of Granada was roused, it seemed as if a
jubilee had been proclaimed. Thus far, therefore,
Anne of Jesus, in Andalusia, had been more successful
than was, as we shall see, St. Teresa at Burgos. There
is much similarity between the two histories, and in
each case there was an Archbishop from whom
consent had to be wrung against his will. The prelate
whom St. Teresa had to deal with was, as we shall
see, somewhat more stubborn than the Archbishop of
Granada. He had begun, nevertheless, by promising
his consent.

When, in the course of the day, Don Luis and the
Licentiate Laguna went to visit the Archbishop,
they found him still discontented. When they
asked him how he came to act as he had done
in giving his permission, he said he could not
help it, he had felt forced against his will. He
would give nothing to the convent, he was
already unable to help those which already existed.
At the same time, the Religious were deprived of
much of the aid which they might otherwise have
received, by the fact that they were the guests of
Doña Anne de Penalosa, who was well known for her

great charities. But through some reason or other she gave them very little. The Discalced Friars, themselves in great straits on account of the prevailing scarcity, were their best friends. It is said that Anne de Penalosa was taken in by the joyous expression on the faces of the nuns, and thought that they had abundant resources from other quarters. Thus it was that for seven months which they passed in her house they had to live upon very little. They observed their Rule with the most perfect fidelity. Don Luis de Mercado, who lived under his sister's roof, never saw them with their veils lifted.

They experienced, it may be said, all the other hardships which can be felt most keenly by a religious community. They could take no postulants. Lady after lady applied, to the number of two hundred. Every one had something about her which prevented her admission. They could not find a house. It was not till the August of the year in which they arrived that Father Jerome Gratian succeeded in hiring one for them, which they then entered, leaving their good hostess, Anne de Penalosa, in desolation, but greatly enriched by our Lord with spiritual gifts in return for her hospitality. Their want of success in gaining subjects was compensated in another way. The priests and preachers in the city were interested in them, and came to say Mass for them and preach to them. Thus their example gradually began to influence the members of the religious communities, so that it was said, by a person of high authority, that a great change for the better had been wrought throughout the city. Thus the sufferings and apparent want of means in the new community were fruitful in other ways, and their example of cheerfulness and patience under the cross would have been less prolific of good, if their history had been a tale of uninterrupted and dazzling success as far as it met the eye. Our Lord chose for them the most exquisite kind of perfection, and took care not to spare them some of the choicest trials and sufferings which He allots to those most dear to Him.

While they were being thus tried in His providence, they received some very singular consolations. One of them was certainly the confidence with which they looked forward to the future, which was confirmed by some special promises of protection and help received by Anne of Jesus in answer to her prayers. Nor was she the only one in the little community who felt her communications with her Divine Spouse to be more intimate and special than in any former period of her life. It was common among them to feel the Presence of our Lord in the Blessed Sacrament in an unusual manner, almost as if it were visible. This favour was so remarkable, and so ordinarily granted to them, that they could not help speaking of it to one another in their conversations. It began from the moment when the Blessed Sacrament was placed in the tabernacle, and remained continually. Here we shall leave Anne of Jesus and her Sisters, in order to carry on the story of the "twin foundation" of Burgos. For this, however, we must go back considerably in the order of time.

The account given by St. Teresa in the *Book of*

the Foundations of the beginning of her convent at
Burgos, is very long, and we must endeavour to supplement it here and there, as well as to summarize the
narrative. It was the last of her works of this kind,
and one of the most difficult, although when it was
first thought of it seemed likely to be accomplished
with ease. The first idea seems to have arisen in the
minds of some of her devoted friends, the Fathers of
the Society of Jesus. She tells us that more than six
years before the time at which she wrote the account,
"directly after the foundation, certain members of the
Society of Jesus, men of great godliness, learning,
and spirituality, and long professed, said to me that
it would be a great service rendered to our Lord if a
house of this holy Order was founded in Burgos." It
was therefore suggested to her about the beginning of
the troubles in the Order, which preceded the separation of the Discalced from the Calced Carmelites.
She says that these troubles made the foundation
impossible. It is well to recall this fact, because,
although it was nothing wonderful for the Fathers
of the Society to wish for, and help on with all their
power, the advance of St. Teresa's Reform, there
happened, in the course of her foundation at Burgos,
to be a conflict of interests, of which she speaks with
some contempt as having been made a handle for
the creation of serious complaints against her, and
for a foolish attempt to sow discord between the
Society and her Reform.

Later on, when she was in Valladolid in 1580,
before she went to found at Palencia, the new Archbishop of Burgos came that way. He was Don

Christoval Vela, formerly Bishop of the Canaries; and he was on his way to take possession of his new see. Mgr. Alvaro de Mendoza, the former Bishop of Avila, and now of Palencia, in which city she was about to found, had been commissioned to give the pallium to the Archbishop, who received it from him at a monastery outside the town of Valladolid. Teresa had asked the Bishop of Palencia, who was always ready to advance the cause of the Carmelites, to obtain from the Archbishop leave for her to found a home in Burgos. The latter, who was a native of Avila, and remembered the foundation of the Convent of St. Joseph, willingly promised the permission. He said he had wished to have a foundation while he was in the Canaries. St. Teresa thought that this promise was enough, as the Council of Trent did not exact a written permission. It turned out that she was over-confident.

In the *Book of the Foundations* she goes on to refer to her great unwillingness to make new foundations at this time, and that our Lord spoke to her in one of the "locutions" which are mentioned in her letter to the Bishop of Osma to encourage her.

He asked me, as if reproaching me, what was I afraid of? Had He ever failed me? "I am the same, fail not to make these two foundations." As I said, when giving an account of the former foundations, what courage these words gave me, there is no reason why I should say it over again here. All sloth departed from me at once, and that makes me think that the cause of it was neither my illness nor my old age, and so I began at once to make arrangements for both foundations, as I said before. It was thought better to make the foundation of Palencia first, because it was nearer, and because the weather was so severe and Burgos so cold, and also because it would please the good Bishop of Palencia. It was therefore done, as I said before.

She tells us that she might have gone on at once to Burgos from Palencia, but that the foundation of Soria, which was near at hand, and presented no difficulties, was offered in the meantime, and she thought it better to take that first. The Bishop of Palencia did not object, but thought it well that she should write to the Archbishop of Burgos to explain how matters were, and, after Teresa had left for Soria, he sent a Canon to Burgos on purpose. The Archbishop on this wrote a very kind letter to Teresa, as well as to the Bishop, putting himself entirely in his hands. The Archbishop was not quite the same man, when on his way to Burgos, and again after he had taken possession of his see. His mind was possibly already under the influence of ecclesiastics on the spot, who had a great regard for what are called "vested interests." The Archbishop added in his letter that he must take account of what he knew about Burgos, and that she must come with consent of the town. If the town refused, his hands would not be tied, but that he remembered the foundation of St. Joseph's, and the great trouble which that foundation, without the leave of the town, had occasioned, and he wished to have everything of the kind avoided in Burgos. He also said that the convent must have a revenue secured, which was a condition Teresa would not like, and therefore he mentioned it.

In fact, the Archbishop was already beginning to draw back. St. Teresa, as we see from her letter to Canon Reinoso, printed in a former page, discerned the coolness which had come over him, and, with her great experience of the manner in which good people are used by the devil to oppose designs that promise well for the glory of God, saw the coming trouble before any one else was conscious of it. It need not surprise us that in the history of these foundations opposition should frequently be found to come from the prelates of the Church, and those prelates excellent men in every way. Convents and monasteries were springing up on every side, and were sometimes a great drain upon the charity of the faithful, and any pinching need which they might experience would involve a recourse to the Bishops in the first instance. Just at this time we learn from St. Teresa herself that three or four Religious Orders were seeking to make foundations in Burgos, and the story of Anne of Jesus and her little colony at Granada, where the foundation was actually contemporaneous with that of Burgos, will illustrate the history before us. St. Teresa tells us that she at once determined to hold back, but without giving as her reason for doing so any distrust of the Bishop. "I wrote to the Bishop of Palencia entreating him that as the summer was nearly over, and my infirmities such as to disable me from being in so cold a country, the matter might rest for the time. I did not raise any doubt as to the Archbishop, for the Bishop was already put out at his making difficulties, after having expressed so much good-will, and because I did not wish to make a quarrel, for they are friends. And so I went from Soria to Avila, not at all minded for the present to go to Burgos so soon, and my going to St. Joseph's at Avila was very necessary for certain reasons."

At Palencia, Teresa had met a pious lady living in Burgos, Catalina[1] de Tolosa. She had come to Palencia to place two of her daughters in the newly-founded convent, and she had already two others in the convent at Valladolid. She was a widow and very wealthy. At the time of her meeting with Teresa, the foundation of Soria does not seem to have been under consideration, and the foundation of Burgos was thought to be quite certain, the Archbishop having given his consent, as was supposed. Teresa asked her to hire a house in Burgos for her, that she might take possession at once when she came.

She thought this matter was at an end when she went to Avila, as Doña Catalina was made aware of the delay and its causes, and Teresa had asked her no more than to hire a house for her in case she came. But the good lady would not let the matter rest, and understanding that the consent of the town was the sole impediment, set herself to overcome the difficulty without delay.

She had two neighbours, persons of importance, and great servants of God and very desirous of the foundation, a mother and daughter. The mother's name was Doña Maria Manrique, who had a son a Regidor,[2] called Don

---

[1] Catalina is the Spanish form of Catharine, and as St. Teresa constantly uses it, we take the liberty of using it also, as well as the name most familiar to us.

[2] The "Regidores" were the members of the Corporation, answering to our Aldermen.

Alonzo de San Domingo Manrique, the daughter was
called Doña Catalina; they both spoke to him that he
might propose it in the Corporation. He asked Catalina de
Tolosa what foundation he was to say that we should have,
for that without that they would not grant it. She said she
would bind herself to give us a house if we lacked one, and
to support us, and at this same time made a petition to that
effect signed with her name. Don Alonzo set about it so well
that he got what he wanted from all the Regidores, and went
to the Archbishop, taking the licence in writing. When the
mother wrote to me immediately they began the negotiation
telling me that it was in hand, I took it as a joke, for I
knew how averse they are from admitting convents founded
in poverty, and as I did not know, nor did it ever occur to
me that she would undertake it, I thought we were far from
the end of the business. Nevertheless, one day, on the
octave of St. Martin, as I was commending the matter to our
Lord, I thought what could be done if the leave were given,
for as to my going to Burgos with all my infirmities, so cold
a place, and cold being so bad for me—I thought I should
not be allowed to, it would be rashness to take so long a
journey, so nearly broken by the hardships I had suffered in
coming from Soria, as I have said, and that the Father
Provincial would not allow it. I thought the Prioress of
Palencia could do very well if she went, that all was easy,
and she would have little to do. As I was thinking thus, and
quite determined not to go, our Lord said to me these words,
from which I knew that the licence was given: "Make no
account of the cold. I am the true warmth. The devil is
exerting all his force to hinder the foundation; you take My
side that it may be made, and fail not to go yourself, for it
will be of great profit." With this I changed my mind, for
although nature sometimes resists in a matter which costs
much trouble, the determination to suffer for so great a God
does not fail, so I said to Him that He was not to take

account of my feeling so weak, in commanding me whatever was for His service, and with His favour I could not
fail to do it. It was then snowing; what made me most
afraid was my bad health, for if I had had health, nothing
could have seemed much to me. It was this that tried me
so much commonly during the foundation : the cold has
been very little, at least what I have felt; in truth, I thought
I felt it as much when I was at Toledo. Our Lord has well
kept His word which He said as to this.

She tells us that a few days after this she received
the licence of the Corporation, together with letters
from the two ladies urging her to come without delay.
There was fear of new obstacles. The Minims (of
St. Francis of Paula) were seeking to found a monastery, and a little before the Basilian Fathers had
established another. The Carmelites of the Mitigation had for some time been applying. There were
therefore many rival claims. The town of Burgos
was famous for its charity and religion, for which
St. Teresa praises God much. It had lost much of
its former prosperity and splendour, and yet it freely
admitted all these religious houses. She says she
had often heard of its charity, but did not think it
was so great as she found it. But the Archbishop,
considering all the inconveniences which might result,
was against their foundation, thinking that they
would injure the convents and monasteries already
depending on alms. She thinks the devil may have
had some hand in it, desirous of preventing the great
good which these religious houses do.

Teresa says she would have gone at once if she
could, for she thought she was more bound to prevent

the loss of so good an opportunity, as the good ladies who were doing so much. Our Lord's words taught her to expect some great opposition, and yet it was not clear from what quarter it could come. Doña Catalina said that her own house was the one they were to take possession of, and that the Corporation and the Archbishop had given full leave. Whence was the difficulty to come? She sees in this an instance of the light often given to Superiors in such cases, for Father Gratian had asked whether the Archbishop had given his leave in *writing*. She answered that she was told the whole matter had been communicated to him, and that he had approved of the licence being asked of the town, and said nothing against it, and we were certain what he would say. Father Gratian determined to go with her. His Advent sermons were over, he had to visit Soria, which he might do on the way, and he wished to be able to take care of Teresa on the winter journey.

Teresa left Avila, never to return, on January 2, 1582, although till the very few last days of her life, she was looking forward to seeing it again, as she intended herself to take part in the ceremony of the profession of her dear child Teresita. She took her as a companion to Burgos, for the sake of keeping her away from her relatives, who were at this time, and to the very last, tormenting her with the proposal that her brother Don Lorenzo's will should be quashed, in order to the enrichment of his son at the expense of the Convent of St. Joseph, to which he had left a part of his fortune. Teresa had with her

also, of course, her faithful lay-sister, Anne of St.
Bartholomew, Thomasina of St. John Baptist, a nun
she had taken from the Convent of Alba de Tormes,
to be Prioress at Burgos, another lay-sister, Mary of
St. John Baptist, from Avila. The weather was very
bad. Teresa suffered much from inflammation of the
throat. She rested a few days at Medina del Campo.
The Prioress, Albert Baptist, was ill of a fever and
pains in her side, and was unable to receive Teresa at
the door, as usual. Seeing she was absent, Teresa
went straight to the infirmary, and asked her how it'
was that she was ill when she came? She touched
her side, and told her to get up, as she was well, and
come to the refectory. The Prioress rose up quite
well.

St. Teresa rested in Medina for a few days, and
left it on the 9th. The day before her departure she
wrote to the Licentiate Don Dionysio Peña, chaplain
of His Eminence the Cardinal of Toledo, giving an
account of the happy state in which she had found
Doña Elena, the niece of the Cardinal. She is well
and is getting plump. She is as much at home as if
she had been a Carmelite many years. She speaks
of her journey as undertaken unexpectedly, but
"some good people of Burgos have so great a desire
for a convent there, that they have got leave from
the Archbishop and the town," and she is on her way
with some Sisters to put the design into execution.
It will cost her much trouble, for she had not done it
when she was so near, at Palencia, but went back
first to Avila, and at this time the journey is a great
effort to her. She begs his honour to pray to His

Divine Majesty that it may be for His glory—in that case, the more one suffers the better. His honour is also to let her know how his illustrious lordship the Cardinal is, and how he is himself. It is certain that the more of these convents there are, the more are the subjects of his most illustrious lordship ; let him commend them to our Lord. He is not to forget them in his Holy Sacrifices. There is also a greeting sent to Doña Luisa de la Cerda, her old friend. She says that she leaves for Burgos (by Palencia) on the morrow.[1] The, letter was no doubt occasioned by her visit to Doña Elena Quiroga, at Medina del Campo, and perhaps Teresa did not forget that she had applied and was to apply again for leave to found in Madrid, which was under the jurisdiction of the Cardinal of Toledo.

Teresa left for Valladolid on the next day. She took with her two nuns for the new foundation, one of whom was Catharine of the Assumption, daughter of Catalina of Tolosa, and the other Catharine of Jesus. Agnes of Jesus, whom she took from Palencia, made up the number to nine, counting Teresa herself and Anne of St. Bartholomew, as well as Teresita. Father Gratian and another Father, who joined them here, made up the little company. The roads were dreadfully bad, on account of great floods. The Fathers had often to trace out the way, to secure the safety of the carriages, or to drag them out of or through the mud when they had stuck fast. As they drew near Burgos, the danger increased. The River Alançor is there swollen by several lesser streams

---

[1] Letter ccclxxxiii.

joining it, and the road threads its way through their various courses. At a place called the Bridges the floods had entirely hidden the track, and yet a step off the right road would plunge the carriages into deep water. St. Teresa does not tell us what her companions afterwards revealed. She got out and bade them follow her, while they begged that they might first go to confession. She bade them take courage, as they were labouring for the glory of God—what could be a greater happiness than to die martyrs for His love? She would go first—if the stream swept her away, they were to go back to the last inn. She went in, and her foot slipt, but she was held up by an invisible hand. "Ah, Lord," she cried, "when will you cease to sow our path with difficulties?" An answer came, "Do not complain, for it is so that I treat My friends." "Ah, Lord," she replied, "that is why you have so few." She went on, and passed the point of danger, and her companions followed. A little further on, they were able to hear Mass and go to Communion, and her tongue, which was affected by her paralysis, became free. Sometimes the carriages were so fast in the mud that the mules of one had to be harnessed to the other as well as its own. Gratian was invaluable, he was so courageous and calm. At "the Bridges," however, even he was alarmed. She tells us that she was all the time suffering from fever, and could not swallow anything without pain.

Before leaving Palencia, St. Teresa had written to Doña Catalina de Tolosa to apprize her of her coming. The letter is dated the 11th of January, and

begins by apologies for not having started before.
She had got the Prioress of Valladolid to write to
Doña Catalina as soon as she arrived. Illness had
kept her four days. When she grew a little better, she
set out for Palencia, " fearing your honour, and those
other my ladies, whose hands I kiss many times. I
beg their honours, and your honour too, not to blame
me for the delay. If you knew what state the roads
are in, perhaps you would blame me more for having
come." She is a little better, but still unwell, which
she hopes will not last long. The Father Provincial
would not let her start till he saw her better, although
he desired it much, "and kisses your honour's hand,
and desires much to make your acquaintance." Then
after some arrangements about means of communication, she says they mean to start on Friday (which
would be the 19th). Then she lays down particularly
what must be done when they arrive. His Paternity
wishes them first to visit the Crucifix of Burgos.
Then they will inform Doña Catalina, as before, and
come to her house as secretly as possible, and, if
necessary, will wait till night, when Gratian is to go
to ask the Archbishop's blessing, that the first Mass
may be said the next day, and till that is done, her
honour must believe Teresa, that it is better that no
one know anything of their coming. It is always her
way to observe this secrecy. Whenever she thinks over
all that God has done for them, she is astonished, and
sees that it is all prayer. May God be praised for
all. She is bringing Catalina's daughter, Catalina of
the Assumption, and it has been no little matter to do
it, there has been so much opposition. She speaks of

the number of which their party consists, eight in all. Doña Catalina is not to trouble about beds, they will manage well enough for themselves. " These angels " —Catalina's daughters—are well and joyous. The letter concludes with good wishes and greetings.

They arrived at Burgos on the 26th of January— a few days after Anne of Jesus and her companions reached Granada. They first went to venerate the famous Crucifix, and then went at once to the house of Doña Catalina de Tolosa. It was as much of a convent as the house of such a lady was likely to be, who had already given four daughters, and was ready to give a fifth, to Carmel, while her two sons were soon to follow the example of their sisters. She had prepared a suite of rooms for the nuns, and there was a large hall close by in which the Fathers of the Society had said Mass for the first two years of their settling in Burgos. Father Gratian was to say Mass there, and the whole apartment was so arranged that the nuns could perfectly observe the rules of enclosure. But the foundation of Burgos was to be the last made by Teresa, and its history was to be a succession of crosses. They began at once. Doña Catalina had prepared everything she could think of to receive her guests well. Among other things, a large fire had been lighted that they might dry their clothes after the rain, which had been falling in torrents. The smoke and heat made Teresa so ill, that the next day she could not hold up her head. She was obliged to receive the friends who came to visit her in bed, and a little grating was arranged within which she had to converse with them through a veil.

T 3

It was most annoying, because the day was to be one full of business which she must attend to.

Early in the morning Father Gratian went to the Archbishop to announce their arrival and beg his blessing. The Archbishop received him with indignation. "Why had they come without his leave?" When Gratian urged all that he had said about Teresa's coming, he replied that he had meant her to come to deal about the business, not to bring a number of nuns with her, as if the business were already settled. Gratian said the magistrates had given their consent, which was what the Archbishop wanted, and therefore there was nothing more to be done but to begin the foundation, that Don Alvaro de Mendoza, who had been consulted by Teresa whether it would be well for her to enter the city without first informing and asking the Archbishop, had said that his Grace had told him that he desired the foundation, and that therefore the application need not be made before she was there. The Archbishop told Gratian he would not give his permission till they had a house of their own and a certain income, otherwise they might go back—"as if," Teresa says, "the roads were open and the weather good!"—and she breaks out into a beautiful passage about the manner in which God rewards those who love and labour for Him with great crosses.

It was clearly impossible for Teresa and her companions to fulfil the conditions exacted by the Archbishop. Neither would he even let them stay where they were, under the only circumstances that could make a temporary sojourn tolerable. For he would not permit Mass to be said for them in the house of Doña Catalina de Tolosa, where they.might have used, we have just seen, as a temporary chapel, the large room in which the Fathers of the Society had said Mass for two years. It was an immense inconvenience for cloistered nuns to go through the streets to hear Mass in a church ; but this was all that they could do, and Teresa had to content herself with this privilege on Sundays and feast-days, on other days going without Mass at all. She had many friends, some of them influential ecclesiastics, who pleaded in her favour, but the Archbishop was inflexible. At last he allowed them to begin the foundation as they were, undertaking to buy a house as soon as possible, and to migrate into it. He required sureties for this. They had no lack of friends to be their sureties, and Doña Catalina undertook to furnish the revenue. Nearly a month passed in this way, during which they could only hear Mass on Sundays, in a public church and in the early morning. Doña Catalina furnished them most liberally with all necessaries, and gave up, as has been said, a part of her house that they might live retired, according to their Rule. Thus matters continued for the first month of their residence in Burgos. St. Teresa was all the time suffering from fever.

Teresa tells us that Father Gratian was lodged meanwhile with a college friend of his, a Dr. Manso, a canon and preacher in the Cathedral. Gratian was getting anxious about his stay, as he had to preach the Lent in Valladolid, and the time was drawing on. At last the sureties required by the Archbishop were found and the endowment secured, and success seemed at hand. It was not so, however. After a month of parleying, Teresa received a note from the Vicar-General, saying that the leave for beginning the foundation could not be given till the community had a house of its own—the Archbishop did not like it to be made where they were, the street was too noisy and the place damp. There were also other objections, which she tells us she did not understand, and they were made by the prelate, or by those who at present guided him—"as if the matter were now discussed for the first time." The upshoot of all was that there was to be no more discussion, and the Archbishop must see them in a house which he approved before he allowed them to begin.

All this time the nuns were going out through the streets to Mass. They found for this a quiet chapel apart in the parish church, but still for cloistered nuns it was a great burthen. Father Gratian seemed to have made up his mind that they must abandon the affair and go away. He was in a great hurry, as he had to leave for his sermons. His state of mind was the chief distress to Teresa. Our Lord seemed to say to her one day, *Ahora, Teresa, ten fuerte*—"Now, Teresa, be brave!" She set to work to encourage Gratian, and begged him to leave them in Burgos and go to his work.

With some friends of his, who exerted themselves much, he managed that a very small lodging should be found them in the Ospedale of the Conception, where the Blessed Sacrament was kept and Mass said daily. Here they were met with fresh difficulties, for a lady had arranged to go and live in the same part of the Ospedale after some months, and a room which was to be hers opened into one of those which the nuns were to have. She was not satisfied with having the key, she would have a regular barrier made. The people of the Ospedale, too, made their objections. They thought the nuns intended to take possession of the whole place. A legal document was signed before a notary, obliging the nuns to go out when they were told. Teresa was afraid, but Father Gratian made her do it. After all, they only got one room and a kind of kitchen. But Fernando de Matanza, one of Gratian's friends, the Administrator of the Ospedale, gave up to them two more rooms, which they could use as parlours, which they thought a great charity. Another gentleman, Francisco de Cueva, who held a place of some importance in the town, and had much influence in the Ospedale, befriended them greatly. They moved into their new abode at the end of February, having been a month or more with Doña Catalina de Tolosa.

Teresa speaks most gratefully and affectionately of this good lady, who had done and was doing so much for her. She was extremely afflicted at all the opposition and delay, and although this Ospedale was at a distance from her house, she came to see them every day, and provided them, as before, with all that they wanted. As soon as he saw the nuns in a place where they could hear Mass, Father Gratian let himself be persuaded to go away, leaving them an injunction to get a house of their own as soon as possible—a thing not very easy, as the event showed, in Burgos. His friends took up the cause of the nuns when he was away, but were careful not to mention them to the Archbishop till there was something satisfactory to tell him. The nuns had gone to the Ospedale on the eve of St. Mathias, and nearly a month was spent in hunting for a house. How one was at last found, St. Teresa may herself relate.

They told me of a house belonging to a nobleman, which had been for sale for some time, and, though there were so many Orders looking for a house, it pleased God that none of them liked this, and they are all astonished at it now, and some are even very sorry.

She heard such a bad account of it, that she set the thought aside.

One day when the Licentiate Aguiar, one of the friends of our Father's already mentioned, who had been making a careful search everywhere for a house, was telling me that he had seen some, and that no house fitting for us could be found in the whole city,—and when I was thinking it impossible to find any, judging by what people said to me, I remembered this one which I have just spoken of as being given up, and thought that though it were as bad as it was said to be, it might be a refuge to us in our necessity, and that we might sell it later.

Aguiar came into the plan, and went at once to see it. He found a tenant in possession who would not show it, not wishing it to be sold. But Aguiar liked its position, and it was resolved to treat for it. The owner was away, but a cleric in the city had power to deal for the sale. It was arranged that Teresa should go and see it. She thought it quite cheap at

the price asked for it. The day after, the cleric in
charge met the licentiate at the Ospedale, and it was
agreed between them to carry out the purchase. She
was told she was giving five hundred ducats more
than it was worth, but she thought differently. She
had some scruple, because the money to be paid was
not her own, but the Order's. It was before Mass,
on the eve of St. Joseph, and the priest who acted
for the owner had promised to come back after Mass.
The nuns prayed to St. Joseph that they might have
a house on his feast, and our Lord told Teresa not
to hold back for money. In short, the contract was
then and there made, and the house bought for
thirteen hundred ducats.

As soon as it was known, the usual hubbub of
opposition and criticism arose. The cleric who acted
for the owner had much to go through. But the
owner and his wife, who were communicated with at
once, were glad that their house should be a convent,
and ratified the sale on that ground, though, as
Teresa said, they could not do otherwise. A third
of the money was paid at once by Catalina de Tolosa,
although there were some hard conditions inserted in
the contract. The people who had refused the house
were extremely sorry at their own blindness.

The truth is [she says], as soon as I saw it, with everything therein as if prepared for us, it seemed to me a dream
—everything was done so quickly. Our Lord repaid us
well for what we had gone through, when He brought us
into a Paradise—for the garden, the view, and the water,
seemed nothing else. May He be blessed for ever!
Amen.

An amusing feature in the history is that the Archbishop professed himself very glad of the success of the nuns. "He thought it was due to his obstinacy, and he was right." Teresa took care to get into the house as soon as possible. She was warned that there was a design to keep her at the Ospedale till certain deeds were completed. The man who lived in it did not want to go, and she had some trouble. She went in, notwithstanding, occupying one room, and setting up a "grille" and a turn. This made the Archbishop angry again. "I did all I could to soothe him, and as he is a good man, even when he is angry, his anger passes quickly away." She excused herself about the "grille" by saying that it was "only what is done in the houses of persons who live in retirement—we had not put up a cross." Nothing could as yet induce him to grant the licence.

There were great fears he would not sanction it, but Dr. Manso and the other friend of the Provincial, of whom I have spoken, was very much with him, watching opportunities to remind him of us and to importune him. For it pained him much to see us living as we were doing, because in the house itself, though it had a chapel which had never been used for anything but Mass while the former owner lived in it, he would never allow us to have Mass said, but we must go out on festival-days and Sundays to hear it in a church which we were very fortunate in having close by, though after we had gone to our house, until the foundation was made, a month went by, more or less. . . . We had not a little to suffer in drawing up the deeds, for at one time they were satisfied with sureties, at another they would have the money paid. Many other difficulties were raised. In this the Archbishop was not so much to blame. It was a Vicar-General who fought hard against us, and if God had not changed his mind at the time, whereby he became another man, it seemed as if the matter would never be brought to an end. Oh, the distress of Catalina de Tolosa! that can never be told. She bore it all with a patience that amazed me, and was never weary of making provision for us. All the furniture we required for fitting up the house she gave us—beds, and many other things besides: our own house was amply provided, and as to anything we might need, it seemed as if we were not to be in want of anything, though her own house might be so.

Teresa is never tired of singing her praises, and she says that some founders had given more of their substance, but no one had the tenth part of the trouble which this lady had to bear.

She has mentioned in a word or two only, after her manner, what seems to have been a chief cause of the opposition—the Vicar-General, who "fought hard against them." Probably there was a great deal of opposition of which St. Teresa could have told us, as well as his. It would be interesting to know how the good Vicar-General "became quite another man," for we may be fairly certain that it was in consequence of some influence of her own which was brought to bear on him. From what we hear of her at this time, it seems as if there was almost an invisible but most efficacious "effluence of sanctity" in her which no one could resist. But we know that there are some states of mind in which men can resist anything, as the presence of our Lord Himself was unavailing to bend the hearts of the Chief Priests.

The sojourn of St. Teresa and her nuns in the

Ospedale seems to have been arranged by Divine
Providence, not only in order that they might suffer
the longer, but that what St. Paul calls the " fragrance "
of their holy lives and examples might be scattered
throughout the city in a way which would become
impossible, when they were shut up in their own
convent. Some anecdotes of this time will show
the effect of her presence in Burgos. She was
soon to leave this world, and it seems as if our
Lord used the common fame of her sanctity to
make people anxious to see her and converse with
her, before the cloister shut them out. The poor
patients in the Ospedale got to know that a Saint
was among them. She went down into the large
hall in which they lay, and visited them one by
one, and over and over again in the case of those
who needed the most consolation. They said the
mere sight of her was a relief. One poor sufferer
could not refrain from crying out piteously in his
pain, and disturbing the rest. Teresa went up to
him, and he was silent. She exhorted him to suffer
patiently for the love of God, prayed by his bedside,
and he was cured. Another time Doña Catalina had
sent her some fine oranges—for in her pain Teresa
had expressed a desire for one. But she went down
into the hall and gave them all to the sick, and when
reproached by her nuns, she said she had wished for
them in order to give them away. It was the same
with some fine lemons that were sent her. One day
her Religious complained of the miserable garret in
which she had to sleep, the roof of which let through
the air and rain. She bade them think of our Lord's

place of rest on the Cross, and compare her lodging with His.

There were many religious communities in Burgos, and they came to know that Teresa was in the city. She was pressed to visit them, and she could not refuse. The Canon Manso, afterwards Bishop of Calahorra, testified in the Process in 1610 that " Mother Teresa caused great spiritual profit to the other convents of religious women in Burgos, both by her great reputation for sanctity, religion, and severity of life, and by her conduct and heavenly conversation. After having visited all the convents of the city, conversing with and consoling the nuns therein, she left them so much edified, that many and very particular changes of life and manners and improvements were seen and experienced in the souls of those Religious, as was public and notorious in the city of Burgos. This was specially the case in the royal convent of Las Huelgas de San Bernardo. Mother Teresa de Jesus only entered it once, but to see her habit, her poverty, her humility, her devotion, her simple and open manners, her thoughts and words so filled with the love of God, the spirituality of her conversation, her fervent zeal for the salvation of souls, and the wholesome advice that she gave as to the strictness with which religious persons ought to treat themselves in order to be more pleasing to God—this alone, in this one visit, I know reformed almost the whole convent, and I know it because I was the Canon Lecturer of the Cathedral of the city of Burgos, and I was in communication with the most grave and religious persons in that convent, and I heard them say what I have now said, and many other things in confirmation thereof which I do not remember." He mentions that he knew Teresa when she came to the house of Doña Catalina, and conversed with her through the curtain when so unwell, and was inspired with great awe and respect, thinking her a great saint and friend of God, and his reverence and fear "made his heart sink within him and his hair stand on an end," and from that time he always was convinced she must be a great pillar of the Church.

The account given of Teresa by the Doctor Antonio de Aguiar, who was very useful to her, is much to the same purpose. He too had been a fellow-student of Father Gratian, and had been called in by him to attend Teresa, when she arrived at Burgos in so poor a state of health. He visited her at once, while in the house of Doña Catalina, but came to know her more intimately when she went to the Ospedale, and afterwards to the house which she purchased, which was obtained by his means. He relates the whole story of the manner in which the purchase was effected. Afterwards, when the house was being put in order for the nuns, he saw her constantly, and she told him at various times almost the whole history of her foundations, leaving out, of course, what related to her preternatural favours. He says the church of the house was made out of the stable, and the mangers served to hold the Missal and cruets. She told him that all her convents were in poor and miserable situations, and that she had come to Toledo with a single coverlet and mattress and a very small supply of money, and yet within a few days had bought a house which cost her nine thousand ducats, and from that time God had always shown them the greatest favours and mercies. She excused herself one day from coming down to see the work and the plans, which he was superintending, saying that she was occupied in writing the history of the foundation of that place, and that his charity would be commemorated therein, which God would reward, and one day there would be much profit from the reading. In fact, she seems to have taken especial care to write immediately the history of her last foundations. Aguiar mentions some instances of her charity and her love of poverty.

We may now turn for a short space of time to the letters which belong to this period, before the leave was given for the actual foundation in the house which Teresa had acquired. These letters will illustrate the story which has been given.

On the 6th of February, Teresa wrote to Mary of St. Joseph, at Seville, sending her letter by Don Pedro de Tolosa, a son of her hostess, Doña Catalina. She had then been twelve days in the city, and she tells Mary that nothing is yet done in the way of foundation. "There are certain contradictions. Things go on much in the same way as they did in Seville. I consider how much God is to be served in this convent, and all that occurs will be for the best, and make the Discalced more known. This place is a royal city, and perhaps if we came in quietly no one would think about us, so this trouble and contradiction will do us no harm, and indeed some ladies are disposed to enter as nuns, although the foundation is not made." She begs prayers for all this. Thus, whatever happens, she sees God's will in it, and the good which will follow. Then she recommends the bearer of the letter, as the son of the lady in whose house they are, and who has been the cause of their coming to Burgos. She has already four daughters in their convents, and two more that are likely to enter. She begs Mary of St. Joseph to send her by the bearer the money she owes to the convent at Avila, for charity's sake. She begs her to be particular about this, and to send the whole sum, for she has pledged herself in writing to pay it this year. She says, "I shall be very much annoyed with your Reverence if you send it the same way as the other sum. It will be safe in Don Pedro's hands." The "other sum" we know had been misappropriated by Doria's brother Horacio. She is to show Don Pedro every kindness and charity she can, as it is owing to him and his mother, and nothing will be lost by it. She tells her that Gratian is there, and very useful in their troubles. Teresita, too, is with her. She mentions how the family wanted to get her out of the convent, and she did not dare to leave her. She is very good and perfect. She praises the nuns she has brought with her. She complains of her throat, which makes it difficult for her to masticate, but hopes to be better soon.[1]

On the 1st of March we find Teresa writing to her friend the Canon Martin Alonzo de Salinas, of Palencia. She says they are getting on well in the Ospedale. It reminds her of the good work which

[1] Letter ccclxxix.

his honour is doing in a similar place at Palencia.
It is a great thing to have such work in hand. It
gives her great consolation to see the poor cared for.
God be blessed! The Archbishop has sent some one
to visit her and see if she has anything to ask. He
says that, for the sake of the Bishop of Palencia and
her other friends and herself, he will give the licence
in the end, when they have a house of their own, and
they are not to return where they were before. She
speaks of some Fathers who have a complaint against
her, but the language is not clear. There were three
Orders seeking a foundation in Burgos at the time—
the Calced Carmelites, the Minims, and the Basilians.
As some of the people of whom she speaks say that
their Order is the same as hers, and that they will
do nothing till she has got a house of her own, it
looks as if the Carmelites were meant. She speaks
of a house which they might have for eleven thousand
ducats, including an annual charge of six hundred, in
a bad position, which they are greatly desirous of
getting; but it does not seem clear that this was the
house they ultimately took.[1]

We have next a fragment to Mary of St. Joseph,
chiefly valuable for the affectionate manner in which
St. Teresa speaks of her, and the esteem for her she
shows. She tells her that if a foundress has to be
chosen after her own death, she is the one that ought
to be chosen. Yes, and even while she is alive. She
knows more, and is better than herself. This is the
truth. She has a little experience besides. As for
herself, she should be thought of no account, so old

[1] Letter ccclxxx.

and worthless is she. This is very strong language.
Perhaps at this time St. Teresa was under the miscon-
ception as to the proceedings of Anne of Jesus at
Granada, of which we shall speak presently.[1]

On the 18th of March, after the house was secured
to which they were to move, Teresa writes to Father
Ambrose Mariano, who seems to have been near
the Duke[2] or Duchess of Alva, perhaps at Pastrano.
She asks him to get for her a Brief from the Nuncio
giving leave for them to have Mass in the house.
They have got a good one, and the Archbishop
approves of it much. But she and all of them are
afraid there will be some more delays, and though
there is a church hard by, it is a great trouble for
them to have to go out to hear Mass. So she writes
to him to petition the Nuncio, and to get a letter
from the Duchess backing her petition. Mariano is
to read her letter to the Duchess and send it on, and
then to send the application to Father Nicolas or
Juan Lopez in Madrid, and give any directions that
may be necessary to have the matter despatched.
She understands there will be no difficulty. There
is a chapel in the house which has never been
used for anything but to say Mass. Where they
first wished to found, there was a hall in which
the Jesuits had kept the Blessed Sacrament for
fourteen years, and yet the Archbishop would never

---

[1] Letter ccclxxxi.

[2] Letter ccclxxxii. "The Duke" is mentioned in this letter, but
the Duke of Alva died in Portugal, which he had just conquered for
Philip II., in February of this year. The duke may mean the Duke
of Huescar, the son of the great duke.

let them have Mass said. He is full of good words, and says how much he now desires this and that. One would think there was nothing more to ask for. There is some evil influence at work—the devil is evidently much opposed to the foundation, and he must not be let to have his own way, now that the nuns have a house. With the leave just asked, they can wait any time, and the licence will be given out of mere weariness.

There seems to have been some trouble with Father Antonio. " His proceeding gives me so much pain that I have determined to write to him the enclosed. If your Reverence thinks he will not be much provoked, seal it, and the others, and send them." It would be of much use to us if we had "the enclosed," as it probably would enable us to understand many things at which we can now only guess, and to have besides another letter of St. Teresa's. A few months later we find her telling Father Gratian that Antonio is good friends again with her.

Doña Catalina de Tolosa, as has been said, had two daughters in the Novitiate at Palencia, Mary of St. Joseph and Isabel of the Trinity. Some of the difficulties about the foundation at Burgos were because the Archbishop would not let the purchase be made, as we understand, out of the dowries of ladies that became nuns in the convent—wishing, probably, that they should be reserved to supply a yearly income. These two novices, therefore, came to the aid of the foundation at Burgos by renouncing their portions, both from father and mother, in favour of Burgos, and the next letter we have from Teresa is

U 3

to thank them for their generosity.[1] She says she is always glad to hear from them, but her occupations prevent her from always answering. She is rejoiced at their becoming foundresses, for so they are, and without this help, she does not know how to manage to buy the house. Their mother would gladly give the money, but she cannot do more than she is doing, and it has been the ordinance of God that their "charities" should do this. The Archbishop does not wish the foundation to be made till they have a house of their own, and, on the other hand, there was no capital to buy one. So they see how things would have been without them. They are to praise God, then, that they have been the authors of so great a work ; not all deserve the favour which He has given to them and their mother. She does not mind the troubles they have passed through. They have seen in it all how much the foundation annoys the devil, and it will give the house greater authority. She hopes that now the Bishop will give leave. What we suffer must never afflict us, since the grace is so great. Their little sister Elena had been with St. Teresa since she went to the Ospedale. St. Teresa hopes she will be a great nun. Her niece, and Mother Thomasina—the future Prioress—greet them much. They thank them for what they have done, and will commend them to God.

These letters illustrate the narrative which has been given of the affairs of this foundation of Burgos up to the time of the purchase of the house, and a little after it. But in the meantime the Archbishop

[1] Letter ccclxxxiii.

fell back again into his policy of delay, and of course the application to the Nuncio for a Brief allowing them to have Mass said in the new house could not be answered immediately. St. Teresa found herself again, apparently, defeated. She hoped all through that the issue would be what it ultimately was, but it was not the less vexatious to be so continually put off. So she took the step of appealing to her firm friend, Alvaro de Mendoza, the Bishop of Palencia, to whom it was that the Archbishop of Burgos had in the first instance promised the permission which he so long withheld. The Bishop of Palencia was in great indignation at the non-fulfilment of the promise made to him. He took, says St. Teresa, "any harm done to us as done to himself," while the Archbishop all the time seemed to think that he was doing no harm to them at all. Teresa asked the Bishop to write again, saying, that as they had now a house, and had complied with all his conditions, he hoped that he on his part would do as he had promised.

The Bishop complied, and sent his letter open to Teresa. She saw it would make matters worse, and Canon Manso thought it better not to deliver it. It was kind and friendly, but there was language in it so plain that it might have made the Archbishop angry, especially as the Bishop had already sent him some messages which had roused his feelings against him. The Archbishop reproached St. Teresa, saying that as Pilate and Herod had been made friends at the Passion, having been before at enmity with one another, she had made those who were friends before become enemies. To this she quietly replied that his

Grace saw what sort of a person she was. But she again used her powers of persuasion with the Bishop of Palencia, and asked him to write another and most friendly letter, setting forth how much the glory of God would be advanced by the permission. The Bishop of Palencia did as he was asked, but told her that what he was now doing for her was harder than all he had before done for the Order. The letter, however, had its effect, helped on no doubt by the prayers as well as the great influence which her character and manner must have had on all with whom she had to deal. The Archbishop gave way. He was probably charmed beyond measure by finding that his old friend could write in such a strain after so much delay and so many refusals, and in this way the strong pressure brought by Teresa to bear on the Bishop of Palencia, in order to induce him to write kindly and charitably, seems to have been the decisive force which achieved the victory.

"In a word," she says, "the Bishop's letter answered the purpose in such a way—Dr. Manso was pressing it at the same time—that the Archbishop granted the licence, and sent the good Hernando Matanza with it, whose pleasure in bringing it was not little. That day the Sisters were very much disheartened—they had never been so before—and the good Catalina de Tolosa so much so, that she could not be comforted. It seemed as if our Lord would lay His hand more heavily upon us at the moment He was about to give us joy—and I, who had not been without hope hitherto, had none the night before. Blessed and praised be His Name

for ever, world without end. Amen." Dr. Manso
had leave from the Archbishop to say Mass the next
day, and to reserve the Most Holy Sacrament. He
said the first Mass, and the High Mass was sung
by the Father Prior of St. Paul's, of the Order of
St. Dominic, to which, as well as the members of the
Society, our Order has always been greatly indebted.
The Father Prior sang the Mass, with very solemn
music played by men who came unasked. All our
friends were much pleased, and so was nearly everybody in the city, for they were all very sorry to see
us in the state we were in, and thought so ill of the
conduct of the Archbishop that I was at times more
distressed by what I heard people say of him than I
was at what I had to bear with myself. The joy of
the good Catalina de Tolosa, and of the Sisters, was
so great, that it kindled my devotion, and I said
unto God, "O Lord, what other aim have these
Thy servants but that of serving Thee, and dwelling
within a cloister for Thy sake, out of which they are
never to go forth?"

We might be sure that St. Teresa did not fail to
write a joyous and graceful letter of thanks to the
Bishop of Palencia after the termination of the difficulty. We have it still, and it is the last of those
addressed by her to him that survives. It is written
on Good Friday, April 13th.[1] She tells him that the
Archbishop was so pleased by his letter that he at
once made haste to try and finish the matter before
Easter, without any one asking him, and he wished
himself to say the first Mass, and bless the church.

[1] Letter ccclxxxiv.

She expects that for that reason they must wait till the "last day" of Easter, for all days up to that are occupied.

She tells him some formalities have been accomplished which were quite new to her. The parish authorities had been cited to say if they would lose anything by the convent. They replied that, on the contrary, they would do all they could to help them. It is considered now to be a finished thing, and she has sent to thank the Archbishop. God be thanked! for it seemed impossible to all, though she says she has always had confidence, and so had suffered less than others. All the Sisters kiss his lordship's hand, for he has taken them out of a great trouble. She wishes his lordship could have seen their joy and the way they praised our Lord! Be He for ever praised, for having given his lordship the great charity that was needed to make him write the letter to the Archbishop. The devil saw what good it would do, and so opposed it with all his might, but he got little by it, for it belongs to our most powerful God to do what He wishes. The remainder of the letter is full of compliments and good wishes. The first Mass is still to be said on the "last day of Easter," perhaps before.

We have several letters of St. Teresa after the foundation of Burgos had been accomplished, and she did not leave the city till the end of July or the beginning of August. She had to suffer in the course of May from a very dangerous inundation, of which we shall have to speak, as well as of other matters of importance. But some of the letters may at once be shortly dismissed. The first, dated April 18th, a few days after the last, is a letter of compliment to Don Padrique Alvarez de Toledo, Duke of Huescar, the son of the great Duke of Alva, who died in Portugal in this spring. He had married the year before this, as has been said, without the King's leave, and he and his father had been disgraced and imprisoned in consequence. His wife was about to give birth to a child, and Teresa's prayers had been asked for her safe delivery. The note we speak of is an answer to these requests.[1] Another note is to Canon Manso, her friend and Gratian's, telling him that the latter— who seems to have returned to Burgos after his Lenten course of sermons was over—had been suddenly summoned to Soria by his own father, who was on his way to Rome, and wished to see him. Gratian had been obliged to leave in a hurry, and so, to his great regret, had missed seeing Manso. Teresa takes the opportunity to tell him that he has all her nuns as his daughters now, and herself in particular, a poor creature, whom he must not forget. She tells him there is to be a clothing, at which the " most illustrious " will officiate—meaning the Archbishop. The clothing must have been that of Elena, the youngest daughter of Catalina de Tolosa, and another novice, of which we shall hear directly.[2]

Another short letter is to Leonor de la Misericordia, of whom we have already heard, at Soria, telling her that Gratian is to be there, and advising her to open the whole of her soul to him, for her greater consolation. There are some bits of news

[1] Letter ccclxxxv.   [2] Letter ccclxxxvi.

about the family of Doña Maria de Veamonte. She says also that she might talk with Gratian about the "matter of Pampeluna." It seems that there was a design of founding a convent there, and, in fact, Leonor herself went there.[1] We have also a note to Pedro Casademonte, in Madrid, containing nothing of importance, but showing Teresa's anxiety to found there. She sends him some letters from Granada.[2] Then comes what, all things considered, is a touching fragment of five or six lines.[3] It is not known to whom it is addressed. It merely says that "our Father" (Gratian) was here last week, that he is well, and has gone to Soria, and thence starts on a round, probably of visitations. "It is a pain to me, because we shall be a long time without knowing about him." So the hurried departure of Gratian from Burgos to meet his father at Soria, was his real parting from Teresa in this world. When she fell ill on her road to Avila, he was away, and it was Fra Antonio of Jesus, the first friar of the Reform—who had been lately out of sorts with her—who gave her the last sacraments.

St. Teresa concludes her account of the foundation of the Convent (of St. Joseph of St. Anne) at Burgos, by explaining what was probably in her mind when she wrote the letter to Canon Reinoso at Palencia which will presently be inserted. It refers to some disputes that were likely to be raised concerning the money given by Catalina de Tolosa as the endowment of the convent.

Some time after the house was founded, it was thought by the Father Provincial and myself that the endowment

Letter ccclxxxvii.   Letter ccclxxxviii.   [3] Letter ccclxxxix.

furnished by Catalina de Tolosa had certain inconveniences which might end in a lawsuit for us, and in some trouble for herself. We preferred trusting more in God, that we might not be the cause of giving her the smallest annoyance. So to save her, and for some other reasons, we all before a notary renounced the property she had given us, with the sanction of the Father Provincial, and sent her all the deeds. It was done very secretly, lest it should come to the knowledge of the Archbishop, who would consider it a wrong done to himself, though it was really done to the convent. For when it is once known of a house that it is founded in poverty, there is nothing to be afraid of, because everybody helps it. But when the house is thought to be endowed, there is evidently a risk, and it may have to remain for a time without the means of living. Provision for us after the lifetime of Catalina de Tolosa was made. Two of her daughters, who were to make their profession this year in our Convent of Palencia, had renounced their property in its favour. This renunciation she made them annul, and make another in favour of this house. And another daughter of hers, who wished to take the habit here, left to the house her portion from her father and from her, which was the same as the income she was giving us. There was only this inconvenience, that the nuns do not enjoy it at present. But I have always held that the nuns will never be in want, because our Lord, Who sends incomes to convents which depend on alms, will raise up people to give us much for this house, or will find means to maintain it. Though no house was founded in this way, I have begged our Lord from time to time, as it was His will the foundation should be made, to come to its relief, and supply what is necessary for it, nor did I wish to go away till I saw whether any entered as nuns. One day, thinking of them after Communion, I heard our Lord say, "Why doubt? This is now done. Thou mayest safely go," giving me to understand that the nuns would never be in want of that which might be necessary for them. I felt as if I were leaving them amply endowed, and have never been anxious for them since.

She adds that the Archbishop and Bishop of Palencia remained very good friends—that the former gave the habit himself to Elena of Jesus, the youngest daugher of Catalina de Tolosa, and to another nun who came in, Beatrix del Arceo Covarrubias, a widow, and that the support necessary to the convent had never failed up to the time at which she wrote. It is easy to see in the last passage which we have quoted from the *Book of the Foundations*, that there may have been some foundation for the gossip about the Carmelites and the Fathers of the Society, to which the following letter refers, but which, however, was entirely false as to the motives and conduct imputed to St. Teresa. Doña Catalina had left some of her property to the College of the Society by will, and this property was apparently now charged with the income of the convent. With Father Gratian's consent, the nuns renounced their claim, and the deficiency was supplied, as to the future, by the renunciation of the two nuns at Palencia, daughters of Catalina, which was made in favour of the convent at Burgos. But this was kept secret, lest the Archbishop might object,—and reasonably so, from his point of view,—and in the meantime Teresa did not mind if a few tongues were let loose about the injury the new convent was doing to the good Fathers.

The letter to Canon Reinoso was as follows :[1]

JESUS.

The grace of the Holy Spirit be ever with your honour ! It always gives me pleasure when I see a letter of yours, and it is plain to me that I cannot often have this consolation. I know your honour is aware of this. Yet it is a grief to me that I can have no more than I have.

By the letter that goes with this, which the Mother Prioress will show your honour, and which I am writing to the Father Rector, Juan de Aquila, your honour will see something of what is going on with the Society. In truth, it appears that a quarrel in form is beginning. The devil is hatching it, by getting faults to be laid to my charge, with very great accusations, for the very thing for which I ought to be thanked, and it is said that of their own body witnesses can be produced in some of the matters—it is all a question of those ill-omened self-interests—what I say, what I desire, what I work at—it is much that they do not say what I think. As I believe that it is all a lie, I see clearly that the devil must be concerned in this entanglement.

As Teresa here refers to a letter which is directed to the Rector of Palencia, and we do not know what that letter contained, we are unable to see how far she thought it well to speak plainly as to what had been done. The gossip which may have been moderate enough at Burgos, might be swollen into larger and darker proportions at Palencia. The only question is whether Teresa had thought fit to tell the Society at Burgos what she had done in secret, for fear of the Archbishop's knowing it. When she says that charges are made against her for something that she ought to be thanked for, it seems clear that she refers

to the renunciation just mentioned. She had volun-
tarily given up her claim to the property which had
been made over to her, although she had not said
what she had done. Her language is that of
a person who knows perfectly what foundation in
appearance the complaints against her had, yet how
untrue they were, and how every one would know
them to be untrue directly the facts were known.
It is this that accounts, as we think, for her strong
expression about the lie.

The second part of the letter may or may not be
a continuation which refers to the same persons. The
letter is written to Canon Reinoso, that he may do
something in the matter. "Your Reverence," she
says, at the end, "will see and apply what remedy
you think well." It seems, therefore, that the persons
referred to were, as has been said, at Palencia, and
therefore not at Burgos. But the second part of the
letter evidently refers to persons at Burgos.

Lately, they told Catalina de Tolosa that they did not
wish to have anything to do with the Discalced, because of
our way of prayer. The devil must have a great interest
in setting us at variance, since he takes so much pains.
They said also that their General was coming hither, and
had already disembarked.

She remembers that he is a friend of Don Francisco, and perhaps the trouble might be set at rest by
his means, the truth be known, and silence be ordered
by authority, because in truth it is a pity for such grave
people to occupy themselves with childish trifles such
as these. It is uncertain, on the face of the letter,

whether St. Teresa is here speaking of the Society
or of the Calced Carmelites. The word "Descalças,"
without the addition of "Carmelites," seems to imply
the latter. For there were "Discalced" Franciscans
—and probably of other Orders—as well as Discalced
Carmelites, and the omission of the word "Carmelites"
would be most natural if the persons spoken of were
themselves such. It was much more likely that the
General of the Carmelites, who about this time was
so far on his way to Spain as Genoa, should visit that
country, than the General of the Society. Not long
before this time Father Everard Mercurian, the
General of the Society, had sent a Visitor from Italy
to Spain, where he had also visited some of the
Provinces, with much fruit, by means of Father
Balthasar Alvarez and others. But, of course, we
cannot be certain that the rumour St. Teresa speaks
of did not refer to the Society, merely because it was
improbable, and even absurd. There would be no
difficulty at all in deciding that it must refer to the
Carmelites, except that there is no express transition
in the words of the text.

In the evil days after the Suppression of the
Society, and perhaps before, this letter was made
use of by its enemies as an argument that St. Teresa
was opposed to it. It was by no means the only
weapon of the kind which was thus forged. It is
enough to say that if the interpretation put on the
words was certain, they only refer to a false impression current among some members of the Society in
a particular College, on a very unimportant matter, in
which they were mistaken through ignorance of the

facts. St. Teresa's love and friendship for the Society
in general, and for those of it whom she came across
in particular, are far too prominent features in her
history to be obscured. It may be added, that the
scene of the imagined disagreement could hardly
have been worse chosen. Burgos was a place to
which the Society had urged her to come, and the
Fathers there helped her in so many ways. It is
said that Father Ripalda had himself put it into the
head of Catalina de Tolosa to found the convent,
and throughout the whole story of the foundation
the Fathers of the Society are her fast friends. On
the other hand, we know enough of the history
of the Reform to be sure that its enemies would, for
a time at least, most naturally be found in the ranks
of the older Observance of the same holy Rule.

In the account of the foundation at Burgos which
St. Teresa has left us, there is no mention of the
danger to which she and her community were exposed within a few weeks after the happy issue of
their struggles with the Archbishop. The danger
came from a sudden swelling of the River Arlanzon
on which Burgos stands. The house which the nuns
had bought lay in a suburb of the town, which was
exposed to sudden inundations, and it appears to
have been hemmed in between the stream and a hill
which projected towards it. The inundation took
place on the feast of the Ascension. The convent
was an isolated building, cut off by the hill from the
rest of the town. There had been much rain, and all
the streams which feed the Arlanzon were swollen.
The inhabitants of the nearest houses abandoned

them, and fled for safety to the city. Teresa did not like the nuns to leave their cloister, and she was probably ignorant of the danger which resulted from the configuration of the ground.

The house was old and creaky. The cell in which St. Teresa placed herself had gaps in the roof through which the sky and stars could be seen. The rising flood soon covered the lower storey, and the waters seem to have been prevented from flowing freely out by the fastening of the doors. St. Teresa had the Blessed Sacrament taken to a higher storey, but they did not think of any measures for their own safety. They went on with their litanies as the flood increased, from six o'clock in the morning to midnight. St. Teresa was absolutely exhausted, and begged Anne of St. Bartholomew, whose narrative we are following, to see if she could get her a morsel of bread. All the provisions were under water. One of the novices, a stout and robust girl, went into the water up to her waist, and fetched a morsel of soaked bread, which Teresa took. It seems that the flood had subsided elsewhere, and some bold swimmers— the nuns took them for angels—managed to dive so as to be able to unfasten some doors and let the water flow out. The house was full of big stones, which filled eight carts.

Anne tells us that she and Teresa had two coverlets between them, and that she used secretly to put them both over Teresa, in order that she might be warm. She tells us also of her care to wash linen and clothes for Teresa, who was wonderfully fond of neatness and cleanliness in everything. Anne used to watch her opportunity to get a little sleep by Teresa's side, who thought she was sleeping in her own cell. We shall have to draw again upon this faithful attendant's narrative.

There are a few more letters of St. Teresa—nearly the last of which we shall have to speak—written during her stay in Burgos. But we must not forget Anne of Jesus and her companions at Granada, of whom we have said nothing since the beginning of the narrative of the foundation of Burgos. If we have had little to tell of them, it is because things remained for several months with them in the same state as when we heard of them last. The "foundation" which was permitted, in their case, in the house of Doña Anna de Penalosa, did not, for some months, make any real advance. At least there is silence about it to us, and, what was more important then, there was a great silence to Teresa herself and, as it seems, to Father Gratian. A great deal of mischief may be done in Religious Orders by want of communication between Superiors and subjects. St. Ignatius was wont, when he sent Fathers out on any mission, to give them few instructions, but to require constant communication with himself. Anne of Jesus may perhaps have neglected this most important part of her duties as foundress—a capacity in which she had not had experience.

Thus came about what we may certainly count among the special favours in the way of suffering imparted to this community, a kind of suffering which they clearly could not have expected, and which must have been felt by them most keenly. Among the letters of St. Teresa in this last year of her life, there is one which must have given great pain to her spiritual children at Granada. It is written from Burgos in May, 1582, when she was within six months of her holy death. Burgos was at a great distance from Granada, and the means of communication in those days, even between cities of considerable importance, were most precarious.[1] Andalusia was almost a foreign country as regards Castile. Moreover, letters, as we have frequently had occasion to see in tracing what remains of the correspondence of St. Teresa, might be written regularly, and yet might never reach their destination. There were perhaps, also, some particular circumstances about the foundation of Granada which made it easy for Teresa to misunderstand the condition of things in the southern city. We have mentioned that Father Gratian had divided the Province committed to his charge into two Vice-Provinces, each under a Superior of its own. He could only have done this by his own authority, and he had at the same time committed to St. Teresa a special authority over all the convents of the Reform. Such a state of things might have led to many misconceptions as to the immediate authority to which Anne of Jesus and her nuns in Granada were subject.

There is also the utmost uncertainty in regard of

---

[1] We find frequent allusion to the difficulty of communication in the letters of St. Teresa. There seems to have been some places between which there was a regular post. This is called in her letters an *ordinario*. Between other places it was necessary to send a *proprio*, i.e., *mensajero*, or special messenger. It cost a good deal, naturally, to send a special messenger.

the time at which Anne became formally the
Prioress at Granada.   In the foundations which had
been made by Teresa herself, she had generally
appointed a Prioress when she had completed the
foundation and was about to depart.   Nothing of
the kind was possible in Granada, and St. Teresa
seems, at all events, to have been very imperfectly
informed of what was being done.   The nuns at
Granada seem to have acted for themselves, and
chosen Anne as Prioress.   Generally these elections
were made in the presence of the Provincial, or were
confirmed by him.   We have mentioned the possibility of the lack of means of communication, and
perhaps some of Anne's letters failed to reach
their destination.   Perhaps, also, Teresa heard of
what was being done from other sources, badly
informed as to the facts.   All these things, taken
together, probably produced in her mind the im-
pressions under which she wrote the celebrated
letter to which we refer, a letter extremely characteristic and valuable to us, and indeed to students
of religious history in general.   It shows us of what
sort were the things which she thought deserving of
blame, as well as the pure zeal and strong charity
of its writer.   But we need not fear to think
that the letter in question was written by St. Teresa
under a certain amount of misconception, and conse-
quently that it seems to impute to Anne of Jesus
conduct of which she was not guilty.   It is needless
to say that, if such was the case, it may have
produced poignant grief to those to whom it was
addressed.   It is certain, however, that St. Teresa

-seems to speak of some of the facts for which she blames the nuns at Granada, as if she had no doubt at all that the allegations were true.

The letter is dated Burgos, May 30, 1582, and was addressed to the "Prioress and Religious of the Convent of St. Joseph at Granada."[1] It is therefore not a private letter, in the sense in which St. Teresa's letters were generally private. In the course of the letter, however, St. Teresa addresses herself to Anne of Jesus alone. It is probable that she kept in view the fact that she was speaking to a whole community, and therefore there is much of what seems a certain stiffness and even sternness about some of the language. It is also to be remembered that Teresa had just seen Father Gratian for the last time, and may have heard from him some strong opinions, even if she were not enjoined to use severe words.

JESUS.

The Holy Spirit be with your Reverences. I have been amused at the fuss which you make in complaining of our Father Provincial, and your neglect in informing him about yourselves, since the first letter in which you told him that you had made the foundation. You have done the same with me. His Paternity was here on the feast of the Cross,[2]

---

[1] Letter cccxci.

[2] The 3rd of May. If it be the case that Father Gratian was at Lisbon on the 19th of February, he must have returned to Spain some weeks after. But it seems pretty clear that on the 19th of February he was at Burgos, which city he left only to preach the Lent at Valladolid. The Chronicle of the Reform says that he went to Lisbon *despedida ya nuestra Santa Madre*—that is, after the death of St. Teresa. The mission to the Guinea coast, mentioned above, must have been in 1583 at the earliest, whatever may have been the case as to the foundation in Lisbon.

and he knew nothing more than what I told him. I had
had a letter from the Prioress of Seville, telling me that
she had heard you had bought a house for ten thousand
ducats. As you are so well off, it is not much that your
patents were so strict.

Teresa seems to mean by this that the nuns at
Granada had complained of being tied down too
much in the permissions which had been given them
by Father Gratian, which were limited. But the
rumour which the Prioress of Seville reported was
certainly false. It may have been founded on the
large sum of money offered as security, to the owner
of the house which their friends had endeavoured to
rent for them. St. Teresa was not only misinformed,
but the information was directly contrary to the facts.
It must be supposed that the permissions of Father
Gratian did not allow them to finish the purchase
without reference to himself or to St. Teresa. Their
doing this would have been properly noticed under
the circumstances, and may have been made a matter
of complaint in the letter from Seville which St. Teresa
had received. She goes on—

But you seem, then, to be so clever in not obeying,
and this matter has given me no little pain for the bad
appearance it will have in all our Order, and also for the
custom which may grow from it of the liberty taken by
Prioresses in such matters, and there is evidently no lack
of excuses that may be made for it. And when once you
had formed the opinion which you have of those gentlemen
who have helped you, it was a great piece of indiscretion to
go in such a large number.

We may remember that on the first occasion on which St. Teresa left the Convent of St. Joseph at Avila for a foundation—that of Medina del Campo—she had fallen into the mistake of taking with her too many nuns, and that much inconvenience was the result. There seems to have been the same mistake made about the foundation at Granada. But it must be remembered that the most brilliant hopes were held out about that foundation, which were believed by the Father Vice-Provincial. In the letter to Father Gratian,[1] written from Avila when the nuns were leaving for Granada, St. Teresa enumerates those who were to go, and it does not seem that Anne of Jesus exceeded the number fixed by her. She speaks as if Anne of Jesus might be put out by the number being taken so much from convents[2] other than her own at Veas, with whose inmates she would have had it all her own way. St. Teresa speaks as if she had in some measure departed from Gratian's instructions, and had had some scruple about it. There may thus have been some mistake. It is very likely that the representation about the bright prospects at Granada—which were so exaggerated—led to the sending of many more nuns than were required. These representations did not come from Anne. It does not seem certain, therefore, that Anne was to blame, going as she did to Granada with assurances that a house would be ready for them.

But it appears that when the nuns found them-

---

[1] Letter ccclxvi.

[2] "De mal se ha de hacer a' Ana de Jesus como lo quiere mandar todo."

selves in such strait quarters—and even these provided'
for them out of simple hospitality—two of the nuns,
those from Seville, were sent back, as well as the two
—old lay-sisters—from Villanueva.   Teresa complains loudly of this.   She says the sending back the
nuns from Seville was a mistake just after their
journey, no short one, and she is astonished at the
hardness of heart shown to the others.   It would
have been better to send back some of those who
had come from Veas, and even some more with them,
considering the great burthen that was laid upon
their charitable entertainers.   They should not, in
fact, have come from Veas, as they knew they had
not a house of their own.

St Teresa may mean by this that as they were to
begin in a hired house, the full number for which
permission was granted should not have been taken.
The knowledge that the house which was promised
them on lease would be denied them, did not come
to Anne of Jesus till after she had left Veas for
Granada.   This is a point of which Teresa was
ignorant.   But we can hardly doubt that if St. Teresa
had been in Anne's position, one of the first steps
she would have taken would have been to send
back those who were not absolutely needed for the
foundation, to the nearest house, and that house would
have been Veas. It seems that what annoyed her most
was that Anne, having to reduce her numbers, sent
away the strangers from Seville and Villanueva before
her own nuns, although these would have had less
far to go, and that she thus made the community very
like an offshoot from Veas, which was what St. Teresa

wished it not to be. Anne appears, from what St. Teresa says, to have acted as she did out of fear, lest the Archbishop might withdraw his licence as soon as he knew that some of the nuns had been sent back. This fear Teresa ridicules, and she says the Archbishop could not do so.[1] But Anne may not have shared this confidence. Teresa certainly speaks as if she was under the impression that there had been some lack of obedience in the proceeding, and we must leave the matter as it is on account of our want of knowledge of all particulars. She says it would be better that the convent should have been broken up, than that there should have been a beginning made in the Order of want of obedience.

Our gain does not consist in there being many convents, but in the fact that those who live in them are saints.

She then speaks of some letters which have now been sent to her from Granada for the Father Provincial. She fears it may be six weeks before they can reach him for certain. He has left Burgos for Soria, and is going about everywhere on his visitation. She does not know when they will have certain information where he is. She is pained to think that when her poor Sisters who have been sent back get to Villanueva, he may be there. The place is so small, and what has happened will be talked about by every one. The Sisters might have been sent to Veas, which was near Granada, till Gratian had been informed. They had no leave to go back, they were

---

[1] " Reidome he del miedo que nos pone que quitara el arzobispo el monasterio. Ya el no tiene que ver on el," &c.

"conventuals" of the new house by his order. She
blames Anne for not having informed him of the
number she took with her, and whether she had taken
(from Veas) any lay-sister.   Her impression seems
to be that more had been taken from Veas than had
been allowed, and that one of them was this lay-
sister. How the facts were we cannot tell. She
speaks as if no more account had been made of
Father Gratian than if he had not held the office of
Superior.

She speaks of the nuns that had come from
Seville as having suffered much from troubles,
different indeed in character from those of which
some of the nuns of Granada complain. They have
had a kind of martyrdom to go through. After all,
when people are in good health and have something
to eat, it is not quite a death for them to be rather
pinched in their lodging. Beatriz of Jesus tells the
Father Provincial that they are expecting the Vicar-
Provincial to take back the nuns of Veas and Seville
to their homes. For those of Seville—they are not
expecting it—it is a good distance, and by no means
convenient. The Provincial will see whether the need
is so very great. As for those of Veas, she says her
mind is made up.

If it were not for the fear I have that I might be helping
you to offend God by disobedience, I should send your
Reverence a strong precept—for with regard to all the
Discalced Nuns, I am in the place of the Father Provincial.
In virtue of this, I say and command that, as soon as
possible, when there is a convenient occasion of sending
them, the nuns from Veas go back whence they came,

except Mother Anne of Jesus, and this, even if they have already passed into a house of their own, unless they have a good income certain, such as will deliver them from the needs in which they are; for in no way is it good to begin a foundation with so many together, and there are many other reasons why what I say is convenient. These last days I have been commending the matter to God, for I was unwilling to answer your letter so very soon. I consider this order of mine to be for the glory of God, and the more it pains you the more so will it be. It is altogether foreign to the spirit of my Discalced Sisters to have any attachment to creatures, even to their Prioress, and they will never advance in spirit if it exists. God will have His spouses free, and bound only to Himself; and I do not wish this house of yours to begin going on in the way that has been at Veas. I can never forget the letter that was written to me from thence, when your Reverence left your office. No unreformed nun would have written it. That is the way factions and other great troubles arise, only we do not advert to them early enough at the beginning.

It appears that these last sentences contain the key to the mind of St. Teresa when the letter was written. What she is afraid of is far more the too great attachment of the nuns to their Superior, than anything else. The nuns at Veas had this defect in her eyes, and Anne of Jesus naturally did not see it. Letters had been written about her from one of her nuns to Teresa, to which the latter refers as proof of the existence of this feeling. By the steps which Anne had taken—or which St. Teresa thought she had taken—she had increased the very danger to which Teresa was alive. If this be considered, together with the apparent misconception

under which she wrote, that Anne had taken more
nuns from Veas with her than were permitted, the
tone of the letter is easily understood. She softens it
a little as she goes on.

So for this once, for charity's sake, follow my
opinion; in time, when things are better settled, and
the nuns more detached, they may come back, if it is
so convenient. In truth, I do not know who they are
who have come to Granada, it has been kept so secret
from me and from our Father. I did not think your
Reverence would take so many, but I imagine they
are all much attached to your Reverence. The spirit of
obedience indeed—a person is put in the place of God,
and you have no repugnance to loving her! I ask your
Reverence for His sake to look that you train up souls to
be Brides of the Crucified. Crucify them then that they have
no wills of their own, and have no childish attachments.
Remember that you are beginning in a new kingdom, and
your Reverence and the others are under an obligation to
behave as men of fortitude, and not as silly little women.

There is then a passage of some length, dwelling
upon one of the letters which had been written from
Granada, and which had made her angry. It appears
that the nuns there had no authority to make
their election of Prioress, and had been complaining that their election, which had fallen, of
course, on Anne of Jesus, had not been recognized
by the Provincial, who had continued to call Anne by
the title of President, not of formal Prioress. Teresa
explains, after some time, that Father Gratian had
acted in this according to the usual rule, as he had
not yet held the election himself. But she breaks
out :

What does it matter, my mother, whether the Provincial calls you President, or Prioress, or Anne of Jesus? It is plain, unless you were put over the others, you would not have been spoken of except as all others were who have also been Prioresses before. You informed that good Father so little about your affairs, that he did not know whether you had made an election or not. It has made me feel ashamed to see my Discalced Carmelites take to such childish follies—and not merely to think of them, but to speak of them—and Mary of Christ is the one to make so much of this matter![1] Either your troubles have made you lose your senses, or the devil has begun his infernal work with our Order. That Mother praises you for your great magnanimity—as if it would have been less if you had put up with the humiliation! God give my Discalced Nuns humility, obedience, and submission : without these, other fine qualities are the beginnings of many imperfections.

I remember just now that you have written to me before, that one of those you brought with you from Veas had some relations in Granada who gave you some help. If it is so, I leave it to the conscience of Mother Prioress to keep this one at Granada, if it seems good ; the rest must go back. I can well believe that your Reverence will have great difficulties in this beginning of things. Do not be frightened —so great a work cannot be done without them, and they say well the reward is great. May it please God that the imperfections which I commit in such a work may not cause an increase of chastisement rather than of reward! This fear I have always with me. I have written to the Prioress at Veas to contribute something towards the expenses of the journey. There is certainly a great want

[1] Mary of Christ was the late Prioress at St. Joseph's, Avila, mentioned in St. Teresa's letter to Father Gratian as having been so eager to go to Granada. It was her government that let down the observance at St. Joseph's so low, with the assistance of the confessor.

of what is convenient. I tell you that if Granada was as near Avila as some places, I should be very glad that my nuns should come back, and this may be done in time, with the favour of our Lord. So your Reverence may say that in making the foundation, when there is no longer need for them there, as you will have nuns of your own, they can return to their own house.

Teresa then explains that the title given to Anne was no mistake and no slight.

I wrote a short time ago to your Reverence at some length, and to the Mother, and to Fra Juan of the Cross, about what is done here, and so now I don't think it well to write more to all. May God grant that your Reverence may not take it ill, as when Father Provincial called you "President." Here, before our Father came and held the election, we called the Superior so, and not Prioress. It is all the same thing. There is a thing I have always forgotten when I was writing.

She goes on to say that she has been told that at Veas, even since the Chapter (of Separation), the nuns go out of cloister to adorn the church. She says not even the Provincial can give leave for this, as the Pope has forbidden it, *Motu proprio*, under excommunication, not to speak of the Constitutions. At first it was some trouble, afterwards the nuns were very glad. They may not even go out to shut the door which opens to the street. The Sisters from Avila must know this, and she is surprised they did not tell the others. The Prioress is to see that this is kept to. God will send people to adorn the church, and all will be provided for that is necessary. We have seen already how much St. Teresa insisted on

.this rule,, which seems not to have been known before.

When I think over the trouble you' must give to your hosts, I cannot help feeling it much. I wrote the other day that you were to look out and get a house, though it be not a good one or cheap ; if it be a bad one, at least you won't be so straitened ; and if you were, it is better you should suffer than your hosts, considering all the good they have done you. I am writing to Doña Anne (Penalosa), and would I could find words to thank her enough ! The Lord will not let her lose, which is the great point.

She ends by telling them, if they want anything of Father Gratian, to write as if they had not already written, for the letters they have sent may be long in reaching him. She adds also that the nuns may stay at Granada till his Reverence has been informed of the whole matter, and settles what is best. No one has written to him or told him why the nuns have not been sent. " May God give us all light, for without that there can be little well settled ! "

We may remark that the last sentence of this letter looks as if St. Teresa relented at the end as to her severe precept about the nuns of Veas being sent back. In fact, it seems as if the order was never executed. Probably the circumstances of the community at Granada were somewhat improved by the time the letter reached that city, and it was written apparently under an impression as to those circumstances which, if it had ever been perfectly accurate, had ceased to be so by the time at which the letter was written. In the letter St. Teresa speaks of the improbability of the Provincial, Father Jerome Gratian,

being able to reach Granada before the winter. But
in fact the letter was written at the end of May, and
in the month of August Father Gratian was on the
spot.   The Vicar-Provincial, Father Diego of the
Trinity, had died of the plague in Avila in the month
of May.   Father Gratian immediately set about the
search for a house, and succeeded in renting one from
Don Alfonso de Alarcon. The good gentleman and
lady, Don Luis de Mercado and Anne de Penalosa,
who had given the Carmelites so opportune a shelter,
could hardly bear to part with them, and continued
to help them in many ways, and the latter was
rewarded by our Lord with many signal spiritual
favours.   Anne of Jesus fell seriously ill soon after
the change of dwelling, and was apparently near her
last moments when St. Teresa died, as we shall have
to relate, at Alba de Tormes.   St. Teresa appeared to
her at the moment of her own death, and she was
restored to health.   When they had been in the new
house six months, novices began to apply.   But this
is not the place to dwell upon the history of this
flourishing branch of the Reform.

It is quite open to us to think that the letter
of which we have been speaking was written by
St. Teresa without full knowledge of the facts, and
that she would have spoken far less severely had she
known them.   However, we have said that she seems
to have relented, before she ended the letter, as to
some of the matters on which she insisted.   She may
also have seen later on that some of the judgments
which she expressed were too severe.   Yet it still
remains true that this letter is one of the most

valuable of all that proceeded from her pen, and that it lays down principles which may perhaps easily be lost sight of even among spiritual persons, but which are yet of the highest importance for the students of religious life.

No sooner is St. Teresa well freed from her anxieties about the foundation at Burgos, than we find her again pushing on her favourite plan of a convent at Madrid. This has been frequently mentioned in the letters of the last year or two. There can be no doubt of the obvious utility of such a foundation, not merely to those who might be immediately affected by the presence of a Carmel in the capital, but also to the Order throughout Spain. Now that the new Province was founded, it was very necessary that there should be some "headquarters." It was more necessary as regards the friars than as regards the nuns, but a convent of the latter once founded, it would not be difficult, perhaps, to secure a monastery for the friars. From the glimpses which we catch of St. Teresa's forebodings as to the Province, it is natural to conclude that she would have been glad to see the Provincial settled in some important monastery for a good part of the year, where he might be in constant communication with his Definitors, unless when he was engaged in the visitation of house after house, during which he was necessarily much alone. In a letter written at this time to Gratian, she tells him freely of the complaint made against him, that he did not like the company of friars of importance. This would have been one of the evils to be remedied by foundations at Madrid. It was a fault of character in Gratian, possibly aggravated by the want of cordiality with which he was met on the part of men of eminence among his subjects. Whatever was the reason for the evil, a great evil it certainly was.

Teresa writes on the 4th of June, on the subject of the foundation at Madrid, to the chaplain, Peña, who seems to have been her ordinary channel of communication with the Cardinal of Toledo. She wishes him a happy feast—it was Whit Monday— and says, apparently in answer to some remark of his, how much she should like to be in Madrid, near his illustrious lordship the Cardinal, whom God preserve for many years. She has had bad health at Burgos, but does not wish to move from it till she goes to Madrid, and she has written to the Cardinal to that effect, and that she may have no more journeys, on account of her old age and exhaustion. It appears that the Cardinal thought of putting off the foundation till the King's return from Portugal. Some say this will be soon, others later. She thinks their business will be best done if the foundation was made before than after, if the Cardinal liked. She believes that God will give the most illustrious prelate light for what is best, and that he desires to show her favour, and so she will not tease him. But, as the Canon has so much to do with him, and as she understands this thing to be for the service of our Lord, she does not wish to fail in any diligence on her part. Therefore she puts his lordship in mind of the matter, being very certain that God will soon

give him light that what is best may be done, and
at the best time. The foundation, as we know, was
delayed for four years, and at last accomplished by
Anne. of Jesus in 1586, accompanied by St. John of
the Cross.[1]

Our next letter from Burgos is dated June 25th,
and is addressed to Father Gratian. It is imperfect,
with one or two large gaps. At this time Gratian
was thinking of going to Seville, from which she
strongly dissuades him, on account of the plague
which was there. He went a little more than a
month later, although for a moment he was prevented, apparently, by the Definitors. The letter
also speaks of the poverty in which they found themselves at Burgos—a fact easily explained when we
remember that they were supposed to be better
founded than they were—and of the need of a friar
to say Mass for them, who she suggests should be
a certain Fra Felipe. Then comes a little bit of her
skill in managing. The Prioress of Toledo (Anne
of the Angels) has written to her to say she is very
ill, and Teresa has a scruple about leaving her there,
as the climate of Toledo is death to her (*verdadera-
mente la mata la tierra*). She thinks that the nuns
are certain to elect her again—they would never
think of anything else. But notwithstanding that,
she wants Gratian to take Anne of the Angels to
Avila, which was her native place. Two good results
would be gained. They would see if her health was
improved, and they might appoint a President in her
place, and without her being Prioress they would see

---

[1] Letter cccxcii.

how she managed. It would be an embarrassment at Avila, if Anne was ill, but, on the other hand, do much good if she were well there, and they owe it to her at Toledo, for they have received a small sum from her every year from Avila. She has laboured much for the Order, and it afflicts Teresa to let her die as she is. She tells Gratian that the nun in question thinks that she is not in his good graces, because she had been pulled up about some expenses, and she thought she was considered wasteful, whereas Teresa had only meant her to be careful to save up, in order to get a regular income and build the church. Teresa apologizes to Gratian for the trouble which the nuns give him. As we find her writing to Anne of the Angels at Toledo, in the August of this year, it does not appear that the proposal came to anything.[1] Yet it seems a thing to which attention ought to have been paid.

There is a short letter of Mary of St. Joseph, the Prioress of Seville, in which St. Teresa shows her anxiety for the nuns during the epidemic there. She has been in perpetual alarm about them. Fra Diego is dead, she knows, but, thank God, Fra Bartolomeo is left. She takes the part of Mary of St. Joseph, who had been blamed, it seems, by Anne of Jesus, for sending her nuns to Seville in a carriage. Teresa says she should have been glad if she had even sent them in a litter, if there was no other way. Mary is not to mind what people say of it. She speaks of the house at Burgos as well settled and paid for, and she will soon be setting off for Avila.[2]

---

[1] Letter cccxciii.   [2] Letter cccxciv.

On the 7th of July, Teresa writes a short note to Leonor de la Misericordia, who has been ill at Soria. Teresa bids her take the little comforts and remedies which the nun gave her, without scruple. It is obedience that is to make it of equal merit to her whether she has them or not. Teresa says they would have done badly not to give them to her. She is afraid she shall not see her soon. The Cardinal (Quiroga) has written to her that he will give leave for the foundation when the King returns, and September is the earliest time that can be looked for. "Your charity is not to be troubled at this. It will be as much consolation for me to see you as for you to see me. If it be not now, God will order it in another way." She has taken some medicine, and cannot write with her own hand.[1]

The last letter from Burgos is written on the 1st of July to Mary of St. Joseph at Seville. It contains little that need detain us. Teresa's anxiety about the nuns at Seville is still evident, but she trusts to the prayers made for them, and she is so glad to hear that they have not even a headache among them. They must not be ready yet, since our Lord spares them when He takes so many at Seville to Himself. She speaks of Pedro de Tolosa, who reports well both of them and the city, where things are getting better than they were. They are to pray much for him and Doña Catalina, who has been the making of the house. Teresa herself hopes to leave for Palencia at the end of the month, for Gratian has promised the nuns that she shall spend a month with

---

[1] Letter cccxcv.

them. Then she will go to Avila to profess Teresita, who desires it much ; her year is nearly up. ' She desires some especial prayers for her—earnest prayers. "Let them consider this as a matter of necessity, for though she is a good little thing, after all she is a child."[1] The letter ends with excuses for not writing more.[2]

NOTE TO CHAPTER X.

The letters of this chapter are as follows :

1. (ccclxxvii.) *To Doña Catalina de Tolosa.* From Palencia, January 11, 1582.

Mentioned at p. 287.

2. (ccclxxviii.) *To Beatris de Ahumada, her niece.* Uncertain date.

A fragment, congratulating Beatriz at her stay with her cousin at Avila.

3. (ccclxxix.) *To Mary of St. Joseph, at Seville.* From Burgos, February 8, 1582.

An account is given, p. 302.

4. (ccclxxx.) *To Martin Alonzo de Salinas, Canon of Palencia.* From Burgos, March 1, 1582.

An account is given, p. 303.

5. (ccclxxxi.) *To Mary of St. Joseph, at Seville.* From Burgos, March 17, 1582.

An account is given, p. 303.

6. (ccclxxxii.) *To Father Ambrose Mariano.* From Burgos, March 18, 1582.

An account is given, p. 304.

7. (ccclxxxiii.) *To Mary of St. Joseph and Isabel of the Trinity, novices at Palencia.* From Burgos, March, 1582.

An account is given, p. 306.

---

[1] " Miren que lo ha de menester, que aunque es bonita, es nina e fin."

[2] Letter cccxcvi.

8. (ccclxxxiv.) *To Don Alvarez de Mendoza, Bishop of Palencia.* From Burgos, April 13, 1582.

An account is given, p. 309.

9. (ccclxxxv.) *To Don Padrique Alvaro de Toledo, Duke of Huescas, afterwards of Alva.* From Burgos, April 18, 1582.

An account is given, p. 311.

10. (ccclxxxvi.) *To Pedro Manso, Canon of Burgos.* From Burgos, May, 1582.

An account is given, p. 311.

11. (ccclxxxvii.) *To Leonor de la Misericordia, novice at Soria.* From Burgos, May, 1582.

An account is given, p. 311.

12. (ccclxxxviii.) *To Pedro Casademonte.* From Burgos, May 14, 1582.

Mentioned at p. 312.

13. (ccclxxxix.) *To a person unknown.* From Burgos, May 18, 1582.

Mentioned at p. 312.

14. (cccxc.) *To Canon Reinoso, Palencia.* From Burgos, May 20, 1582.

A full account is given, p. 315.

15. (cccxci.) *To the Prioress and Religious of the Convent of Granada.* From Burgos, May 30, 1582.

An account and commentary are given at p. 323.

16. (cccxcii.) *To the Licentiate Peña, Chaplain of the Chapel Royal in Madrid.* From Burgos, June 4, 1582.

An account is given, p. 336.

17. (cccxciii.) *To Father Jerome Gratian.* From Burgos, June 25, 1582.

An account is given, p. 337.

18. (cccxciv.) *To Mary of St. Joseph, at Seville.* From Burgos, July 6, 1582.

An account is given, p. 338.

19. (cccxcv.) *To Leonor de la Misericordia, at Soria.* From Burgos, July 7, 1582.

An account is given, p. 339.

20. (cccxcvi.) *To Mary of St. Joseph, at Seville.* From Burgos, July 14, 1582.

An account is given, p. 339.

CHAPTER XI.

Last Journeys and Letters.

ST. TERESA left Burgos towards the end of July, 1582. She would have bent her steps directly to Avila, but for the order of the Provincial, Father Gratian, who yielded to the petition of the nuns of the newly founded convent of Palencia to have their Mother with them for a month. Teresa left, as Prioress at Burgos, Thomasina Baptista, whom she had taken from Alba de Tormes. The nuns at Burgos noticed that she parted from them without her usual efforts to keep down the tender feelings which came over her at such times, and which she usually repressed, lest their manifestation should give great pain to her Sisters. She let them kiss her hand, which also was unusual with her, and she also gave them her blessing. The parting was naturally a time of much emotion, for the restraints of religious life bring with them, in ordinary cases, a great compensation in the form of mutual affection, and with those who had now for some months shared the trials and witnessed the heavenly virtues of St. Teresa, the moment of parting from her must have been extraordinarily touching. She was never to see them again.

We have few incidents of this stay at Palencia,

which we may suppose to have been a time of peace and rest. But Teresa was almost entirely worn out She found her cell fresh and cool, and the whole house in good order. Here, at all events, there was no longer any battle to fight with the Bishop, as had been the case at Burgos—nor were there the insulting words and cool reception which awaited her when she passed on towards Avila, pausing at Valladolid.

The first letter which we have of this time is to Thomasina Baptista, just now mentioned as having been left as Superior at Burgos.[1] The letter is an affectionate answer, in the first place, to some questions about the convent arrangements. It seems that Doña Catalina was for the time residing in or perhaps near to the convent. The opening in the parlour that had been made for her to use is to be closed whenever she goes, and she is to have a room provided for her if she comes back, but its window is not to command the garden—*ya basta lo que nos han visto.* They have had enough of being seen. Teresa's own throat is better. Her room fresh and nice. The nuns are very good indeed. The Prioress is always to give her greetings to her friends when she sees them.

Then there are some provisions about the washing —two Sisters will do, at least they do at Palencia. Then she is full of good news from Nicolas Doria. He writes that he has met the General at Genoa, and has been most cordially received. The General has made him his Procurator for those of the Reform, all that goes to him is to pass through his hands. (This

[1] Letter cccxcvii.

arrangement did not quite please the friars in Spain.) Doria's brothers—important people probably in Genoa —have paid the General great attention. As Doria went to the Calced monastery, they thought there he had left the Reform, and tempted him to do so by offering to elect him Prior! Teresa is evidently much encouraged by all this. She orders special services of thanksgiving, a procession and prayers. " Now we have all we want, except to become saints, and serve God for His favours." She cannot end her letter without compliments to her friends, and especially " our Doctor "—Aguiar, we suppose, is meant—and she wishes the good news which makes her so joyous to be told to him.

We may perhaps remember Doña Teresa de Laiz, the foundress of the convent at Alba de Tormes, in 1571. It is curious to find a letter to her about her convent after so many years, and still more so when we consider that it was there that St. Teresa was, so soon after this time, to die. The convent does not seem to have been in a very flourishing condition —perhaps the good foundress was apt to meddle too much. The letter is an answer to one which Teresa de Laiz had written to St. Teresa, probably trying to get back Thomasina Baptista, who had been made Prioress at Burgos. Teresa tells her that she can do little in the matter. She has been talking to Thomasina, and has been told by her that from head to foot she is troubled at the thought of going back. She gives such reasons relating to the peace of her soul, that no Superior would think of ordering her to do so. She is now in a good, large house, and if

Doña Teresa wishes her well, she ought to rejoice at it, and "not seek to get back one who does not wish to be with your honour." For Teresa herself, she is so wishful of doing what her correspondent likes, she would be glad to meet her wishes in all. For the love of God, don't let her honour be hurt, there are nuns enough in the Order who can supply the place of Thomasina. She asks her also not to think of having back Juana of the Holy Ghost, the former Prioress, for she too has written to her to say that for her life's sake she would not go back to Alba. She does not understand these nuns—it seems no one will remain Prioress there, they all avoid it.

She then implores Doña Laiz to consider that it is her house, and that God cannot be served in disquiet. Her honour should not pet them in any way. If they are what they seem to be, what can a Prioress do! But there are childish ways and attachments among them, such as ought not at all to be with Discalced Carmelites, nor indeed exist in other houses of the Order. She can put her hand, more or less, on those who disturb the others, and she hopes, if she has health, to set things right when she can go there to see into the matter. She has been much pained, because she understands things which ought not to be done or known have been communicated to friars of another Order, and talked about by seculars outside the place. The nuns have done great harm to the Order by their childish ways and imperfections, thinking all are like themselves. She begs her honour, therefore, to be at rest, and wait till the Provincial goes there. It is a favour she asks for herself—for any one who goes there will be the servant of her honour. She would have remedied many things already, if she had known what was going on. She begs the letter may be shown to Sanchez Davila, her cousin, and the chaplain. He is to reprove the nuns who give trouble, and not let them communicate so frequently. People ought not to think it such a light thing to trouble a whole convent, and tattle with externs in a way that may do so much harm to those whom people look up to as good. "Ah, señora, where there is a good spirit, how differently things go on! God give it us, and preserve your honour to us for many years in all the health I desire for you."[1]

This is a strong letter, and there must have been some great mischief at work, which Teresa had possibly learnt from Mother Thomasina Baptista. It seems from a letter, given presently, and written in answer to a communication from her cousin Sanchez Davila, the chaplain of the convent, that she afterwards came to think less unfavourably of these nuns. Yet this was the convent of all others which Providence had chosen to be the dying place of St. Teresa, and the resting place of her remains. Perhaps the mere fact of her dying among them was enough to correct the mischief that she feared. The letter is dated on the Transfiguration, the 6th of August. We have another letter to Thomasina Baptista, written a few days later. The chief point in it tells how Teresa dealt with the proposal of a pious lady who knew their poverty at Burgos, and desired to go about begging for them. Of course this would

---

[1] Letter cccxcviii.

have revealed the whole secret of their condition, and would have alarmed the Archbishop. Besides, the Constitutions say that they may beg only when there is a great necessity. This does not exist in their case, for Catalina de Tolosa has declared she will gradually pay up the portions of the novices her daughters. There is another very kind message to Aguiar the physician—she feels the want of him very much. She is to write to him, and to Canon Manso. She envies them such a confessor. She has heard from Gratian at Almodovar. He is well, but she begs they will pray that he may not go to Andalusia, as he is likely to do,—and, indeed, as in fact he did. He wishes Teresa to be at Alba and Salamanca before going to Avila, and she has written to Alba to say she will perhaps be there in the winter. This letter is dated the 9th of August.[1]

She writes soon after, still from Palencia, to Sanchez Davila, at Alba de Tormes, who had evidently written to her about the nuns' affairs. She speaks of the troubles she has had to suffer at Burgos. His letter has given her great pleasure, but she had not much time to enjoy it. All is well ended. Glory be to God! She should like much to be where he is, for she wants to talk to him about things which are better dealt with so than by letters. The things in which our Lord wishes her will to be done are few—let His will be accomplished, that is the real matter. Possibly she wished to talk over the state of the convent at Alba with him, and also the trouble she had to get Juan de Ovalle and his wife's consent to leave Beatriz in

---

[1] Letter cccxcix.

Avila till her return. But as she was so determined, they let her have her way. God preserve his honour, who takes such pains to help them in everything, and she hopes he will succeed in setting things right for them. He probably was their best friend in Alba. This letter is dated the 12th of August.[1]

Before the end of August, her month at Palencia having expired, St. Teresa passed on to Valladolid, according to the injunctions of Father Gratian. Soon after her arrival, she wrote to Anne of the Angels, Prioress of Toledo—whom we have lately heard of as ill—on a few matters of business. The Bishop of Palencia, who was going to Toledo for the Council convoked by Cardinal Quiroga, seems to have been the bearer of the letter. Teresa recommends his lordship, her great and first benefactor, to the attention of her convent. Then follow some directions about certain changes in the house, which Diego Ortiz, the founder, wished to make. He was always changing plans, and although St. Teresa was pleased with his proposal, she foresees some trouble with him—Anne is to do the best she can. She says she does not know when she shall get away from Valladolid, the business and the troubles these are killing her. There may have been something to set right in the convent, but the chief crosses which she had at Valladolid seem to have come from her family, who were now pressing the matter of Don Lorenzo's will. She hopes to be in Avila at the end of the month. But she alters this before the end of the letter. She will stay where she is till "Our Lady of September"

[1] Letter cccc.

—the Nativity—then for the rest of that month, at Medina del Campo. She also repeats before the end some remarks about Diego Ortiz and the plans, apparently for the church. This letter is dated the 26th of August.[1]

The day after, Teresa writes again to Thomasina Baptista, Prioress of Burgos. She compassionates her trials. One of the nuns is quite out of sorts, but Teresa says it will pass, it is only a temptation. The nun is not to write to any one, except herself and one other, and if she writes, the letters are not to be sent. She is glad the Rector (of the College of the Society) has been to see them. He is to be received with great kindness, to hear the Prioress's confession sometimes, and to be asked for sermons. This does not look like a breach between the Carmelites and the Society at Burgos. The rest of the letter is taken up with kind messages. St. Teresa never seems to forget her kind physician Aguiar. She cautions Thomasina not to put too much upon the novices at first. "Though you are my superior in virtues, yet I have more experience." This letter is dated the 27th of August.[2]

On the 1st of September she writes to Father Gratian, who had gone to Andalusia.[3] She tells him that she does not think his reasons for going sufficient. He had enough to do at home, ordering the studies of the newly installed students at Salamanca, forbidding them to hear the confessions of devout women (*beatas*), and the like.

He might have left the Andalusian convents for a

---

[1] Letter cccci.   [2] Letter ccccii.   [3] Letter cccciii.

couple of months, and put those of Castile in order.
She does not know his reasons, and she has been so
sorry for his going that she has lost her desire to
write to him, and she should not even write to him
now but for an urgent necessity. Then she speaks
about her ill health,—which she seems, as in other
letters, to connect with the phases of the moon.

She then speaks of the trouble which has been
raised by the mother-in-law of Don Francisco,
Beatriz de Mendoza y Castillo. She was bent on
upsetting the will. Teresa says she has not justice
on her side, but as many people tell her she has, and
she is a peculiar lady, Teresa herself rather inclines to
a compromise which has been recommended, for the
sake both of Don Francisco and the nuns themselves.
St. Joseph's at Avila will lose something, but the
claim is eventually secure, and she hopes in God the
inheritance will come to it. (So, in fact, it did, as
Don Francisco died without issue.) It has given her
great trouble. But Teresa, her niece, is well. She
is much afflicted that Gratian is not coming, it is only
now they have told her. She says that she herself is
in part consoled, because it will teach Teresita how
little dependence can be placed on any one, except
God. She adds that she herself has benefited by this
thought.

Considering all the circumstances, this is strong
language for St. Teresa to use to Father Gratian, and
this is the last letter of hers to him that is preserved.
But there is graver disapproval implied in what
follows. She goes on to speak of a letter she has
had from Fra Antonio of Jesus. She has been

surprised at his writing in a way that implies restored friendship, as it appears that he had some quarrel with her. However it be, let Gratian on no account name another for the elections—probably the elections in the various convents and monasteries of Priors and Prioresses, which had to be held, in Gratian's absence, by the Vice-Provincial. " It is not the time," she says, "to be making houses in Rome." This seems to have been one of the plans of expansion for the Reform, which was not able to man its own houses in Spain. " Your Reverence has a great dearth of men, even at home." It appears he was for sending Father Nicolas away, as some thought, on that pretext. She says Nicolas will be a great loss to him. He (Gratian) cannot possibly attend to so many things alone. Fra Juan de la Cuevas told her so, when she spoke with him sometimes. He has a great desire to see Gratian succeed in all, and loves him much, which has put her under obligations to him.

" He also told me that your Reverence was breaking the rules, which have laid down that when you are left without a Socius you are to choose another—I do not know whether he said with the consent of the Priors,—and that he thought it impossible you could be able to do the work, and that Moses took to help him I don't know how many. I told him you had no one to choose, you could not even find Priors, and he said the Socius was the principal thing. Since I have been here I have been told that they note in your Reverence that you do not like taking about with you a person of importance. I see

it is because you cannot find one, but, as the Chapter
is soon coming on, I don't want them to have any
imputation to cast on your Reverence. Look to it,
for the love of God, and be careful how you preach in
Andalusia. I never like to see your Reverence there.
May God spare me the evil of seeing what you wrote
the other day about people who have suffered persecution ; and, as your Reverence says, the devil is not
asleep. As long as you are there I shall suffer much.
I do not know for what purpose you are to stay so
much at Seville, and you are not to come back till
the Chapter, which has added to my anxiety more
than it would if you returned to Granada. The Lord
guide all to His greater service ! There is certainly
great need of a Vicar there in Andalusia. If Fra
Antonio does well here, your Paternity can be looking
out to appoint him to that post. Don't think of
making yourself an Andalusian, you are not the person
for them. In the matter of preaching, too, I beseech
again your Reverence much that you take care to do
it very well, though it be but little." The Chapter
spoken of as coming on was a General Chapter of the
Reform in the course of the next year.

In the rest of this letter St. Teresa passes on to
other matters, but what has been already paraphrased
is enough to show us a good deal of her mind as to
Gratian. After her death, attempts were made, by
alleged visions of her, and in other ways, to represent
her as having changed her opinion of him at the end
of her life. There can be little doubt that a good
deal has been done in various ways to blacken his
memory, and his unfortunate expulsion from the

Order was accompanied by various allegations which might seem to justify it. In itself, it was an act of extreme severity, to say the least, but it could not have been possible if the conduct of Gratian had not given some pretext for it. When a similar threat was made against St. John of the Cross, he told a friend in the Order not to be troubled, for they could never take from him the habit unless he was incorrigible and disobedient, and he was ready to amend in anything in which he had been in fault, and submit to any penance that might be imposed on him.[1] This perfection of humility was wanting in Gratian's conduct when his time of trial came, but the fact does not prove all the charges against him.

Whatever may be thought of the justice or injustice of the measure meted out to Father Gratian, both in his lifetime and after his death, the letter before us does not show any change in St. Teresa's opinion of him. It is not the first letter, by any means, in which she has found fault with him, even seriously. It is enough to show that she retained all her affection for him, and also that there are certain points as to which she, very frankly indeed, expressed her disapprobation. Anne of St. Bartholomew has been quoted as confirming the fact of St. Teresa's change. We do not think there was a change, and as Anne of St. Bartholomew was so constantly with her, and wrote her letters at her dictation, we may take her testimony as not implying more than the letters justify. The fact seems to be, that the defects in Gratian's character, which prevented him from govern-

[1] Fra José de Jesus Maria, *Vida de S. Juan de la Cruz,* l. iii. c. 20.

X 3

ing the new Province in the most perfect way, were not more than what St. Teresa had seen in him almost from the first. But his new position, after the separation from the Mitigation, brought out these defects more prominently, and he seems all along not to have attached the value and importance to the admonitions of St. Teresa which they deserved. The result was disastrous, and it was made more so than it would have been by the strong and imperious character of those who became, in the years that followed, Superiors of the Reform, representing different principles and other methods of procedure and government. But that he was always high in the esteem and regard of St. Teresa cannot be questioned, any more than that he rendered inestimable services to her Reform.

The rest of this long letter refers, as we have said, to other matters. The friars at Valladolid are all ill, and therefore, as it seems, the patents appointing Fra Juan de Jesus Prior to some other place have not yet been given him, because he is the only strong one there, and it would be inhuman in him to leave them. The monastery enjoys a very good reputation in the town. As for Salamanca, she has more troubles. May God put an end to them! She has no time to go there and get to Alba and Avila for the profession of Teresita, but she has met where she is with Pedro de la Vanda—the landlord of the house they lived in—and Señor Manrique, and the house has been rented for another year. She complains a good deal of the proceedings of the Prioress, Anne of the Incarnation. There is a proposal at Salamanca to put the nuns into a house which the students of the Carmelites now occupy, and this Teresa strongly opposes. She goes at length into the reasons, and ends by saying: "For the love of God, be careful what you do there. Don't listen to nuns, if they are set on anything, they think they see a thousand good reasons for it. It is better for them to take a small house and be poor in it, and begin humbly—they can afterwards get into a better position—than remain with a great debt on them. If I have sometimes anything that consoles me for your Reverence's departure, it is because I see you free from these troubles, and I had much rather have them alone."

"Oh! my Father," she says at the end, "what anguish I have had these last days!" She speaks, probably, of her family troubles. "The news of your good state of health has made it pass away." She sends kind messages to the nuns at Seville, and begs them to take care of him. There are kind messages to St. John of the Cross, and from Anne of St. Bartholomew.

The next letter is a repetition of one we have already inserted, to Anne of the Angels, Prioress of Toledo. St. Teresa probably wrote it twice over,[1] thinking that the first might go astray. She writes again on the 5th of September, from Valladolid, to Sanchez Davila, her cousin, the chaplain of the convent at Alba de Tormes.[2] As we have said above, a letter from him about the state of the convent has given her much consolation. God preserve him, for the convent

---

[1] Letter ccciv.   [2] Letter ccccv.

will never lose while he remains, and he has explained
away much that seemed blameworthy.   She tells him
to be in all things a father to her nuns, who speak most
highly of him.   They are, after all, good souls, and
God helps them always, though the devil disturbs
them with occasions for faults.   Blessed be God's
name in all things.   She hopes to see him soon, as
she will pass that way.   She sends a kind message
to Teresa Laiz.   She has received a letter from her
which has consoled her.   Everything will go well.

The latest letter of all which exists that St. Teresa
wrote, is addressed to Catharine of Christ, the Prioress
of Soria.[1]   It is a calm, quiet letter, giving advice or
direction on a number of such details as must occur
in the government of any house.   Catharine of Christ,
the Superior of Soria, to whom it is written, is one
of the " Venerables " of Carmel, and was very highly
esteemed by St. Teresa.   Father Gratian objected to
her nomination as Prioress because she could not
write, and St. Teresa told him she was a great saint,
and that nothing more was necessary for government.
She speaks in this letter about the profession of two
novices, one of whom seems to have been Leonor de
la Misericordia, of whom we know something already.
The other is very young, and Teresa approves of her
profession being put off.   Catharine is not to be
frightened at her having little fits of temper, such
people are often more mortified in the end than
others.   There is a gap in the letter which makes it
less intelligible than we could wish.   She would be
glad indeed to be at Leonor's profession, she would

[1] Letter ccccvi.

like that better than many other things she has to do.
But it appears there were impediments. Apparently,
Leonor had been speaking again of the foundation
in Pampeluna, which was proposed. St. Teresa was
adverse to it, on account of the want of income and
the distance from the other houses. Let things go
on for a time, and let devout people come forward,
and if the thing be of God, He will move them to it
with more force than at present. She herself will
stay but a short time at Avila, for she must go to
Salamanca, and perhaps the foundation of Madrid
may take her away. Catharine may write to her at
Salamanca. (But she never reached either Avila,
Salamanca, or Madrid.) She is glad of a postulant
for Palencia. She ends by begging Catharine to be
careful that the little novice, who had to wait for her
profession, did not think that the delay came from
a desire to give Leonor, who had been a great
lady in the world, any precedence over her. Leonor
is far too humble to think of such things. The
letter is dated from Medina del Campo, the 15th of
September.

We are told that Catharine of Christ became the
foundress of Pampeluna, the project of the convent
there having succeeded a year or so after this. Leonor
seems to have accompanied her Prioress, and lived
long and holily in the country to which she belonged.

No one can read these last letters of St. Teresa
without seeing that she was still in full vigour of
mind,—as wise, as prudent, as charitable, and as
zealous as ever for the glory of God. We know
that her bodily health was quite ruined. She was

sent about to this place and that place in a way
that showed little regard to her wishes or her
strength. Indeed, as we shall see, but for what
looks like an accident, she might have breathed her
last outside the walls of any of her convents, and
before she found her final resting-place at Alba de
Tormes, she had left two convents in succession
because her presence was unwelcome to those who
owed all to her. Such was the cross which she had
to bear to the last. Yet she is always bright, always
resigned, always content, always full of charity.
Externally, her way from Palencia to Valladolid,
to Medina del Campo, to Alba de Tormes, was
indeed a Way of the Cross, during which her Divine
Spouse added, as it were, the finishing touches to
the perfect representation of Himself which He was
forming in her soul.

Perhaps Teresa went to Valladolid, expecting that
her sojourn there would be as pleasant as that at
Palencia had been. Her first letter from Valladolid
is dated, as we have seen, the 26th of August, and it
is an answer to one she had received while at Palencia.
She then expects to leave it after the 8th of September. It was at Valladolid that she wrote her last
long letter to Gratian. She was waiting there, as she
says to Thomasina Baptista, for a letter, probably
from him, and was anxious on many accounts connected with the government of the Province. He
had gone to Seville against her advice, which he
too seldom took. There are many other topics of
the same sort touched on in that letter which were
not consoling. She mentions in it the matter which

really gave her most pain, but she speaks with great moderation. It almost seems as if she was going to yield somewhat as to the will of her brother. She certainly mentions that she is inclined to a compromise. No one would gather from that letter to one with whom she was usually so open, that she was suffering so much from her family. The Prioress of Valladolid was Mary Baptist, the niece of St. Teresa, the Maria de Ocampo whose generous offer of a part of her fortune had been the providential beginning of her aunt's Reform.[1] She could not but be very dear to her aunt, but there was something in her character of stiffness and narrowness, and we do not find Teresa as expansive with her as with Mary of St. Joseph. She was probably an excellent soul, just a little priggish, and the talk about the family honour carried her away. Her defects of character came to the surface at a most unfortunate moment, for St. Teresa was already half stricken to death when Mary Baptist showed temper and rudeness to her. Probably she had very seldom done so in her whole life, and we may be sure that nothing was left in Teresa's heart but the tenderest and most forgiving love.

The convent at Valladolid was founded by a brother of the Bishop of Avila, and Mary Baptist had been made Prioress at Doña Maria's request, and seems to have held the post ever since. She most likely entered heart and soul into the attempt to get Don Lorenzo's will set aside, and it seems that the family had to some extent assembled

[1] See vol. i. p. 142.

at Valladolid, in hopes of producing an effect
upon Teresa by their joint entreaties. Doña Beatriz,
the mother of the young bride, was a very energetic "mother-in-law." It seems that Teresa did not
let them know at once how far she was inclined
to yield. It was at Valladolid, we are told, that a
lawyer, brought in to argue with Teresa, told her that
she was not what she appeared to be, that many
secular persons would behave in a more perfect
manner than she did, and the like. Teresa simply
thanked him for his charity, and prayed that God
would reward him. Anne of St. Bartholomew explains
the position of St. Teresa by telling us that the con-
tention urged on her was that the will of Don Lorenzo
was null and void, which was a very different thing
from asking her to consent to modifications. But
Mary Baptist gave her the greatest pain of all by the
language she used to her aunt, and, if Anne's memory
is to be trusted, she actually went so far as to tell her
to leave the convent.[1]

It is at least certain that at the moment of leaving,
St. Teresa made a short address to the nuns, full of
all her sweetness and wisdom. It has been preserved
by her biographers.

[1] The dates of the letters prove that Teresa at all events stayed there
longer than she intended. The letter to Catharine of Christ, the last in
the whole collection, was written a week after the day she had named
for her departure in a former letter, which was the 8th or 9th of
September. Anne of Bartholomew adds, that when they were leaving
Valladolid, the Prioress plucked her (Anne) by her habit, and said, "Go
away, and don't return here any more." It is difficult to doubt a
direct statement of Anne of St. Bartholomew. But it may perhaps be
thought that as her deposition was taken many years afterwards, there
may be some inaccuracy in it in this and in one or two other matters.

My daughters, I go from this house full of consolation, from the perfection I see therein, and from the poverty, and the charity which all have to one another.   If it goes on as it is now, our God will help you much.   Let each one strive that not one point of what is perfect in Religion be lost through her.   Do not perform your exercises out of custom, but make in them heroic acts, and each day of greater perfection.   Make it your practice to have great desires of virtue.   From them you will make great profit, even although you cannot carry them into effect.[1]

[1] Don Vicente de la Fuente, *Obras de Santa Teresa*, t. iii. p. 172.

NOTE TO CHAPTER XI.

The letters of this chapter are as follows :

1. (cccxcvii.) *To Thomasina Baptista, Prioress of Burgos.* From Palencia, August 3, 1582.

An account is given at p. 343.

2. (cccxcviii.) *To Doña Teresa Laiz, Foundress at Alba de Tormes.* From Palencia, August 3, 1582.

An account is given at p. 344.

3. (cccxcix.) *To Thomasina Baptista, Prioress at Burgos.* From Palencia, August 9, 1582.

An account is given at p. 346.

4. (cccc.) *To Pedro Sanchez Davila, at Alba de Tormes.* From Palencia, August 12, 1582.

An account is given at p. 347.

5. (cccci.) *To Anne of the Angels, Prioress of Toledo.* From Valladolid, August 26, 1582.

An account is given at p. 348.

6. (ccccii.) *To Thomasina Baptista, Prioress of Burgos.* From Valladolid, August 27, 1582.

An account is given at p. 348.

7. (cccciii.) *To Father Jerome Gratian.* From Valladolid, September 1, 1582.

An account is given at p. 349.

8. (cccciv.) *To Anne of the Angels, Prioress at Toledo.* From Valladolid, September 2, 1582.

A repetition of Letter cccci. p. 348.

9. (ccccv.) *To Pedro Sanchez Davila, Chaplain of the nuns at Alba de Tormes.* From Valladolid, September 3, 1582.

An account is given at p. 356.

10. (ccccvi.) *To Catharine of Christ, Prioress at Soria.* From Medina del Campo, September 17, 1582.

An account is given at p. 356.

CHAPTER XII.

Alba de Tormes.

WE have seen that St. Teresa must have left
Valladolid with a heavy heart, that her beloved
niece, Mary Baptist, had no small part in increasing
her afflictions. It is a mistake into which we are
constantly falling, that the natural sorrows of the
saints are less heavily felt by them because they are
saints. This is an echo of the gross and rude opinion
that would make our Lord's sufferings the less intense
because He was God, or the dolours of our Lady less
piercing, because she knew that her Son would rise
again on the third day. Sanctity makes the heart
more tender, it bares it to a hundred wounds which
more common hearts would hardly feel. Worldliness
and sin harden hearts, not sanctity. It may be
said to be Teresa's characteristic among the great
saints, that she was quick and sensitive and deep in
all natural holy affections. Our Lord used this
feature in her character for His own glory in more
ways than one—most conspicuously in the crucifixion
of which He made her in consequence capable from
those whom she held nearest and dearest.

With a heavy heart, then, she set out with her
little pair of companions—Teresita and Anne of

St. Bartholomew — for Medina del Campo. She
arrived at Medina, it seems, on September 16th.
The Prioress of Medina, Albert Baptist, who had but
lately witnessed the miraculous cure of one of her
nuns by the touch of St. Teresa, appears to have
added her own contribution to the sorrows of her
Mother at this time. Anne of St. Bartholomew
tells us that, worn out as she was, and arriving
in the evening, Teresa noticed something in the
house about which she admonished the Prioress,
who took offence. Teresa was deeply grieved at
finding, here also, that her spiritual children were
learning no longer to pay her the obedience which
was due, and left the room. That night she ate
nothing, and could not sleep, and left the next
morning without having taken any food. Her
departure was an act of great obedience, as Fra
Antonio of Jesus, who was Gratian's Vice-Provincial
for the time—Gratian being absent in Andalusia—
had already written to her, enjoining on her to alter
the line of her road, which would have been in the
direction of Avila, in order to pay a visit to the
Duchess of Alva at Alba de Tormes. The Duchess
was a good pious lady, a great friend and admirer
of Teresa, and she had but lately become a widow.
She had obtained a promise from the Superior that
Teresa should always go and stay with her when
she visited Alba de Tormes, the castle of which place
was the ducal residence. The Superiors of St. Teresa
seem to have treated her somewhat inconsiderately,
for without consulting either her wishes or the state
of her health, they were very ready to give in to

these applications from the great people of the world. In the present case, Teresa was ready enough to go to Alba de Tormes soon, and we find that she had already written to the convent to say she was coming, though she probably meant that she would be there after going to Avila for the profession of her niece. Anne of St. Bartholomew tells us that she had a great repugnance to paying this visit just then, but that she obeyed without a remonstrance.

Father Antonio of Jesus came himself to meet her. The Duchess knew that she was ill and weak, and had sent a carriage for her use in the journey. It would have been as well if she had sent some food also. Antonio of Jesus was not great as a purveyor. But, as has been said, she left without eating, and she had taken no food the night before. They arrived at a place called Peñaranda, and Teresa begged for some food, she was nearly fainting. Anne of St. Bartholomew could lay her hand on nothing but some dried figs, and though she gave money to a person to go and fetch some eggs, there were none to be had. Anne burst into tears when she found she had nothing better to give her. But Teresa said that the figs were good, and that many poor people were worse off, and that all these things happened by the will of God. The next day they tried to dine in another village, where there was nothing to be got but some herbs cooked with onions—food unfit for her in her condition, but which she was obliged to eat.

It was not till towards evening that they reached Alba de Tormes. It had been arranged that Teresa should visit the Duchess before going to the convent, but she was so weak that Father Antonio took her straight to the convent. It was the convent the site of which St. Teresa liked, because from the hermitage in the garden, and indeed from the window of her cell (when she was there in 1574), she could see the River Tormes and enjoy an extensive view. The view from the castle was magnificent, taking in the great plain of Avila and the mountains beyond.[1] Teresa had little time or strength to occupy herself with the prospect. The nuns got her to go to bed at once. She said it was twenty years since she had gone to rest so early. From the first, the doctors thought her recovery desperate. But the next morning she was up as usual, and went to Communion, and for a few days, till the 29th September, the feast of St. Michael, she assisted as far as possible at the exercises of the community.

As Teresa was unable to move, the Duchess of Alva—the widow—came to visit her. The doctors had ordered the application of some remedy which smelt very foully, and Teresa was fearful lest her visitor should be annoyed by it, and apologized when she came. The Duchess declared that what she smelt was of a most delicious fragrance. On the day of St. Michael, Teresa went to bed soon after making her Communion, but had herself moved into a cell on a higher floor, which had a little window opening into the church, so that she could hear Mass. But the doctors soon judged this to be too cold for her, and on the 2nd of October, two days before she

[1] See Plasse, *Souvenirs du Pays de Ste. Terese.* Paris, 1875.

died, she was moved again downstairs. Perhaps it was this little cell on the higher floor, of which she spoke with so much joy in her letter of 1574. As long as she was there, she was occupied with the Blessed Sacrament, for we are told that she spent . the whole night between the 1st and 2nd of October in prayer. The next day she asked Father Antonio to hear her confession. After this he begged her to ask of God that her life might be prolonged. She answered she was no longer necessary in this world.

"From this moment"—we paraphrase the account of the last hours of St. Teresa from the pages of her first biographer[1]—"she began to give holy advice to her Religious. She had always done so, but now, when she was about to leave this world, she did this with greater zeal and greater marks of love than ever. On the 3rd of October, the eve of the feast of St. Francis, she asked that she might receive the Holy Viaticum. She could hardly move herself; when she was obliged to do so, two nuns helped her. While she was making preparation for the coming of the Blessed Sacrament, she joined her hands, and said to the nuns who stood around her, 'My daughters and my mistresses,[2] pardon me the bad example which I have given you, and do not learn from me, who have been the greatest sinner in the world, and the one who has been the worst to keep her Rule and Constitutions. I beseech you for the love of God, my daughters, that you keep them with great perfection, and be obedient to your Superiors.'

"When she saw the Blessed Sacrament enter her

---

[1] Ribera.　　[2] " Hijas y señoras mias."

cell, and found herself in the presence of the Lord
and Master she had loved so much, a kind of
complete transfiguration came over her. Before, she
had been deeply cast down, and in a state of deadly
prostration, unable to make the least movement.
Now she raised herself and sat up without any one
helping her. She seemed to wish to dart from her
bed, and it was necessary to hold her back. Her
face became full of beauty, and glowed with love.
It was no longer what it had been. No one could
look at it but with reverence. She seemed clothed
with supernatural youth, all traces of old age had
passed away. She knelt, with her hands joined, as
if she were already in Heaven. Seraphic love seemed
to shine forth from her soul, the joy of Heaven glowed
in every feature, she was like a pure white swan,
singing, at the end of her life, a strain of sweetness
and melody such as had never been heard before.
Her Beloved was before her. Her addresses to
Him were full of the loftiest thoughts, and their
tenderness and sweetness touched all present, and
penetrated them with devotion. 'O my Lord and
my Spouse, the hour so much longed for is come,
it is time that we should see one another. My
tender Lord, behold the moment of my departure,
blessed be Thou a thousand times, and let Thy will
be done! It is time for me to leave this place of
exile, it is time for my soul to be made one with
Thee, and to enjoy all it has desired!'

"The great matter of supreme thankfulness to her
was that she was born a child of the Church, and
died within her bosom. Often she said, 'After all,

Lord, I am a child of the Church.' She asked pardon
for her sins, and said she hoped to be saved by the
merits of our Lord Jesus Christ. She begged the
Sisters to ask this favour for her from our Lord, and
she asked pardon from them with great humility.
When the administration of the Holy Viaticum was
over, the Sisters asked her to speak some words of
edification, but she always refused. From time to
time she simply told them to keep their Rule and
Constitutions well, and always obey their Superiors.
What she was meditating during this time was
evident from her frequent ejaculations of contrition
and humility. *Sacrificium Deo spiritus contribulatus,
cor contritum et humiliatum, Deus, non despicies. Ne
projicias me a facie Tua, et spiritum sanctum Tuum ne
auferas a me. Cor mundum crea in me, Deus!* The
ejaculation, *Cor contritum et humiliatum, Deus, non
despicies*, was the most frequent of all, until she lost
the power of speech."

At nine o'clock, the night before she died, she
asked to receive the Last Unction, which she did
with great piety, reciting the psalms and joining in
the litanies and prayers. Once more, when the holy
rite was over, she gave thanks to God for making
her a child of the Church. Father Antonio then
asked her if she wished her body to be taken to
Avila. But she seemed displeased at the question,
and answered quietly, "Had she a will of her own?
Would they not give her a corner of earth there?"
The night seems to have been passed in much pain,
during which she kept repeating her favourite ejaculations. St. Francis' day drew on, and at seven in

Y 3

the morning she laid herself on her side, "in the attitude in which St. Magdalene is painted," with a crucifix in her hand which she held even after her death till the time of her burial.

Two days before the day of her death, she had said to Anne of St. Bartholomew, her constant attendant, "Daughter, the hour of my departure is coming." This was taken afterwards as meaning that the exact time of her death had been revealed to her. Anne of St. Bartholomew says that for the last two days she never left the room, the nuns bringing her what was wanted, and she giving it to Teresa. In the evening of the last day, Father Antonio bade her go and get some food, but Teresa began to look round as if she wanted her, and when Father Antonio asked her by signs whether it was so, she intimated that it was. When Anne returned, Teresa showed by the joyfulness of her countenance how glad she was. She placed her own head in Anne's arms, and so it remained until she breathed her last. "Our Lord," Anne tells us, "at last allowed her to become aware of His own presence in great majesty, and with a number of saints in His company, and the vision lasted for the space of a *Credo*, until she was perfectly calmed and soothed, so that she said to Him that, as she had seen the glory which Teresa was to share, she would rather ask that she should not be kept from it for her sake a moment longer." When the process was commenced for the canonization of St. Teresa, her dear niece, Teresita, who was a silent witness to the whole scene, and who was thus compensated for the loss of her aunt's

presence at her own profession, stated that the vision
of our Lord's presence which Anne was said to have
had at that time was so reflected in her face, in
so much splendour and light, filling the whole cell,
that she saw the nuns gazing at Anne rather than
at Teresa, unconscious of what they were doing,
until the glory faded away when Teresa died. She
seemed to be seeing and speaking of the most
wonderful things of God. She remained thus till
nine in the evening, when her soul at last left her
body.

Anne of Jesus tells us that she was at that time
very ill at Granada, and had just received the last
sacraments, after which she asked to be left alone.
She saw close to her a nun who wore the same
habit with herself, but there was so great a brightness
around her that she was unable to distinguish her
features. The brightness was most splendid on her
forehead. She kept looking at her, and conceived
an immense respect and value for the religious vocation in all its least ceremonies and regulations, and
she felt a desire to speak to the nuns on the subject,
and say how little a thing it would be to lay down
life itself for the least of them, and how great was
the glory reserved for those who faithfully observed
them. Thinking that the vision was meant as a
warning that her end was approaching, she sent
for the two oldest nuns, those from St. Joseph's at
Avila, to tell them, and ask them to send for her
confessor. She had received in the vision an intimation of certain matters which required to be set
right in one of the convents. She began to get

better at once, and was nearly well when the news came that St. Teresa had died at that time.

The body of St. Teresa after her death remained as flexible as when she was alive, the flesh supple and white as alabaster, her face beautiful, and without wrinkles. A fragrance seemed to exhale from all her limbs, unlike any earthly scent, and so strong that it was necessary to keep the window of the cell open. It filled the whole convent, and clung to all the things she had worn or used. The nuns remained with the sacred body all the night, and the next day, until ten in the morning, when the burial took place. One by one they went to kiss the feet of their Mother. Everything belonging to her became a relic. Antonio of Jesus claimed her habit. The body was placed in a wooden coffin, in the habit of the Order. A cloth embroidered in gold was laid over it to do it honour, as she had seen in spirit when she was for four days thought to be dead at the age of twenty, and would have been buried but for her father.[1] There were two choirs for the nuns, one above the other, on the Gospel side of the altar, with "grilles" into the church. Under the grille of the lower of the two, and in the thickness of the wall, a deep vault was dug, for Doña Teresa de Laiz was anxious to make it impossible for the sacred body to be removed. In this excavation the remains were placed in a wooden coffin, and covered with an immense quantity of stones, lime, and earth. The body had not been opened or embalmed. The inhabitants of the little town came in crowds to witness the ceremony, to

[1] Vol. i. p. 37.

see the face of the blessed Mother, and to take away as relics little objects of piety which had touched her The High Mass preceded the funeral.

The same day, Teresa appeared in glory to one of her nuns, Catalina of Jesus, one of the foundresses of the convent at Veas,[1] telling her that she enjoyed the presence of God, and would be of more use to her Order in Heaven than she had been on earth. Teresita and Anne of St. Bartholomew did not, apparently, stay many days at Alba after the decease of the Saint. Anne wished to be fixed at Alba that she might be near her remains, but St. Teresa appeared to her and told her to go where her Superiors bade her. A prodigy which continued long was immediately noticed by all,—the fragrance which has been already mentioned was continually perceptible, notwithstanding the great mass of materials which had been accumulated over the body. It was this, to all appearance, which led to the exhumation of St. Teresa's remains, nine months afterwards, by Father Gratian, when it was found that the coffin had been broken, that the lime had destroyed much of the clothes in which it was wrapped, and that it was only by a marvel that the limbs themselves had been preserved. Oil continued to flow from the body and all that it had touched. This visit was kept secret, and two years after, at the order of the Chapter of the Reformed Carmelites, the body was transferred to Avila. But Sixtus V., in 1589, commanded that it should be restored to Alba de Tormes, where it has rested ever since.

[1] Vol. i. p. 94.

Instead of relating at length the history of these translations, and of tracing the various relics of St. Teresa which remain in different convents of her Order, we may close this biography with the story of two souls, very dear to her, about whom, in different ways, she was anxious at the time of her death. The histories of Anne of Jesus, Mary of St. Joseph, Anne of St. Bartholomew, and others among the nuns, and those of St. John of the Cross, Father Gratian, and Ambrose Mariano, among the Friars of the Reform, belong to the annals of the Order, and it would be too great a task to sketch them at the end of this volume. But the two souls of whom we speak were not to attain celebrity, as it is commonly understood, and their lives may be considered to belong as sequels to the narrative of St. Teresa's life.

We shall first speak of the bright girl whom we have mentioned as " Teresita," whose profession was to take place at Avila when her aunt reached that much-loved home. Teresita was born in 1568, and was therefore now in her fourteenth year, perhaps in her fifteenth. The close companionship of her aunt which she enjoyed during the long expedition to Burgos and the return from that city, must have been more to her than many years of novitiate. And to have been present at her holy death, to have seen the reflected glory which filled the cell in which she died during that last scene, must have been a treasure to her memory greater than even the having received the veil of the professed from her hands or to have knelt in her presence to make her vows. Teresita hastened to Avila, and on the 5th of

November she took her vows with great consolation
and joy. After her aunt's death, she was naturally
looked on as a treasure representing her, and attempts
were made to have her in other convents. It is said
that Mary Baptist, in particular, asked for her at
Valladolid, but Mary of St. Jerome, who succeeded
as Prioress at Avila, objected. The body of St. Teresa
was at that time in the convent at Avila, and Anne
of St. Bartholomew was asked to pray to St. Teresa
and ask for directions. The answer came that Teresita
was never to leave Avila. The prophecy came true,
although the attempts to have her removed were
frequently made.

She filled the offices, first of Sacristan and then
of Mistress of Novices. Her example, says the same
historian, was enough to persuade all to follow what
she taught, for they always saw her lessons practised
first in her own person. She was most exact in all
community duties, which she performed always with
great devotion. Her silence was continual, her morti-
fications rigorous, her observance of poverty most
exact, her reverence for sacred things extreme, her
care of the least details of Rule perfect. She always
disciplined herself before Confession and Communion.
Her confessors were astonished at her purity of conscience and her humility. She seems to have acted
on the same principles which her aunt mentions in
her letter to the Religious of another Order who
wished to pass to Carmel,[1] for she always esteemed
others for their goodness, and saw in them what was
holy, and praised and loved them, and thought it a

[1] Letter cccxii.

great privilege to place herself at their feet and
occupy herself in serving them.   Our Lord tried her
with many tribulations, dryness, temptations, and
interior discomforts, and in this silent way prepared
her for her crown.   She died in the twenty-eighth year
of her profession, in 1610.   Anne of St. Bartholomew,
who was then in Flanders, saw her at the time of
her death with St. Teresa leading her by the hand,
and another nun at Valladolid, who loved her very
much, saw her at the same time in glory with our
Lady and St. Teresa.

" Teresita " was a soul that had loved the religious
state from infancy, and had known but little of the
seductions of the world.   But there are some other
souls who are called to the same state against their
own inclinations, and in whom the vocation is to be
discerned, with an eye skilled in such matters, by the
very repugnance with which it is received, which
sometimes is a better sign than mere indifference.
We have already said something about the birth
and youth of Teresa's niece, Beatriz.   Teresa had
prophesied to her that, with all her resistance, she
would be a Carmelite, and the fulfilment of the
prophecy took place two years after the death of
the Saint.   The Duchess of Alba, the great lady of
the place, was allowed by a Papal Brief to enter the
cloister and visit the tomb for a novena of prayers,
and she took with her a number of ladies of the town,
Beatriz among others.   Up to that time Beatriz
retained her dislike to the idea of a religious life for
herself, but the many signs of her aunt's great sanctity
which had appeared in the interval since her death

had made on her a great impression of the vanity of the world. We gather from the narrative that her parents were averse to her becoming a nun, as well as herself. The Religious of the convent, probably knowing Teresa's desires about Beatriz, and perhaps somewhat of her own change of mind, had been praying much for her. They looked upon her as a relic of Teresa. When the last day's prayers were over, and the ladies were leaving the convent, they said to Beatriz, "Señora, are you, too, going to leave us?" Now knowing what she said, she replied that she would come "on Friday week."

The words had passed her lips, like those of St. Peter on the holy mountain, when he spoke, "not knowing what he said." She had given a promise. In the interval she was torn more than ever with conflicting motions in her soul. She has left an account of her struggle, in which she says that she once heard a noise in the street, occasioned by a man being led to execution for some crime, and she said to herself that he was happy in having to die only once, whereas she was doomed to die every day of her life. At last she hit upon a scheme of writing to the nuns to say she would keep her promise on the day named, and she meant to drop the paper where her parents would find it, in hopes that they would interfere and prevent her entering the convent. When she went to drop the letter, she seemed to feel invisibly resisted by our Lord. A voice seemed to say she was trusting to man, and distrusting Him. So she told her mother she wished to go the next day—her birthday—to the

Carmelite Convent for Confession and Communion. Her mother merely remarked that she must take care to be up betimes, for Beatriz was not famous, says the chronicler, for early rising. However, she went with a servant early, and the nuns, who were expecting her, took her inside the convent, at which the servant began to cry out that her lady had been made a prisoner, and roused the neighbours. Her parents were opposed to her step, but the Duke and Duchess took part with the convent, and Juan de Ovalle and his wife yielded. She took the habit of Carmel on her twenty-fifth birthday.

Her history in the cloister shows that her self-conquest on entering secured the happiness of the rest of her course. It would take too long for us to recount the whole story. Not long after the beginning of her religious life, her mother, to whom she was tenderly attached, died, and she thus lost her chief tie to the world. The strength and sweetness which were combined in her character were ripened side by side in the atmosphere of Religion. She was strict in observance and gentle to others, and gave universal edification without offence to any. She was the most devout and constant worshipper at the tomb of her aunt, to whom she had recourse in all troubles and aridities, who appeared to her more than once, and gave her most helpful advice. Unlike her cousin Teresita, she passed through many convents, having been sent to found some and to hold office as Prioress in others. When the convent of Discalced Carmelite nuns was to be founded in Rome, she was applied for, but excused herself on account of her health.

She was Prioress in Toledo, Madrid, and Ocana, as well as Mistress of Novices. She died in Madrid February 16, 1639, with the reputation of a Saint, to enjoy for ever the glory which the prayers of her blessed aunt had won for her, and for thousands of others, of whom the catalogue will never be closed till the end of time.

APPENDIX.

Index to Letters.

[1] This letter is at the end of the Book of St. Teresa's Life, written to Father Ybañez in 1561.

[2] The numeration in the text is defective.

z